Register Your Book

at www.ibmpressbooks.com/ibmregister

Upon registration, we will send you electronic sample chapters from two of our popular IBM Press books. In addition, you will be automatically entered into a monthly drawing for a free IBM Press book.

Registration also entitles you to:

- Notices and reminders about author appearances, conferences, and online chats with special guests

- Access to supplemental material that may be available

- Advance notice of forthcoming editions

- Related book recommendations

- Information about special contests and promotions throughout the year

- Chapter excerpts and supplements of forthcoming books

Contact us

If you are interested in writing a book or reviewing manuscripts prior to publication, please write to us at:

Editorial Director, IBM Press
c/o Pearson Education
One Lake Street
Upper Saddle River, New Jersey 07458

e-mail: IBMPress@pearsoned.com

Visit us on the Web: www.ibmpressbooks.com

Praise for *Service-Oriented Architecture (SOA) Compass*

"Service-Oriented Architecture enables organizations to be agile and flexible enough to adopt new business strategies and produce new services to overcome the challenges created by business dynamism today. CIOs have to consider SOA as a foundation of their Enterprise Applications Architecture primarily because it demonstrates that IT aligns to business processes and also because it positions IT as a service enabler and maximizes previous investments on business applications.

To understand and profit from SOA, this book provides CIOs with the necessary concepts and knowledge needed to understand and adapt it into their IT organizations."

—**Sabri Hamed Al-Azazi**
CIO of Dubai Holding, Sabri

"I am extremely impressed by the depth and scale of this book! The title is perfect—when you know where you want to go, you need a compass to guide you there! After good IT strategy leads you to SOA, this book is the perfect vehicle that will drive you from dream to reality. We in DSK Bank will use it as our SOA bible in the ongoing project."

—**Miro Vichev**
CIO, DSK Bank, Bulgaria
member of OTP Group

"Service-Oriented Architecture offers a pathway to networking of intra- and inter-corporate business systems. The standards have the potential to create far more flexible and resilient business information systems than have been possible in the past. This book is a must-read for those who care about the future of business IT."

—**Elizabeth Hackenson**
CIO, MCI

"Service-Oriented Architecture is key to help customers become on demand businesses—a business that can quickly respond to competitive threats and be first to take advantage of marketplace opportunities. *SOA Compass* is a must-read for those individuals looking to bridge the gap between IT and business in order to help their enterprises become more flexible and responsive."

—**Michael Liebow**
Vice President, Web Services and Service-Oriented Architecture
IBM Business Consulting Services

More Praise for *Service-Oriented Architecture (SOA) Compass*

"This book is a welcome addition to SOA literature. It articulates the business case and provides practical proven real-world advice, guidance, tips, and techniques for organizations to make the evolution from simple point-to-point web services to true SOA by addressing such topics as planning, organization, analysis and design, security, and systems management."

—Denis O'Sullivan
Fireman's Fund Enterprise Architect

"The book *Service-Oriented Architecture (SOA) Compass* shows very clearly by means of real projects how agile business processes can be implemented using Service-Oriented Architectures. The entire development cycle from planning through implementation is presented very close to practice and the critical success factors are presented very convincingly."

—Professor Dr. Thomas Obermeier
Vice Dean of FHDW Bergisch Gladbach
Germany

"A comprehensive roadmap to Service-Oriented Architecture (SOA). SOA is, in reality, a business architecture to be used by those enterprises intending to prosper in the 21st century. Decision makers who desire that their business become flexible can jumpstart that process by adopting the best practices and rules of thumb described in *SOA Compass*."

—Bob Laird
MCI IT Chief Architect

"This book is a major improvement in the field. It gives a clear view and all the key points on how to really face a SOA deployment in today's organizations."

—Mario Moreno
IT Architect Leader, Generali
France

"The new potential of service oriented portal architectures did vastly change our business model. On the road there we had to recognize, based on abstractions, the opportunities that are supporting this new business philosophy. Additionally we needed to develop a roadmap to allow redesigning our IT systems. For both objectives the 'SOA Compass' provided valuable help: it gets rid of prejudices about SOA and provides orientation for the reader's project plans."

—Thies Frahm
CIO of businessMart
Stuttgart, Germany

Service-Oriented Architecture (SOA) Compass

The IBM Press developerWorks Series represents a unique undertaking in which print books and the Web are mutually supportive. The publications in this series are complemented by their association with resources available at the developerWorks Web site on ibm.com. These resources include articles, tutorials, forums, software, and much more.

Through the use of icons, readers will be able to immediately identify a resource on developerWorks which relates to that point of the text. A summary of links appears at the end of each chapter. Additionally, you will be able to access an electronic guide of the developerWorks links and resources through ibm.com/developerworks/dwbooks that reference developerWorks Series publications, deepening the reader's experiences.

A developerWorks book offers readers the ability to quickly extend their information base beyond the book by using the deep resources of developerWorks and at the same time enables developerWorks readers to deepen their technical knowledge and skills.

For a full listing of developerWorks Series publications, please visit: **ibmpressbooks.com/dwseries**.

WEBSPHERE BOOKS

IBM® WebSphere®
Barcia, Hines, Alcott, and Botzum

IBM® WebSphere® Application Server for Distributed Platforms and z/OS®
Black, Everett, Draeger, Miller, Iyer, McGuinnes, Patel, Herescu, Gissel, Betancourt, Casile, Tang, and Beaubien

Enterprise Java™ Programming with IBM® WebSphere®, Second Edition
Brown, Craig, Hester, Pitt, Stinehour, Weitzel, Amsden, Jakab, and Berg

IBM® WebSphere® and Lotus
Lamb, Laskey, and Indurkhya

IBM® WebSphere® System Administration
Williamson, Chan, Cundiff, Lauzon, and Mitchell

Enterprise Messaging Using JMS and IBM® WebSphere®
Yusuf

ON DEMAND COMPUTING BOOKS

Business Intelligence for the Enterprise
Biere

On Demand Computing
Fellenstein

Grid Computing
Joseph and Fellenstein

Autonomic Computing
Murch

RATIONAL

Software Configuration Management Strategies and IBM Rational ClearCase®, Second Edition
Bellagio and Milligan

MORE BOOKS FROM IBM PRESS

Developing Quality Technical Information, Second Edition
Hargis, Carey, Hernandez, Hughes, Longo, Rouiller, and Wilde

Performance Tuning for Linux® Servers
Johnson, Huizenga, and Pulavarty

Building Applications with the Linux Standard Base
Linux Standard Base Team

An Introduction to IMS™
Meltz, Long, Harrington, Hain, and Nicholls

Search Engine Marketing, Inc.
Moran and Hunt

Inescapable Data
Stakutis and Webster

DB2® BOOKS

DB2® Universal Database V8 for Linux, UNIX, and Windows Database Administration Certification Guide, Fifth Edition
Baklarz and Wong

Understanding DB2®
Chong, Liu, Qi, and Snow

Integrated Solutions with DB2®
Cutlip and Medicke

High Availability Guide for DB2®
Eaton and Cialini

DB2® Universal Database V8 Handbook for Windows, UNIX, and Linux
Gunning

DB2® SQL PL, Second Edition
Janmohamed, Liu, Bradstock, Chong, Gao, McArthur, and Yip

DB2® Universal Database for OS/390 V7.1 Application Certification Guide
Lawson

DB2® for z/OS® Version 8 DBA Certification Guide
Lawson

DB2® Universal Database V8 Application Development Certification Guide, Second Edition
Martineau, Sanyal, Gashyna, and Kyprianou

DB2® Universal Database V8.1 Certification Exam 700 Study Guide
Sanders

DB2® Universal Database V8.1 Certification Exam 703 Study Guide
Sanders

DB2® Universal Database V8.1 Certification Exams 701 and 706 Study Guide
Sanders

DB2® Universal Database for OS/390
Sloan and Hernandez

The Official Introduction to DB2® for z/OS®, Second Edition
Sloan

Advanced DBA Certification Guide and Reference for DB2® Universal Database v8 for Linux, UNIX, and Windows
Snow and Phan

DB2® Express
Yip, Cheung, Gartner, Liu, and O'Connell

DB2® SQL Procedure Language for Linux, UNIX and Windows
Yip

DB2® Version 8
Zikopoulos, Baklarz, deRoos, and Melnyk

Service-Oriented Architecture (SOA) Compass

Business Value, Planning, and Enterprise Roadmap

**Norbert Bieberstein, Sanjay Bose,
Marc Fiammante, Keith Jones,
Rawn Shah**

IBM Press
Pearson plc
Upper Saddle River, NJ • Boston • Indianapolis • San Francisco
New York • Toronto • Montreal • London • Munich • Paris • Madrid
Cape Town • Sydney • Tokyo • Singapore • Mexico City
ibmpressbooks.com

The authors and publisher have taken care in the preparation of this book, but make no expressed or implied warranty of any kind and assume no responsibility for errors or omissions. No liability is assumed for incidental or consequential damages in connection with or arising out of the use of the information or programs contained herein.

IBM Press Program Manager: Tara Woodman, Ellice Uffer
IBM Press Consulting Editor: Linda Foo
Cover design: IBM Corporation

Published by Pearson plc
Publishing as IBM Press

IBM Press offers excellent discounts on this book when ordered in quantity for bulk purchases or special sales, which may include electronic versions and/or custom covers and content particular to your business, training goals, marketing focus, and branding interests. For more information, please contact:

> U.S. Corporate and Government Sales
> 1-800-382-3419
> corpsales@pearsontechgroup.com.

For sales outside the U.S., please contact:

> International Sales
> international@pearsoned.com.

ISBN 0-13-187002-5
Text printed in the United States on recycled paper at Courier in Westford, Massachusetts.
2nd printing, January 2006

Library of Congress Cataloging-in-Publication Data

Service-oriented architecture compass : business value, planning, and enterprise roadmap / Norbert Bieberstein ... [et al.]
    p. cm.
  Includes bibliographical references and index.
  ISBN 0-13-187002-5
  1. Computer software—Development. 2. Computer architecture. 3. System design. 4. Business—Data processing. I. Bieberstein, Norbert.
  QA76.76.D47S45 2005
  005.1—dc22

                                                                            2005019911

To my wife, Joanna, and my daughters, Katherina, Caroline, and Julia

N.B

To my dad, Chitta Ranjan, and my mom, Sephali, for instilling confidence and believing in me

S.B.

To my wife, Corine, and my daughter, Florence, for their support of my taking some family time to work on the book

M.F.

To my wife, Gillian, and my sons, Simon and Philip

K.J.

To my ever-supportive wife, Sarah

R.S.

Contents

Forewords

Computing has evolved in dramatic ways since the first abstracting systems were developed in the late 1930s and early 1940s. In the ensuing decades, the usual metrics associated with computing have increased by many orders of magnitude: speed of computation, capability to store and retrieve information, capability to transmit information, programmability, and so on. The twenty-first century is witnessing yet another transformation of computing: its immersion into a networked environment. The confluence of computing and communication has produced a fertile environment for innovation and reinvention in computation. This book is about one very important example of new thinking: the so-called Service-Oriented Architecture.

The potential applicability of computers to administrative tasks was recognized very early in their development. The Hollerith punched card, invented in the 1880s by Herman Hollerith, was used in connection with the 1890 U.S. census. Hollerith based his punched cards on the earlier punched card design used in 1804 in Joseph-Marie Jacquard's eponymous loom. Although some of the earliest applications were driven by military needs (for example, ballistics and cryptanalytic computations), after World War II, computers were turned to civilian use in the conduct of business. Payroll, inventory, accounts receivable and payable, sales, production, numerical control, and a host of other business data-processing applications were developed to run on expensive mainframe machines. These so-called data-processing systems were often housed in glassed-in "fishbowls" and were exhibited proudly by their owners as evidence that the company was at the forefront of high-technology application. Programming languages such as Common Business Oriented Language (COBOL) were developed for the business world as a counterpart to Fortran's dominance in scientific and engineering computing. Of course, since that now-long-ago era, many other high-level languages and systems have been developed for business applications.

Many of these business-oriented applications and systems deal with vast databases containing billions and, in some cases, trillions of bytes of information. Modern database technology allows for hierarchical storage structures capable of manipulating and storing terabytes to petabytes of information. (A petabyte is 10^{15} bytes.) In most such systems, the programs that interact with the databases and with each other do so either through the sharing of access to a common data storage system or by direct exchange through application programming interfaces (APIs) on a shared computer. Distributed database systems are federations of database systems that typically maintain multiple copies of data, keeping them synchronized by a variety of pairwise and group coordination procedures. This program-centric view of data structures and file exchanges has dominated the data management scene for decades. Only as networking has become more widespread has this philosophy been given serious reconsideration.

Rather than thinking of database management (local or distributed) as a programming problem involving the programmatic updating of storage structures, a network-centric view of data management sees the interaction among the systems as a layered architecture of services. This is very much aligned with the Internet's architecture, which sees remote systems as servers or as peers in a client-server or peer-to-peer system. In this view, protocol replaces API as the primary mechanism of exchange between programs. The protocol specifies the format of exchanged information and the procedures by which the information is exchanged. The APIs used in one machine need bear no relation to those used in another. All the commonality lies in the procedures and formats for protocol-driver data exchange.

This is a profoundly different way of looking at data handling in a networked environment. Rather than the bulk transfer of an update file that is then run through a local program that executes the database update, the source(s) and sink(s) of the traffic exchange transactions in accordance with agreed protocols. Each machine expects the others to provide services in aid of database management in accordance with the agreed-upon and standardized protocols.

Peer-to-peer data and file sharing operates along these lines—all participants agree on a protocol, format, and representation for the exchanged data. That this is a powerful form of information processing is revealed by statistics that show that up to half of the Internet's capacity is taken up with such transactions.

This book takes the reader, in some careful detail, through the concepts and operational issues associated with the creation of a Service-Oriented Architecture (SOA) for distributed information processing. It is hard to imagine a more important topic in the twenty-first-century information infrastructure. Some important side effects of this reparsing of the data-processing architecture are that business IT continuity will be easier to establish, interenterprise transactions will be easier to implement, security and authenticity of the transacting parties will be easier to establish, confidentiality of the information will be easier to maintain, and the capability to scale the available processing, networking, and storage capacity of the system will be enhanced. Indeed, one expects that service providers will be able to soak up surge demands using shared computing, storage, and network assets, while enterprises need only invest in capacity to deal with their average demands.

SOA and the many other acronyms in this book will become the alphabet by which intra- and inter-enterprise transactions will be spelled out. Of course, the utility of all of this will depend on the development of standards to which all software providers adhere. In the same way that the basic Internet protocols have created a common and widespread platform upon which to build a major new communications and computing infrastructure, so too will the SOA standards create yet another widespread and shared platform for new applications. As this book is released, the effort is still in its infancy, but it should be apparent that a successful implementation of the concepts can have a lasting effect on the capability of enterprise to harness the increasing power of computers, storage systems, and networking.

Vinton Cerf
Chief Internet Evangelist
Google

It is no overstatement that we are at an information crossroads, a critical juncture from which there is no turning back. At this introspection point we understand that, just as the Industrial Revolution transformed our economy and society, we are now faced with the "integration revolution." We are confronting an element in the continuation of the Industrial Revolution that explicitly leverages Moore's law and cheap and massive bandwidth options (cable, wired, wireless). This reform is similar to the way in which global economies shifted with the original introduction of telephony, telegraphs, mainframes, and personal computers. The new mandate sits squarely in between all the pieces of our lives that we are demanding be treated as one. One plug for all electric outlets, one standard for how we view information and multimedia, one mobile phone that operates seamlessly worldwide, and one model for how we respect and meet the diverse needs of business and people. It is at this integration challenge that we find service-oriented architecture (SOA) as our way forward.

The SOA paradigm represents an identifiable, market-analyst-certified solution to the enterprise's business and IT challenges. The core reasons are simply a byproduct of timing. Either the existing enterprise system or technology represents an organic infrastructure that is simply too expensive and complex to manage, or more to the point, it simply fails to offer the capabilities that the myriad new business challenges require. The key term here is "flexible"—flexible business processes, flexible applications, and flexible technology. It may seem trite and even simplistic, but what SOA has effectively done is galvanize a set of major business and technical problems that have been festering for some time now. Coupled with the massive cultural changes occurring in business—mergers, acquisitions, downsizing, and upsizing—while offering a vast array of potential, technology has been limited by two gating factors. First, until SOA became the battle cry, there was no coalescing rubric. Second, the business challenges themselves have changed at such an unprecedented rate that the skills and cultural adaptability simply fell short.

These points may all sound very elementary and even hackneyed; however, do not be misguided into thinking this is accurate. In fact, the very elegance of these complexities is at the heart of what is happening in the technology industry across the board. The business and technical challenges are so demanding, so complex, and so fluid that the means to resolve them and bring value into the mix requires the same degree of adaptability. It is not a marketing slogan, not an easily applied set of slides or quick fixes. It is a fundamental shift in the way the business, commerce, and industry around the world will be required to adapt and change.

In its broadest sense, SOA is the architecture for integration connectedness. SOA is evolving to render the Internet into a ubiquitous utility, readily available for all manner of exchange, commerce, and communication. It is an architecture designed, by its very nature, to enable the diverse and naturally occurring heterogeneity of our systems and infrastructures. It has evolved not just to help systems communicate, but to ensure that they collaborate on multiple dimensions, across an infinitely scalable set of consumer demands: from the simple use of Web-based commerce to the more complex needs of industry verticals.

It is almost mundane to say that much of SOA is based on the same old principles that have been helping us improve software comprehension and flexibility for the last 45 years, namely, through increased modularity and abstraction. The extent of the evolution is important. It is not just another incremental crank of programming models (structured, object-oriented, and others) enabled by an environment with much greater bandwidth and computing power embodied in standardized, global internetworks. The real shift is that we are making fundamental tradeoffs in efficiency in favor of abstraction and modularity to drive significant improvements in economic efficiency and innovation. We are seeing this in diverse examples, such as universal access to products and services with much greater efficiency in supply chains that eliminate middlemen and provide real-time feedback.

IBM has engaged with many enterprise clients on SOA, and our experience shows that after the customer demonstrates value, he is eager to embrace it initially in increments until his confidence has been confirmed. This trend has cascaded across various industries, and the realized business value of SOA serves as a potent catalyst. After a short maturation cycle, the industry will wholeheartedly embrace SOA because it has to and because it is a framework for the solutions businesses require, not because it will create another business and technology Gordian knot that will unravel in the future.

This book provides a blend of broad technical and business guidelines while navigating an enterprise roadmap for SOA. And although many of the issues addressed are designed for use in complex enterprise applications, there is a need to broadly infuse the very significance of this "integration revolution."

We anticipate that you will find this book both helpful and valuable in your path to SOA adoption.

Daniel Sabbah, Ph.D.
General Manager, IBM Rational Software
International Business Machines
Somers, New York, U.S.A.

Jason Weisser, Ph.D.
Vice President, Asset & Integration Technology
International Business Machines
Paris, France

Preface

E arly in 2004, a small team within the IBM Enterprise Integration team was asked to draft an IBM internal SOA cookbook to document SOA engagement experiences and share best practices. By engaging subject matter experts across IBM and infusing our own project experiences, we created the first version of a SOA cookbook. This was well received by the IBM SOA technical community, and a general awareness of this book spread to our key customers. Some of these customers started requesting a formal and public version of the cookbook. This brought us together to distill the internal cookbook and author a SOA book for the general SOA community.

Trademarks and Notices

IBM, WebSphere, CICS, IMS, and Tivoli are registered trademarks of IBM in the United States and other countries. UNIX is a registered trademark of The Open Group in the United States and other countries. Microsoft, Microsoft .Net, .NET, Windows, Windows NT, and the Windows logo are trademarks of Microsoft Corporation in the United States, other countries, or both. Java and all Java-based trademarks are trademarks of Sun Microsystems, Inc. in the United States, other countries, or both. Other company, product, and service names may be trademarks or service marks of others.

The figures in Chapter 10 have been reprinted with the permission of the Standard Life Assurance Company within Section 10.1 (©2005) and the Ministry of Justice of the Government of the Republic of Austria within Section 10.2 (©2002). Figure 2.1 has been reprinted with the permission of Forrester Research, Inc. (©2004).

The opinions expressed in this book are those of the authors and do not reflect the official opinions or positions of IBM or its management.

developerWorks® Link Icons Used in This Book

A.1

Margin icons are used to indicate that links to further resources related to the text are available at the developerWorks Web site on ibm.com. These links are listed at the end of each chapter and an electronic guide is available through ibm.com/developerworks/dwbooks.

Acknowledgments

To write this book, we relied on the advice, expertise, knowledge, and contribution of a number of our IBM colleagues. Most of them are actively engaged in SOA-based customer projects and IBM software product development.

We would first like to thank the key content contributors to this book. With their substantial effort and deep subject expertise, it was possible to give insights into a broad range of SOA topics. **Randy Langel** provided input for Chapter 2, "Explaining the Business Value of SOA." The topic of information and data services was elaborated on by **Mei Selvage** in Chapter 3, "Architecture Elements." **Greg Flurry** and **Eoin Lane** helped articulate the sample assets in Chapter 6, "Enterprise Solution Assets." **Heather Hinton**, a security architect in IBM Tivoli product development, provided content for Chapter 8, "Securing the SOA Environment." Members of the Tivoli team, including **Rosalind Radcliffe, Ingo Averdunk, Sudhakar Chellam, David Cox, Steve Tremper,** and **John Whitfield**, provided content for Chapter 9, "Managing the SOA Environment." We would also like to thank **Derek Ireland** of Standard Life, **Dr. Martin Schneider** of the Austrian Ministry of Justice, and **Anton Fricko** for their help with Chapter 10, "Case Studies in SOA Deployment."

Several technical experts helped review individual chapters. We appreciate their valuable feedback and input—**Jonathan Adams, Yvonne Balzer, Maryann Hondo, Heather Kreger, Rick Robinson**, and many others who were supportive in various subject areas and deserve our recognition.

The team from IBM Press was instrumental in thoroughly reviewing this book and providing overall guidance and feedback. We want to thank them for improving various aspects of the book. **Kevin Davis** and **David Kane** did two rounds of rigorous technical reviews and provided critical inputs. **Ginny Bess Munroe** provided excellent language-editing skills by streamlining the text and Amy Lepore patiently copy edited the chapters. Lori Lyons led the project in the final stages. And finally, **Paul Petralia** provided overall editorial leadership and liaison.

We would also like to thank **Vinton Cerf, Daniel Sabbah,** and **Jason Weisser** for generously donating their time to write the forewords for this book. The work took time from our daytime jobs, and we thank our respective management at IBM for their understanding and for granting us the necessary freedom and support.

Finally, we would like to thank our families and friends for their ample encouragement and support. Thank you for your infinite patience during the last year while this book was being prepared. It would have been impossible without your support and understanding.

About the Authors

Norbert Bieberstein is a solution architect for the IBM Enterprise Integration team and is responsible for the team's worldwide communication. In his dual role, he gained first-hand experiences from customer projects in various industries striving to migrate to SOA-based On Demand solutions. He currently is completing his MBA at Henley Management College in the United Kingdom. In his communication role, he is delivering insight and best practices to IBM and customers in various forms. Norbert co-authored the IBM Redbooks *Introduction to Grid Computing with Globus (SG24-6895-01)* and *Enabling Applications for Grid Computing with Globus (SG24-6936-00)*, wrote the textbook *CASE-Tools* (ISBN: 3446175261), and published several magazine articles on various IT topics. Norbert also worked as a technology manager in the IBM software partner organization, where he led the IBM OMG delegation during UML definition. He also acted as a software engineering (CASE) consultant to the IBM software development labs. Norbert has more than 25 years of experience in information technology and computer sciences. Before joining IBM in 1989, he was an application developer for a regional CIM provider and worked as scientific programmer at Aachen University of Technology (RWTH), where he received his masters in mathematics and geography. He also holds teacher's degrees for higher education in Germany. He lives with his family near Düsseldorf, Germany.

Sanjay Bose is the Design Center leader for the IBM Enterprise Integration team. He has more than 12 years of IT industry experience, primarily focused on creating product architecture and design, articulating technical strategy, and designing enterprise application systems using distributed technologies. He currently leads the design center to identify IBM software portfolio requirements and to develop solution components and assets by engaging enterprise clients and IBM software product development laboratories. His areas of expertise include service-oriented architecture, enterprise service bus, Web services, J2EE, and e-business technologies. Sanjay also worked in product development on the WebSphere Application Server and the WebSphere Portal Server. He has published several technical papers and also has contributed to industry specifications and standards. Sanjay received his bachelor's degree in computer science and engineering from the Indian Institute of Technology (IIT) in Mumbai, India and has completed MBA coursework at the Tepper School of Business, Carnegie Mellon University. He lives and works in Pittsburgh, Pennsylvania.

Marc Fiammante is an IBM Distinguished Engineer, elected to the IBM Academy of Technology in 2003, with wide experience in large project architecture and software development on multiple environments. He is the chief architect of the European, Middle East, Africa, and Asia-Pacific Enterprise Integration Solutions team. Marc has 21 years of experience in IT. He has filed several software domain patents and has published several articles related to e-business technologies. He leads architecture teams in major industry projects. He has architectural and technical expertise with service-oriented architecture, Web services, enterprise application integration, and e-business and object-oriented technologies, including a number of software middleware systems, programming languages, and standards. Marc is a graduate engineer of the Ecole Centrale de Paris.

Keith Jones, PhD, is currently a leading IT architect at IBM Enterprise Integration Solutions, where he focuses on the definition and implementation of service-oriented architectures with leading-edge customers. He has 30 years of experience in the IT industry as a systems engineer, software developer, strategist, systems architect, and author of many middleware publications. Keith's professional interests center on building transactional, message-oriented, and service-oriented middleware infrastructures in support of business processes in a wide range of customer environments. Most recently, these have included infrastructures at major financial services, retail services, automotive manufacturing, online media, and auction enterprises. Keith has a PhD in chemistry and lives with his family in Boulder, Colorado.

Rawn Shah is the Community Editor (and, formerly, the SOA and Web services Zone Editor) for IBM developerWorks. Rawn has 12 years of experience in the IT industry, serving in various roles including positions as a network administrator, an application developer, a vice president of a regional Internet service provider, a columnist, an author, and an editor. He has written more than 280 articles for dozens of technology magazines, including CNN.com, *NetworkWorld, JavaWorld, NC World, Windows TechEdge,* and *LinuxWorld,* and he was directly involved in the release of the industry-leading publications *JavaWorld and LinuxWorld* in the mid-1990s. His interests lie in finding new ways for facilitating the communication and collaboration of technical ideas and processes between distributed audiences and transferring this knowledge in meaningful ways to nontechnical audiences such as business teams. He and his family currently reside in Tucson, Arizona.

developerWorks and SOA

Through the SOA and Web services Zone on developerWorks, IBM helps software developers and architects by providing them with technical content, tools, and resources that enable them to build on demand applications in an open environment. Our goal is to provide new, original content that guides developers both in their thinking and implementation of Web services creation and development of a Service-Oriented Architecture.

A sampling of content includes topics that are about both cutting-edge developments as well as some of the basics:

- **Business processes**—What are the roles of Web services and SOA in creating and managing business processes? How is this particularly relevant for those architecting on demand solutions?
- **Migration**—Is it possible to migrate to a SOA? What are the steps I take to do that?
- **Model-Driven Architecture**—How does the Rational portfolio enable more efficient creation and modeling of services?
- **Standards**—I'm aware of Web services standards, but not sure how to address them in my development process.
- **The Enterprise Service Bus**—Why do I need it?

These comprise just a small overview of the categories that we touch on in the SOA and Web services Zone on developerWorks. We are also aware that some are looking to understand methodology and philosophy of creating certain kinds of systems, and others want practical advice on delivery and implementation. Every month delivers a number of articles, tutorials, downloads, sample code, and community resources that address the broad array of issues related to services development.

Because of IBM's position as the leader in open, cross-platform software development, developerWorks benefits from having access to some of the most accomplished thinkers in the SOA and Web services space. Some of these people are regular contributors through their article series, blogs, and participation in our online forums, Technical Briefings, and Web-based seminars.

We invite you to look around our zone and see for yourself how it might help you with your development and architecture goals:

ibm.com/developerWorks/webservices

Chapter 1

Introducing SOA

"Once an organization loses its spirit of pioneering and rests on its early work, its progress stops."

—*Thomas J. Watson, Sr.*

The increasing pace of the evolution of business requirements and the need for increased revenues and cost optimization are leading corporate executives to deliberately align their IT organizations more closely with their business requirements. The main goal of this convergence is to develop more optimal and operationally integrated business processes that can be implemented by departments, business units, and business partner networks. Historically, this convergence process has been constrained because IT systems have not kept in step with business needs and because the IT infrastructure has inherent operational and developmental limitations, such as proprietary programming interfaces that restrict a system's flexibility. Consequently, the integration challenge demands a technology that can successfully bring together the needs of business and IT into a viable solution that not only makes efficient and effective use of the IT infrastructure, but that is also flexible and adaptive enough to keep pace with continual changes in the organization's business processes and business models.

Integration challenges are often considered to be only a technical interoperability issue. A change to a business need supported by functions that an application provides is considered to be a change to the actual software program, how it is deployed, or how it interacts with other applications. When a new business need arises, organizations order the revitalization, creation, or installation of new applications. However, this view of the integration challenge assumes a prevailing and potentially long-term view of any application, limiting the overall flexibility and agility of the business. Therefore, we need to reexamine the approach to and the source of this challenge to unlock a new way to address the issue of business-driven software changes and implementation.

The prevailing integration challenge in the software industry stems from the very same force that has been the energy of this industry: the diversity of methods and approaches deployed to solve a multitude of essentially technical issues. This positive force has allowed software engineers to tackle increasingly complex problems with new ideas, new methods, and new technologies. It has also helped to speed the growth of most, if not all, other industries with the rise of computerization by exploiting a range of hardware solutions, operating environments, application systems, programming languages, and software development techniques.

Yet it is this same evolving diversity that has allowed the creation and multiplication of barriers among the many solutions that have been developed. The issue of incompatibility among solutions has become a paramount problem, not just because of the technical issues that must be resolved but because it introduces barriers to the way companies use IT to do business and interact with others.

As businesses invest in more complex and more richly featured software technologies, they also separate the world of technical operations from that of business operations. However, focusing only on technical aspects and not considering the organizational or business issues often leads to an information and process-integration failure.

Integration is an old story. In 1967, Paul Lawrence, the Louis Kirstein Professor of Human Relations at Harvard Business School, together with Jay Lorsch, addressed the organizational issues related to departmental efficiency and enterprise integration and defined integration as the "state of collaboration that exists among departments that are required to achieve unity of effort."

Until now, and as noted previously, most solutions for aligning technology and business requirements have been too technology oriented and application focused. Recently, *enterprise application integration (EAI)* technology has been viewed as *the* solution to the business-IT alignment problem. EAI, although it initially solved significant coordination problems, has failed to evolve to address the current complex array of integration issues, and it has often failed to deliver the expected business flexibility.

In addition to a focus on technology-derived solutions, there is the problem of language. There is a clear division between the language used by the business operations community and the technical jargon of the IT community. This makes it increasingly difficult to relate IT operations to business management and to relate technical problems to business issues. Interestingly enough, one of the most common problems of implementing software is not the complexity of creating a technology solution; instead, it is the problem of developing an understanding of the business needs and of what must be implemented to meet those needs.

Therefore, there is a definitive requirement to find an enterprise approach that truly allows both business leaders and IT to meet in the middle. What large organizations really need is a business and architectural framework that identifies how diverse software solutions can interact with each other across technical incompatibilities and that relates software solutions to business-level requirements and business problems.

1.1 SOA to the Rescue

The concept of service-oriented architecture (SOA) offers a framework for better-integrated systems that meet business needs. This concept is a new rationalization of practices and techniques that already exist in process-driven, top-down, bottom-up, and meet-in-the-middle methods of software integration. It has now come to reality with the evolution of technology and the advent of true interoperability.

SOA envisions the implementation of a *services platform* consisting of many services that signify elements of business processes that can be combined and recombined into different solutions and scenarios, as determined by business needs. This capability to integrate and recombine services is what provides the closer relationship between business and IT, as well as the flexibility to address new situations.

The role of the SOA services platform is to provide a foundation for delivering essential business services in a flexible, easily composed, and highly reusable fashion. It is essential that an enterprise adopts a global *ecosystem* approach to building such a platform by providing focus on the lifecycle for business-driven IT services as they are created, evolved, and phased out during the lifetime of the organization and on using a consistent architectural approach to providing flexible and reusable business service delivery.

The need for an enterprise ecosystem view has led to the creation of the service-oriented architecture, through which composite applications can be created, modified, and removed dynamically using services, abstracted from existing applications and data, provided by the platform, or provisioned from external sources.

From a business point of view, an SOA can be expressed as a set of flexible services and processes that a business wants to expose to its customers, partners, or internally to other parts of the organization. In this context, these same services can be recombined and supplemented to support changes to or an evolution of business requirements and models over time. As an example, an auto parts supplier that uses an SOA can expand to support new automobile brands and can integrate new parts catalogs without impacting its existing business processes.

From the technical point of view, SOA defines software in terms of discrete services, which are implemented using components that can be called upon to perform a specified operation for a specific business task. The SOA concept evolves the existing software concept of a *function*—a specific piece of code that performs one particular task—to include the notion of a *contract*, a technology-neutral but business-specific representation of the function. In the auto parts supplier example, a common service might be the "catalog service" that exposes catalogs from different providers in a common way throughout the enterprise.

The concepts of service-oriented software and architectures based on such software have existed in some form for a number of years. We have found service-oriented implementations in COBOL/CICS® mainframe systems, object-oriented C++ systems, and in Java® application platforms. Some of these concepts have evolved from older ideas and from a variety of software technology origins. Thus, with no surprise from an industry that thrives on the diversity of technical ideas, the definition of what constitutes an "SOA" varies widely across the industry.

Before we create a working definition of SOA to be used throughout this book, we must understand the different ways that SOA has commonly been defined and clarify our view of what "SOA" really means.

1.2 Exploring SOA

There are a number of ways to look at the concept of SOA. In its most basic form, SOA is an approach to building software systems that is focused on *how* the software is actually implemented. To understand this approach and implementation directive, we need to look at individual parts of the definition and the *dimensions* of a typical enterprise SOA.

1.2.1 The Term "SOA"

The following are common examples of SOA definitions. Most of these definitions focus on the technical aspects of architecture, although some include business characteristics. These definitions, which we gathered from multiple sources, are interesting because they illustrate the number of different views or expressions of what an SOA is; however, they all tend to coalesce into a common meaning:

- *A business definition:* A set of business, process, organizational, governance, and technical methods to reduce or eliminate frustrations with IT and to quantifiably measure the business value of IT while creating an agile business environment for competitive advantage.
- *Another business definition (introduced by IBM):* A service-oriented architecture provides the flexibility to treat elements of business processes and the underlying IT infrastructure as secure, standardized components (services) that can be reused and combined to address changing business priorities.[1]
- *The widest technical (and rather minimalist) definition:* An enterprise-wide IT architecture that promotes **loose coupling, reuse, and interoperability between systems.**
- *A moderately complex technical definition:* An application architecture in which all functions or services are defined using a **description language** and have **callable**

---

1. In an informal survey of some of its business customers done by IBM in late 2004, the previous definition received an overwhelming 90 percent support from business executives of major industries.

interfaces that are called to perform business processes. Each interaction is independent of each and every other interaction and the interconnect protocols of the communicating devices. Because interfaces are **platform independent**, a client can use the service from any device using any operating system in any language.

- *The least common denominator definition:* A system architecture in which application functions are built as components (*services*) that are **loosely coupled and well-defined to support interoperability** and to improve flexibility and reuse.
- *The narrowest definition:* SOA is a synonym for solution architectures making use of Web service technologies such as **SOAP, WSDL,** and **UDDI.** Here SOA is defined as "any product and project architecture conforming to the W3C Web services architecture (WSA)."

In this book, we elaborate on the principles of these definitions, particularly the first four, and we do not restrict ourselves to the final, narrower definition. For our discussion, we have chosen to adapt the definition of SOA that resulted from a survey of business executives:

> *A service-oriented architecture is a framework for integrating business processes and supporting IT infrastructure as secure, standardized components—services— that can be reused and combined to address changing business priorities.*

In our view, there can be valid SOAs that do not define a single Web service and instead use existing technology such as mainframe transactional or object-oriented systems. Similarly, there are valuable Web service implementation projects that are not valid SOAs because they do not address the business value, true reusability, and flexibility that SOAs can and should provide.

1.2.2 Dimensions of SOA

As we explore the concepts around service-oriented architectures, we need to look at various dimensions: business value, reach and range, and maturity and adoption strategies.

1.2.2.1 Business Value

Businesses today cannot survive, let alone prosper, without leveraging diverse technologies into both their day-to-day operations and their long-term strategy. Enterprises are adapting to broader connectivity and increased revenues, but they also focus on innovation by restructuring applications for greater flexibility and lower costs.

According to the 2004 Global CEO Study, a landmark survey conducted by IBM Business Consulting Services, most CEOs say their companies are neither responsive enough to changing business conditions nor agile enough to pursue new market opportunities. The study claims:

> *"Given the rate at which the market is evolving, it is almost impossible to carry out long-term planning. It is critical to be able to plan on a rolling basis, rapidly and continuously."*

One of the goals of service-oriented architecture is to provide a response to that agile, rolling enterprise vision by delivering a strong business value proposition. Additional business drivers for SOA include the following:

- Anticipating market changes
- Developing new customer, partner, and supplier relationships
- Improving the time to market
- Creating differentiated solutions for higher-value customer and partner interactions
- Reducing operating costs

The business case for SOA that this book explores requires the assessment of business needs and analysis of any identified gaps (see Chapter 2, "Explaining the Business Value of SOA"). This approach also calls for the identification of key differentiating components and nondifferentiating components, with detailed business cases for each opportunity, so that investments can be intelligently prioritized. As an example, a component could be enabled for cross-selling to increase revenue. Another component might be identified as a candidate for outsourcing, which would be made easier by an SOA approach.

1.2.2.2 Reach and Range

The second dimension that will affect architecture is *reach*, where and to whom (employees, departments, customers, or business partners) the SOA will be made available, and *range*, the number or diversity of services made available. The environment—consisting of the technical software and hardware as well as the users of the systems—can affect all stages of SOA implementation, from planning to deployment, by adding or relieving from technical constraints. For example, different services require different levels of security, different levels of reliability, and different levels of data access and information hiding; all of these considerations affect the architecture.

1.2.2.3 Maturity and Adoption Strategies

As previously indicated, the business and architectural concepts behind SOA are in and of themselves not new. For at least five to ten years, large companies have had such concepts involved in their strategy roadmap; additionally, there have been real industry trends related to SOA, such as *componentization*. However, many of these approaches either have not yet emerged from the conceptual stage or are only partially implemented. This makes the dimension of maturity and the strategy for the adoption of this approach a key factor of SOA.

Failure to transfer the vision of such new approaches to the engineering level can be attributed mainly to the fact that existing implementation technologies had limitations that did not allow a successful enterprise-wide deployment of the approach. For example, a single platform might have limited the implementation due to the absence of tools, lack of standardization, or interoperability problems.

Enterprises do not implement service-oriented architectures as *big-bang* projects because there is a valid need for progressive adoption strategies that address the following considerations:

- Making a business case for the adoption of the architecture
- Validating available technologies

- Selecting a business pilot and enabling a line-of-business
- Expanding to the enterprise
- Expanding to the partner network

These dimensions of SOA indicate that a compass with points facing business, organization, architecture, and technology is necessary to approach SOA.

1.3 A Preview of the Service-Oriented Architecture Compass

SOA can fundamentally change the direction taken by an enterprise to development and deployment of business software systems for competitive advantage. Introducing SOA at the enterprise level cannot reasonably be reduced to a single project because it will affect the way that IT responds to the business requirements. When an enterprise starts on its journey to SOA, a compass is an essential navigational instrument for finding the right direction. Therefore, any book on SOA that gives concrete prescriptions for business componentization and technology implementation must be based on a common understanding of SOA—the concepts, recommendations, and best practices.

But to say that service-oriented architectures are here to solve all of our technical and business problems would be, of course, a gross exaggeration. There are numerous other problems that introduce hurdles for interoperability, compatibility, and well-mannered operation among diverse systems. Furthermore, like any other technological system, SOA deployment requires careful business-case evaluation, planning, design, implementation, and management by a properly skilled and talented team to become a successful endeavor.

This book is about making SOA real in terms of justifying action to gain business value, planning for adoption, and developing good strategies for implementation. It also proposes that even if we assume that there is consensus on methodology within a particular organization, a discussion on the nature of business and technical services within an enterprise is needed. This can help avoid misperceptions and misunderstandings, especially when extended to include a wider audience such as business partners.

Building the business case for a service-oriented architecture is not a simple task. The return on investment, as with all reuse strategies, might not be immediate. Of course, business cases are specific to each environment, and Chapter 2 discusses some of the elements that we have found to be valuable in our experience.

SOA has brought some important business and technical concepts into the spotlight. In particular, the significance of coupling software systems and their degrees of isolation is explored in Chapter 3, "Architecture Elements." We also explore implementation alternatives. These identify the programming models, constructs, patterns, protocols, and even the programming language that will be used in a SOA implementation project.

One of the most critical decisions is to avoid placing the SOA project solely in the hands of an IT department and to foster collaboration with line-of-business representatives to get broad support across the enterprise. We share some ideas for SOA team roles and tasks in Chapter 4, "SOA Project Planning Aspects."

It is worth mentioning that conceptual architectures and frameworks defined by corporate IT might sometimes have a dubious reputation at the business level in many companies; this reputation might need to be counterbalanced when an SOA vision is presented. A common statement heard in our experience is, "We have tried this before. Why do you think it will succeed this time? How do we plan for it this time around?" Therefore, the roadmap to introduce SOA into an enterprise and the governance to ensure true reusability and control cannot be overemphasized. We dedicate an important part of Chapter 4 to these considerations.

In Chapter 5, "Aspects of Analysis and Design," we reflect on the important ideas that carry forward from previous technological eras, and new techniques that apply as business requirements are analyzed and new services identified, specified, and realized. We also discuss the role of modeling for service-oriented systems as they are planned, prototyped, and provisioned.

For effectively leveraging SOA, architectural decisions and solution patterns need to be captured and reused across all enterprise projects for maximum impact. We provide guidance on how to document them in Chapter 6, "Enterprise Solution Assets," and share some sample assets.

Our previous discussion about reach and range for service-oriented architectures was intended to direct attention to a number of non-functional requirements found in SOA deployments. Those aspects are discussed in Chapter 7, "Determining Non-Functional Requirements." The concept of SOA does not deliver all necessary means to tackle these issues, but rather, SOA should be regarded within a broader context of an operating environment for on-demand applications, the general blueprint for modern IT.

One important set of non-functional requirements deserves special consideration: the security risks that services can be exposed to and the malicious acts that an enterprise must defend itself against. Security under service-oriented architectures gains new dimensions, for which we offer thoughts and advice in Chapter 8, "Securing the SOA Environment."

Another complex issue is the need to manage and monitor the operational aspects of an SOA-based services platform. The systems management concepts, the new challenges, and distributed management solutions are covered in Chapter 9, "Managing the SOA Environment." Several supportive technologies are discussed that facilitate 24×7 operations with failure toleration at the enterprise level.

To visualize how an SOA project comes to life, we offer the real-world examples in Chapter 10, "Case Studies in SOA Deployment," to illustrate challenges, approaches, and the lessons learned. Finally, Chapter 11, "Navigating Forward," summarizes the guiding principles of planning SOA projects and takes an advanced look at future directions for this innovative approach.

New technologies for networking, computational and data grids, and autonomic computing very nicely complement service-oriented architectures to cover the range and reach dimension. When thinking of the reach of an SOA in particular, there are many new topics that require solutions.

1.4 Summary

This chapter introduced several popular definitions for SOA. We then categorized and clarified them by identifying which characteristics are desirable.

We then discussed the SOA dimensions of business value, reach and range, maturity and adoption strategies, and we illustrated how each of these impacts the work needed for an SOA deployment. Finally, we gave a working list of topics that should be considered by enterprises navigating toward SOA and shared how we elaborate these topics in this book.

Now that you have a basic understanding of what SOA is, let us look at the reasons why one would leverage it. The next chapter covers the value of building an enterprise ecosystem with an SOA approach based on both technical and business justification.

1.5 References

Crawford, C. H. *Toward an on demand service-oriented architecture.* IBM Systems Journal, Vol. 44, 1-2005. http://www.research.ibm.com/journal/sj44-1.html.

Galbraith, Jay R. *Competing with Flexible Lateral Organizations, 2nd Edition.* Addison Wesley, 1994.

Handy, Charles. *The Age of Unreason.* Random House, 1995.

IBM Business Consulting Services. *The Global CEO Study 2004.* IBM, 2004.

Joseph, J., Ernest, M., and Fellenstein, C. *Evolution of grid computing architecture and grid adoption models.* IBM Systems Journal, Vol. 43, 4-2004. http://www.research.ibm.com/journal/sj43-4.html.

Lawrence, Paul R. and Lorsch, Jay W. *Organization and Environment: Managing Differentiation and Integration.* Harvard Business School Classics, revised edition, 1986. http://harvardbusinessonline.hbsp.harvard.edu/b01/en/common/item_detail.jhtml?id=1295.

Lorsch, Jay W. and Lawrence, Paul R. *Organization Planning.* RD Irwin, 1972.

Chapter 2

Explaining the Business Value of SOA

"Small opportunities are often the beginning of great enterprises."

—Demosthenes

Why do some companies survive and others fail?

Corporations are built on the assumption of continuity; they focus on operations. On the other hand, capital markets are built on the assumption of *discontinuity;* their focus is on creation and destruction. The market encourages rapid and extensive creation and hence greater wealth building. The market is less tolerant than the corporation when underperforming over the long term. Some of the key reasons for failure are ignoring higher-value markets, the inability to address more technologically advanced competition, or competition from lower-cost sources.

Consider the following: In 1917, U.S. Steel led the Forbes list and employed 268,000 people. Now it is down to about 21,000 employees. In the same year, there were eight other steelmakers on the top 100 list and 33 other companies in the business of extracting things out of the earth. About 45% of the list was made up of such resource producers. Today, 61 of these companies no longer exist (a 61% extinction rate).

In 1987, U.S. Steel was still on the list of the 100 most valuable companies, but by that year it was in the beginning of a gradual decline. One by one, over a period of many years, the other natural resource companies slipped off the list. Although it might be slow, change is powerful.

Examination of the S&P 500 presents a similar story. Of the 500 original companies of the S&P 500 in 1957, only 74 remained on the list through 1997, an 85% reduction rate. It is interesting to note that such *driving forces* (see Michael Porter[1] under "References" section) still exist today, but the rate of change has increased. In other words, *companies are going out of business at a faster rate today than they were in 1957*, as correlated by Richard Foster and Sarah Kaplan in *Creative Destruction* (Currency Press, 2001). Foster and Kaplan's book indicates that technological and public-policy shifts have consistently destabilized the market, and it is occurring at an increasing rate.

Despite the dotcom bust and major bankruptcies in the United States, this phenomenon occurs worldwide. For example, the current leading steel manufacturer in Germany, Thyssen, has replaced older, well-known names like Krupp and Hoesch, which disappeared in the last 20 years. This rapid rate of extinction leads to the three core questions that will be discussed in detail in this chapter:

1. How do companies survive over the long term?

2. How can companies effectively execute a business plan that incorporates continuous business transformation?

3. How can companies achieve the greatest possible business agility?

Today, enterprises must be more dynamic than ever to survive. They need new, evolved ways of handling the competition, and their IT infrastructures must support them as they face unique challenges they didn't have to face years ago. We believe SOA is the way that companies can develop IT infrastructures capable of supporting dynamic enterprises. However, to understand SOA, you first need to understand the particular forces of change that now affect businesses.

2.1 The Forces of Change

Most companies today are pressured by customers and shareholders to drive up growth by increasing productivity and squeezing costs out of the operation. However, it can be difficult to maximize efficiency if a company is wedded to rigid, expensive, or proprietary IT systems. It may be very efficient with a proprietary system, which might be optimal if that is all the market requires. However, a rigid and proprietary system has disadvantages in terms of effectiveness, which is what is asked for from an enterprise operating in a quickly changing market. In fact, these days agility is the most valuable thing a company can buy itself as an organization—the flexibility to meet new market demands and to seize opportunities before they are lost or before the competition gets there first.

To increase flexibility, companies need to look at business operations as a collection of interconnected functions—discrete processes and services (checking customer credit

---

1. Professor Michael Porter of Harvard Business School's Institute for Strategy and Competitiveness numerous fundamental concepts in competition theory, which have since become well accepted knowledge and practice for about 20 years now.

information, authenticating users, and so on). Company leadership then needs to decide which of these functions are core to the identity of the business or provide aspects to differentiate the business from its competitors. The nondifferentiating aspects can be streamlined or even outsourced to a partner. If a company can mix and match the differentiated functions on demand, or even on-the-fly, in response to changing business conditions, it can have a tremendous competitive advantage in the marketplace.

This is a powerful idea in itself, but to achieve this degree of flexibility in business operations, companies need an equally flexible IT environment. In our view, this indicates the need for an IT environment that can change on demand to the needs of the business. Service-oriented architecture provides a valuable response to this need for flexibility in business operations by providing the core structure of an on-demand operating IT environment.

Proof of this is reflected in findings from recent surveys such as those published by Forrester Research[2] in January 2004, one of which is shown in Figure 2.1. SOA appears on top of the list in Figure 2.1. Furthermore, recent publications by Gartner Group support its growing importance and predict a predominance of service-oriented solutions like SOA and service-oriented business applications (SOBA). Charles Abrams, director of Gartner Research recently stated, "In 2001, we told you that Web services would be where they are now. Now we're telling you that they aren't done yet. Expect their impact to extend across new architectures beyond SOA, all vendor products, and new business models."[3]

Based on Porter's concept of *driving forces* and following his thoughts on competitive advantage, the IBM Institute for Business Value developed an approach to show how IT and business forces drive enterprises to change their operations (see Figure 2.2). These changes allow them greater flexibility, enabling them not just to stay in business but to demonstrate leadership in a global economy.

These forces have led to two complementary trends for business transformation: enterprise reconstruction and industry deconstruction.

2.1.1 Enterprise Reconstruction

Enterprise reconstruction is a trend within a single company to break open the classical vertical silos that are built up over time to support the various business units into hierarchical structures. This trend emerged because of the necessity to achieve highly efficient performance of repetitive business processes in the enterprise. Vertical silos reflect an efficient enterprise with a fixed set of tasks and defined interactions that allow highly repetitive execution. Although efficient, this clashes with the drive toward more dynamically effective operations. The hierarchical nature of vertical silos often hinders reaction time whenever the enterprise needs to implement new services.

---

2.   A survey by Forrester Research to its members of the Enterprise Architecture Council of the Forrester Oval Program, January 2004.

3.   On the Gartner event in Athens, Greece, March 15, 2005.

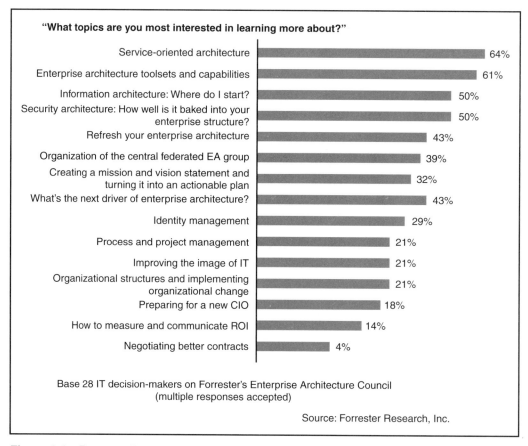

Figure 2.1   Forrester Research, January 2004 survey.

Applying the concept of Porter's value chain to the enterprise shows that horizontal integration maps out the flow of work through the enterprise. As external pressure grows for the business to reorient itself to allow greater customer focus and responsiveness, it has to learn how to display variability and resilience at the same time. This reinforces the trend for enterprise reconstruction.

2.1.2 Industry Deconstruction

While enterprises are busy changing their internal models from vertical silos to horizontally integrated business flows, there is another trend in the industry toward the specialization of businesses according to their core strengths. This specialization lets an enterprise focus mostly on the core of its business. This core business function represents the main expertise, direction, and strategies of the business; it typically also receives the most accolades. Tasks outside the business's core are generally outsourced to third parties to provide the actual

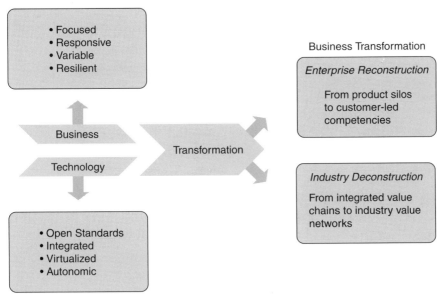

Figure 2.2   IT and business forces force enterprises to become more dynamic.

enablement and delivery. Each of these third parties then focus on improving their own core services. Thus, a network of business partners, each focused on its core competencies and taking advantage of its partners' competencies, together can deliver services to customers in a more flexible and agile manner.

In this way, enterprises in general are moving away from having integrated value chains—a defined set of suppliers and distributors in a sequence of production steps that deliver the end product to the consumer—that are contained wholly within a single enterprise. Instead, they are moving toward new business models with greater cooperation and interaction with their business partners, suppliers, and customers.

2.1.3 The Impact of the Enterprise Reconstruction and Industry Deconstruction Trends

Both of these trends lead to integrated industry networks that are loosely coupled rather than strictly linked together. In this sense, we find a deconstructed industry of services that can be aligned and realigned as needed in a given situation.

This drive toward such a deconstructed, services-aligned industry is self-enforcing; although more services are being offered, these services are better defined and implemented and contribute to a global economy. In addition, there is an interest in outsourcing that will see increasingly stronger competition, not just from larger outsourcing providers but also from niche service providers, facilitated by the standardization of interfaces, service descriptions, and contracts. In the end, a number of general services will become commodity offerings, and efficient players will have to share the market, whereas niche players will have to strengthen their offerings by delivering special benefits to the service consumer.

2.1.4 The Trend Toward Business Components and Services

In most cases, businesses today no longer require a high degree of optimal performance for repetitive processes. Instead, businesses are now measured by their time-to-market and, more significantly, by their reaction to support their customers with flexible, well-suited solutions appropriate to their needs.

Businesses differentiate themselves from competitors by attaching services around their products. These services are increasingly commoditized, which means companies are becoming service providers rather than sellers of products. Just think of how quickly the mobile phone has reached market saturation in many countries. In less than two decades, mobile phones gained a huge share of the population of the developed world, compared to the century it took for land-line telephones to reach similar population sizes.

Customers demand new and more integrated solutions and even more for services around these commodity products. All of these trends bring us back to the question of how SOA can address the needs of companies that face the challenge of transitioning from product-oriented businesses to service-oriented businesses.

2.2 Common Questions About SOA

First let's get to the most basic questions about SOA. To help a business executive understand the value of changing the enterprise's IT infrastructure into a service-oriented architecture, the following questions deserve convincing responses:

1. What is SOA?
2. Why do companies need SOA?
3. What benefits will businesses receive if they implement SOA?
4. What opportunities will companies miss if they don't implement SOA?
5. What is different with SOA compared to previous approaches?

The following sections attempt to provide answers to these questions. We don't provide a prescriptive method; instead, we attempt to highlight the current perspectives from both the business and IT viewpoints. Further, in this book we look in more detail at the conditions for an SOA project (see Chapter 4, "SOA Project Planning Aspects"), and we consider a more formal approach to the modeling of services and common semantics (Chapter 5, "Aspects of Analysis and Design").

2.2.1 What Is SOA?

Chapter 1, "Introducing SOA," adequately provided a technical as well as a business definition of service-oriented architecture. In summary, from the business viewpoint, SOA is a set of business, process, organizational, governance, and technical methods to enable an agile, business-driven IT environment for greater competitive advantage. It provides the flexibility to treat business processes as well as the underlying IT infrastructure as components that can be reused and recombined to address changing business priorities. Thus, in essence, SOA is the map that guides you down the road to competitive advantage.

2.2.2 Why Do Companies Need SOA?

The combination of SOA and Web services is in some ways being marketed as the silver bullet that companies have been looking for to magically solve all business issues of today. There are valid doubts about such claims, which certainly never will come true. Many business issues are not just solved by a specific IT architecture or a certain approach to making business decisions. As long as people are involved, errors are still likely to occur. However, with a foundational architecture like SOA, you can expect to do the following:

- Realize the long-promised potential of utilizing IT to extensively accelerate or improve business
- Justify IT expenses and capital outlays
- Provide nontechnical people with a clear understanding of what IT does, how they do it, and their intrinsic value

Projects that study the possibility for using SOA and its related technologies and methods (see Chapter 5) are of great help to do the following:

- Determine a company's core competencies
- Identify an outsourcing strategy
- Define a plan to reduce the complexity (such as cost) of the company's shared IT infrastructure needs with its trading partner community

From a technical perspective, it is easy to see how the claims of SOA can be realized. With SOA and Web services, incompatible computer systems can communicate without the previous technical complexity or high cost of maintenance. SOA can help attain business agility through the reuse of a company's current IT assets and integrated processes. Finally, SOA makes it easier to create a more direct, measurable association between business assets and services, and IT assets and services.

2.2.3 What Benefits Will Businesses Receive if They Implement SOA?

At a very high level, the answers to the question of what benefits companies receive through an SOA implementation are as follows:

- It saves money, time, and effort over the long term through reuse of "components" and because of the flexibility of SOA.
- It eliminates frustrations with IT through flexible solutions and shorter times to deployment.
- It justifies IT investments more clearly through the closer association of IT to business services.

- It provides business executives with a clear understanding of what IT does and its value.
- It allows the creation of and changes to services incrementally rather than leaving a guesstimate of the development costs, thereby eliminating the classic IT 6-6 answer: "The project will take 6 months and cost 6 figures."
- It provides a business and competitive differentiator, with direct rationalization and relation to how that competitive advantage is implemented in IT.

Other technologies have made these same claims. However, many business leaders, analysts, and technical leaders agree that, with SOA, we have a different situation that validates this in reality. Chapter 10, "Case Studies in SOA Deployment," offers lessons learned from real projects that support these claims.

2.2.4 What Opportunities Will Companies Miss if They Don't Implement SOA?

Implementing business-driven IT with SOA promises to simplify and accelerate business transactions. Therefore, the agility and flexibility options of an SOA allow organizations to better handle business situations like the following:

- Department, intracompany, or intercompany mergers
- Acquisition
- Divestiture
- Product or service rollouts
- Business partner, customer, or supplier changes
- Geographical expansion
- Competitive gains in market share

2.2.5 What Is Different with SOA Compared to Previous Approaches?

SOA is not a new idea. Solutions have been built according to SOA principles for at least a decade, although they have usually been implemented in proprietary (expensive) ways. Although SOA-like solutions have been possible on a departmental or multidepartmental scale, it became extremely difficult to scale these solutions across large enterprises and across multiple companies and partners.

So what's so different now?

Previous SOA-based solutions have a history of successful implementation. Even with their high costs, they still provide economic value and functional flexibility in a company. The principles of SOA can be successfully put together for a single organization or even a few select partners through careful coordination. Software vendors have even tried to establish communities of partners built around their application offerings. However, making this possible on a wide scale in the industry requires well-defined and cross-platform standards implemented in the software offerings of many vendors. The reason the term "SOA" has become so prevalent now is due to the rise of new technologies that make SOA-based solutions much more cost efficient and productive to implement.

This new standard technology is a result of Web services. Open Web services standards are important because they break down the proprietary barriers between vendors and software programs. This is demonstrated by the commitments of major vendors, such as BEA, IBM, Oracle, SAP, and Microsoft, to standardize their respective hardware and software, allowing the sharing of information and data.

2.2.6 Rethinking Components for Business and Applications

As noted previously, the premise of SOA that makes its claims possible is the concept of reusable components. Components are the discrete business processes and services that make up a business. An SOA makes it possible to continually reuse components. Think of it as a mosaic of individual, functional components that can be arranged and rearranged. A company that follows the concept of SOA can build, deploy, integrate, and link applications and heterogeneous systems and platforms together across the organization.

SOA has yet to reach its full potential. Most applications today are still integrated with custom-developed code—they're hardwired, if you will—making it slow, difficult, and costly to rearrange the pieces in the mosaic. What everyone has been waiting for is a way to standardize the *connections* among all those components so that they work the same way everywhere without requiring additional, customized programming, which is costly and can prevent reuse.

The common components and information utilized by and derived from business processes can be reused multiple times in an SOA to give the customer varying experiences. For example, a piece of software is now represented as a service, matching any business component you can identify. This is illustrated in Figure 2.3. In this sense, business services can now be more accurately reflected in coded software.

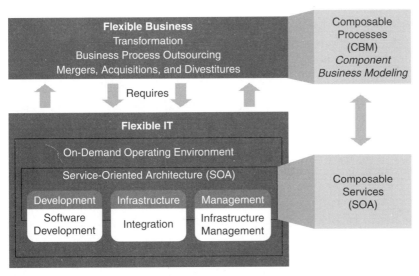

Figure 2.3   Business components interacting with IT components.

To make it possible to rearrange and compose components, your IT systems need to satisfy a number of criteria, mainly an agreed upon set of standards and rules that need to be in place. These include the following:

- *Standards:* Web services for implementation and enterprise, and respective industry standards that apply to the business side; this includes, for example, industry services models as shown in Chapter 5.
- *A common roadmap:* Acts as the master plan to guide your enterprise to a successfully changed and agile business as outlined in Chapter 4.
- *Common information model and industry semantics:* This is necessary to avoid ambiguities and to support understanding between all involved parties (see Chapter 5).
- *Strong governance processes:* Prevents your loosely coupled systems from degrading into anarchy (see Chapter 4).
- *Flexible business processes:* Based on dynamic business process modeling approaches, backed by appropriate methods and tools (see Chapter 5).
- *Business transformation and openness for change as a base:* Changing a business involves changing not just the system but also the people involved, including those on the IT and business ends.

2.2.7 When Not to Implement an SOA

In certain cases, it is better not to implement an SOA because it is not a suitable solution. As with all approaches, there is no one-size-fits-all with SOA. ZapThink.com senior analyst Jason Bloomberg explains, "When Not to Use an SOA"[4]:

- *When you have a homogeneous IT environment.* Theoretically, you might still need an SOA if you want to consider opening services to an external environment.
- *When true real-time performance is absolutely critical,* such as at telephone switches or in other situations that require nanosecond response times. Though as hardware and networks develop, you might find SOA-based solutions here as well.
- *When flexibility is not needed,* such as if the processes of the business are already direct and uncomplicated and do not need change. If there already exist optimized commodity processes, then the organization may not benefit from changing to an SOA.
- *When tight coupling is needed,* such as within a cohesive component or application.
- *If the organization isn't ready for it.* SOA is typically a cross-organization effort. It is rarely likely to deliver immediate business benefits for a single line of business application, such as order entry for standardized products.

---

4. Jason Bloomberg, "When Not to Use an SOA," http://www.zapthink.com/report.html?id=ZAPFLASH-02162004. Jason Bloomberg is a senior analyst at ZapThink LLC in Waltham, Massachusetts.

2.3 SOA Value Roadmap

This section builds a roadmap for how to reach the expected benefits and value of SOA. It describes an approach for how to explain the business value of SOA in nontechnical terms. Superiors in management will likely ask architects to summarize the values of SOA to them.

We also provide a checklist that shows the business issues you need to cover along with suggested approaches for explaining each issue. The checklist lays out the logical business arguments that will paint a full picture of the value of SOA. It starts by examining the business fundamentals of architecture, and it then works through process issues and services (or incremental delivery). This education yields an SOA business value package.

2.3.1 Explaining SOA to Business People

One of the keys to flexible business processes depends on close interaction between the IT department and the business units. This partnership is an absolute necessity for a successful SOA implementation. Currently, in most organizations, after a new business need is identified, the business operations team usually contracts the IT department to build an appropriate application that satisfies the need. Business management does not really care to know the details of how the application is built.

Similarly, the IT department builds the application only to the specifications provided and does not really look too much further into how this impacts the business. Essentially, both sides stay within their own domains, with a wall over which the business operations group throws a project to the IT group, and IT responds with a technical solution. In general, this builds too shallow of a view and understanding across the groups and, therefore, too shallow of a collaborative development process.

The IT industry has long talked about alignment and partnership with the long-term and in-depth needs of the business side, but with such limited collaborations, IT departments have been largely unsuccessful in having strategic impact on their business counterparts. Therefore, it is imperative to find a way to get the two groups cooperating in deeper relationships with each other so that they can better respect and understand the needs of the other.

Hence, educating people on the many business benefits inherent in an SOA is the first step in solidifying an active working covenant between IT and business groups. This relationship is, after all, the foundation from which all else in SOA can be built. As we show in Chapter 5, there are distinct layers of services abstractions from enterprise business components to application components. Keeping the relationships between the layers means providing a base for communication between the various levels on the business and IT sides. Chapter 4 contains a more detailed discussion about the roles involved in changing business and IT toward an SOA.

2.3.2 A Checklist for Business Change Agility

The checklist in this section shows you how to develop a business understanding of SOA. These seven steps should help you explain the technical, operational, and functional underpinnings of SOA, which are explained in greater detail in following subsections:

1. First *unravel the concept of architecture* from its perceived technical underpinnings and explain the business realities of this necessary business function (see Section 2.3.2.1).

2. *Clarify the architect's role* in providing architectural function crucial to business success (see Section 2.3.2.2).

3. Explain why it is better to *realign IT elements around service definitions* or business processes (see Section 2.3.2.3).

4. Emphasize the need to *build an in-depth IT-to-business group dialogue* that leads to a meaningful, constructive, respectful, and regularly engaged relationship between IT and the company's business units (see Section 2.3.2.4).

5. Show how service orientation will *create a digital model of the business* using a top-down approach (see Section 2.3.2.5).

6. Describe how *IT can align with the business via processes and metrics* (see Section 2.3.2.6).

7. Show that *IT can align with business via incremental delivery* (see Section 2.3.2.7).

2.3.2.1 Unraveling the Concept of Architecture

An identifying characteristic of an SOA is that it is a style of IT architecture. Although this might be stating the obvious, the point is to remember that an SOA has all the qualities, demands, and risks inherent in any type of architecture. People are most likely to associate the word "architecture" with a technical connotation. An architect must challenge this view by explaining the importance of architecture to the business and the need to understand architecture from the perspective of a business benefit.

Architecture at a Glance

Architecture involves investment in process, technology, and interface standards. Its purpose is to improve an organization's capabilities by maximizing business agility and reducing the cost of IT development and operations.

The benefits of architectural investments span many projects, not all of which may be foreseen at the time of the original investment. This notion of architecture helps us understand what architects do and many of the challenges they face. Several observations are significant here, as they relate to architecture in general and SOA in particular:

- *Architecture is not a specific set of tasks or skills* because every organization will achieve its architectural goals in different ways. The goal of the architecture group is to select and implement the most effective investments in standards, procedures, technologies, and interfaces to support the organization's *business* goals and *business* processes. The architecture group's deliverables will depend on the types of investments that are most appropriate, given those business goals. This requires the architects to be familiar with business language, issues, and context in order to provide that bridge.
- *Architecture is an investment principle,* as it indicates that you should plan ahead and think through the resulting solution during the early phases of the project.
- *Architecture is a risk.* Not all architectural ideas can be realized as envisioned. There are unpredictable circumstances that can force amendments to a chosen architecture, which may cause higher costs or take away the benefits associated with an architecture style.
- *Architects can never predict all the applications and systems that will use the architecture they create.* Increasingly, the goal of architecture is to support general, organizational business directions rather than specific, planned projects. Architecture is, therefore, a risk. Architects assume that if everyone (or at least a large portion of the organization) follows the architectural rules, there will be future benefits (productivity cost savings, business agility, or reduced time to market, for example). They hope that their architectural plan will continue to have value in the long term, even for projects that were not envisaged at the time they created the plan. The number and type of assumptions that an architect can make will be constrained by many factors, especially the organization's attitude toward risk and how much the architect knows or can guess about the future. The only way architects can have any hope of predicting future requirements is if they are fully engaged with the direction of the business. We emphasize the architect's role, as the understanding of technical implications requires a different way of thinking than that for business.
- *Architecture is a set of constraints.* It is about achieving what is best for the majority. Individual projects and programs need to follow the architectural constraints to allow the whole organization to benefit, despite any individual inconveniences. Organizations that do not have a clear concept of what constitutes the common good cannot implement wide-ranging architectures. Tension is inevitable because it is unlikely that any architecture (set of constraints) will be appropriate for the entire organization; therefore, a conflict-resolution process (governance) must be part of architecture. Conflict resolution will be next to impossible without the architect becoming fully engaged with business management. Business needs impose restrictions and constraints; they also define the service levels required from the IT systems which the architect needs to plan for. To decide on priorities, possible solutions, and compromises, a strong interlock is needed.
- *Architecture is an organic process, not a static document.* Architecture evolves in response to changes in the organization's business goals and the available technologies.

- *The goal of an architectural plan must be articulated.* An architectural plan intended to minimize cost of ownership is not the same as one intended to minimize time to market or to maximize business agility.
- *Architecture is hard to cost justify* because it depends on making bets and assumptions. The true value of architecture is often only proved retrospectively. If system development and operations are cost effective and the organization's business goals can be satisfied easily, then the architecture was well designed and executed. In practice, organizations get the architecture that they can cost justify, which is not always the architecture that will be most beneficial from a business perspective. However, an SOA implementation has the inherent quality of tying IT costs to specific business processes, which are tied to specific business measurements.
- *Architectures are seldom universal.* Different parts of the organization will have different goals and may need different architectures to support them. Any architectural deliverable needs to be scoped; "one size fits all" architectures are seldom successful. For example, a common goal of architecture in areas such as mainframe applications is to promote quality and low cost of ownership. The goal of architecture in fast-moving businesses is usually to promote time to market with acceptably low risk. There is generally a trade-off between the depth and the breadth of architectural investments.

As indicated, architecture is a rather pragmatic approach that needs to adapt to always new and different facts and demands. Nevertheless, there are well-defined principles and concepts that architects apply in their roles to a broad ranging multitude of tasks.

2.3.2.2 Clarifying the Architect's Role

Architects are responsible for a myriad of tasks related to managing the business processes of developing, deploying, and maintaining the architecture. Although the architect's role is crucial to a company's success, it is often rarely noticed or evident to the business people. In the SOA world, architects need to change and expand their knowledge of the business processes of the company, turning themselves into the bridge between IT and the business groups.

Educating people on these changes requires an understanding of an architect's current, non-SOA responsibilities, as it lays the groundwork to elaborate on the expansion of the business duties the architect assumes in a new SOA environment. In fact, SOA architects will need to work so closely with their business groups that you might as well regard them as *super business analysts*.

The following are current tasks of an architect that contribute to business success:

- *Identifying potential architectural investments and cost justifying them.* This requires architects to seek information from their technology and business associates to identify which architectural investments are appropriate.

- *Communicating the architecture and maintenance process to its users and supporting users of the architecture.* This might involve training, publications, Web sites, groupware tools, hotline support, internal consulting, or competency centers, so-called "centers of excellence" (For details, see Chapter 4's section on governance considerations.)
- *Road map management.* Few organizations have the luxury of starting from a blank sheet of paper when defining architectures. In practice, most architecture groups maintain a roadmap that documents the current physical architecture and the desired target architecture, defining how one is to evolve into the other.
- *Conflict resolution and exception handling.* Conflicts between the goals of individual projects and the goals of the organization are inherent in architectures. The absence of conflict might be a danger sign that either the architect is being ignored or there are unsatisfied opportunities for standardization. Exceptions are sometimes required and should be handled by a defined process. The nature of service-oriented architectures allows less strict development efforts that can give rise to such conflicts; these should be detected and resolved early in the project.
- *Deploying the architecture.* Most architectural deliverables are implemented by a process of communication, training, and mentoring. In the SOA world, these deliverables will mirror the company's business processes.
- *Monitoring the effectiveness of the architecture and encouraging or enforcing compliance.* To achieve the SOA goal of business agility, it is imperative that architects regularly consult with the business members of the team.

As enterprises drive toward greater integration across regions, lines of business, and departments, architecture will be increasingly important to the success of organizations and will be recognized as a valuable discipline. A clear definition of the business goals of architecture and the roles of architects is a necessary component of an architecture function.

2.3.2.3 Realigning IT Around Services

To make businesses more responsive to change, business interactions must be represented as services, with individual elements of business functionality performed by IT applications. Three benefits result from this:

- *Loyal customers.* Customers have strong incentives for loyalty when you increase their efficiency and effectiveness. As you more deeply intertwine their processes with yours, you prevent them from going elsewhere.
- *Efficient suppliers.* When you increase your suppliers' efficiency, you can press them for lower prices and offer better prices to your customers while also driving down process cycle time.
- *Lean businesses.* Through flexible outsourcing, your process can seamlessly incorporate value-added features provided by outsourced suppliers. You might even remove steps from your customers' side of the process by integrating some of their other suppliers into your side of the process.

A company can approach business agility deliberately by focusing narrowly on Web services, and this is fine for just a limited number of business interactions. However, services are just the start of a much higher-level vision of business value—the overall responsive, optimized business.

The strategic approach uses Web services to build flexibility end to end across internally and externally connected applications. Incrementally, business services become the core IT deliverable, enabling IT to more readily deliver value.

An aggressive and strategic approach to services will deeply restructure and realign IT around service design and delivery. In other words, IT becomes a *service-oriented business unit*. From planning and requirements through project scoping, design, creation, deployment, and governance, IT work will then revolve around services.

2.3.2.4 IT-to-Business Services Alignment

An improved relationship between IT and business units, coupled with the incremental delivery of business processes via services, allows the "compound growth" of business benefits; one improvement builds on another. This combination can produce some powerful results:

- *Faster response to customer priorities and shifting markets.* As competition, customer demand, and regulatory forces shift the market and drive change to business processes, a company with a well-defined and relatively developed inventory of services is able to more quickly reconfigure its applications to incorporate new and evolved business requirements because there is a high likelihood that a needed service is already available.
- *Faster delivery of business change, both internally and externally.* Aside from customer- and market-driven changes, services can also accelerate internally driven change.
- *Higher end-to-end process value.* When IT responds quickly to internal and external change, the business is encouraged to continually pursue process optimization. When a company continually adds one process improvement on top of another, the cumulative impact can be huge (lower cost, faster cycle time, and better business results).
- *Reduced cost of change.* Besides handling change faster with services, IT can also deliver changes at a lower cost, which further encourages the business to pursue continual process optimization.

Rule of Thumb

When services align with business process steps, they can be changed incrementally as processes change so that IT becomes less of a drag on business change.

2.3.2.5 Creating the Digital Model of the Business

To appreciate the huge impact that services can have, you need to look at what happens over the long term as application delivery efforts adopt a service-oriented model. Over time, as each project builds on and extends the available body of services, it creates a digital representation of the physical world's business processes. In other words, you create a digital model of the business. Chapter 5 provides a closer look at how this digital model of the business can be achieved.

This occurs as a result of the following factors:

- *Businesses deliver services via business processes.* A simple but important starting point is to recognize that every company puts business strategy into action at a business-process level. Through either well-defined, measured processes (such as a manufacturing production line) or uncontrolled, ad hoc processes (such as a special project to brainstorm new market opportunities), business processes are the way things get done.

- *Business processes tie to business measurements.* Critical business metrics reflect either the operation of a business process or the results of the process. They measure the cost and cycle time of a process, such as the work effort, resources, and elapsed time required in converting a lead into a closed sale. Alternatively, they measure what the process produces, such as total or average sales. Furthermore, metrics tie to steps in a business process, as in the number of cold calls that turn into prospects or the total sales coming out of the last step in the sales process.

- *Business process steps are delivered via IT applications.* IT delivers all of its solutions— any application or any infrastructure element—to meet the needs of one or more business processes. Specifically, there are places within any business process where process steps interact with IT assets to capture, transform, or report business data. As with processes, it may be structured, defined data, such as a new order, or unstructured, ad hoc data, such as an e-mail. These interactions are the moments where IT value is delivered to the business.

- *Business process steps must align with the needs of business services.* Within a business process, each interaction with an IT asset is a potential place for a service. If the interface between the process step and the IT asset is framed in terms of the purpose of the process step, and if the interface is open to being invoked through multiple interaction channels (such as a Web application, desktop application, Web services, interactive voice response, and so on), the IT asset is a business service. Because a business service directly serves the purpose of a process step, it is, in effect, a digital representation of the process step. Furthermore, a service provides important flexibility for a process step because, no matter how the interaction channel of the step might change, the service maintains consistent operation of the process step through its encapsulation of the relevant business rules.

When this sequence occurs properly, the individual services model the steps of the business process, building up an inventory of services. Thus, you can appreciatively develop a digital model of your business from this sequence.

As the business changes—as you create new process steps and optimize existing steps by changing who does what and when they do it—many of the underlying services become stable, and the only need for change is in the method of access. Likewise, many new business initiatives can easily leverage the existing inventory of services.

The digital model provides a structure to collect, examine, and align business and IT metrics. The pattern, volume, and content of interactions flowing through your services offer insight for measurement of business process efficiency and results. In addition, services provide a place to allocate IT development, infrastructure, and management costs, providing for additional correlation between IT costs and business process results.

2.3.2.6 Aligning IT with Business Processes and Metrics

As discussed previously—building on the basis of modeling units of business operation—services foster a change in the relationship dynamics between IT and business. IT has long talked about alignment and partnership with the business, but with limited ability to talk in business terms, it has made little impact on business operations. With a strategic approach to services, IT has a chance to change this. In the following paragraphs, we discuss how it can be done.

When the IT unit of an enterprise understands that services allow them to create a digital model of the business, the unit might realize that the proper design of services requires an understanding of the business processes for which the services will be deployed. As the IT organization investigates the possible choices in designing a service, it must deepen its knowledge of relevant process steps and use the business process context to set the scope and semantics of each service.

At this point, IT has a critical choice. It can stay in the role of simply implementing a given set of specifications sent by the business units, whereupon it will go with the process steps as laid out by those units and simply design services to match without really questioning why they are necessary. However, when IT takes the strategic approach to services, it can investigate the process more deeply, looking for opportunities to optimize service value.

To achieve this, IT architects need to be able to converse with the business units in terms of business benefits. Therefore, the IT organization should seek to understand process metrics and examine the impact of different service design approaches on these metrics. Such metrics can be applied by calculating the value of reusable assets and templates used to create services, or via other means of measuring productivity. The componentization of the business and corresponding IT services allows a much more precise metric for implementing solutions than a large project plan, stretching an expanse of time and involving costly development crews in maintaining complex systems.

Doing so expands the view from a focus on pure application delivery to one of business results:

1. Which service design alternatives will yield the greatest business impact?

2. Which alternatives will provide the most positive results for customers and partners?

3. Could alternate interaction channels further improve these results?

4. Could a service incorporate multiple steps, automating interim steps and thereby improving results?

The answers lie in understanding how the various options will affect business metrics. This is a difficult and crucial step in the transition to service-oriented IT. The business might well disdain the IT organization questioning as an intrusion that slows the application-delivery process or because it exposes the business as having no relevant metrics. IT staff might prefer to sit tight in the comfortable role of only taking orders. Learning the vagaries of business processes is an unfamiliar and difficult task, and many techies will view it as extra work that is of little value and even less interest to them.

However, it is not necessary for all IT staff to tackle business processes, rather only enough to make the translation to service design and implementation. Initial business objections can be overcome by stressing the IT organization's need to understand and design toward the intended business value.

For example, the IT group can evaluate the key issues facing the business, such as the following:

1. What are the primary pain points in the process?

2. Where are the weaknesses of the process?

3. How do process volumes vary with business activity?

4. What data would facilitate smarter or faster decisions at any given step in the process?

In pursuing these types of questions, the IT organization can combine its new, deeper understanding of processes with its knowledge of technology and existing applications to offer a fresh perspective on possible solutions. It can then frame its suggestions in concrete terms describing the potential impact on specific metrics, processes, and process steps. Rather than suggesting technical options and expecting the business to translate, it can bring to attention operational suggestions in business terms. This allows the IT organization to take a major step toward having strategic business impact, and if they play their cards right, the mysteries of technology implementation can be elevated into a collaborative business design process.

The improved understanding of business operations is of significant benefit, but the chain of possibilities extends even further. With a business and IT partnership for business design, the IT organization has a bold chance to put its money where its mouth is by measuring its own performance, in part on the actual improvements in business results delivered by IT projects.

Typically, the way IT is measured today—mostly by delivering on spec, on time, and on budget—is only as good as far as the lengths it goes to provide solutions. You can be successful and still miss the underlying purpose: improving business results. To be accurate, the business unit still retains primary responsibility for its business results, but if the IT organization has a stake in the game, it can promote a change in the unit's thinking and give the organization a justified basis for raising questions and issues regarding the business value of a project.

We are aware that many in an IT department will resist such a change due to the fear of stricter control, loss of freedom, and the like. The change of focus from solving technical issues to thinking about the business value might be perceived as a watering down of the traditional development process. Therefore, a good starting point is to close the loop on preproject justifications—as many firms fail to do—and publish visible results of postproject value audits.

IT needs new skills for the transformation toward service orientation. Inserting pure techies into business discussions would probably not result in a stronger connection with the business. Neither will adding a project manager to nail down dates, scope, and commitments help to create that connection. Creating a partnership with the business requires a quick study on who can win business trust by showing keen insight into business issues and clear advocacy for the business. Some of these lessons learned are outlined in Chapter 10.

It takes a focused combination of business knowledge, creative thinking, relationship skills, and technology savvy to build and sustain a business partnership. A company might have to look outside itself for such skills, whereas a larger, comprehensive, and experienced service provider can be of assistance at the center of both business design and IT delivery.

2.3.2.7 Aligning IT with Business via Incremental Delivery

Beyond the IT-to-business alignment based on business design, the digital model aspect of services fosters an alignment toward the implementation of business change. An IT project backlog can become an embarrassment to the IT department and a sore spot for the business. Worse, the IT side might deliver a new application only to find that the business process can only take advantage of a subset of the full design—in other words, the business process was not planned comprehensively in schedule with the deployment of new applications.

When business operations and IT are closely cooperating on design, it is easier to clearly define the change that must occur on both sides to achieve the intended value. In the new SOA model, business and IT collaboratively plan for coordinated, incremental change because of the following:

- *Massive business process change is too risky.* Business process change is difficult. People have to break old routines and learn new ones. Managers must learn to operate and optimize new metrics. Training and reference resources have to change. Each change introduces risk, and the risk compounds for attempts at massive process change.
- *Business changes most effectively in increments toward a vision.* Big change is sometimes necessary, with mergers and acquisitions being a major case in point. However, you can move toward a vision of big change in small chunks that the business can more easily digest. It is easier and less risky to implement smaller changes, plus you can learn from one set of changes to build smarter on the next set.

- *Process impact drives project prioritization.* Measuring and prioritizing business change based on the expected improvements in process results focuses discussion where it should be: on the facts and analysis of options for business change, not on perceptions and emotions about pet projects.
- *Services change in alignment with the business.* With a prioritized list of process changes, IT can focus more narrowly on just the services and interaction channels needed for high-priority changes. IT can incrementally develop, deploy, and manage a targeted set of services while the business is planning and preparing to implement associated process changes. The result is that they come much closer to the goal of changing at the speed of business. With IT and the business operations aligned on delivery timing, there might still be a backlog of ideas for change, but they are likely to be on the backlog of both units.

2.4 The Nine Business Rules of Thumb for SOAs

The knowledge from the SOA business value roadmap can be condensed into the following rules of thumb that we have learned from various projects across many industries:

Rule of Thumb

Rule of Thumb 1: SOA Benefits
There are many business and technical benefits to an SOA, but none is as important as the capability for a company to respond quickly and effectively to business change and to leverage that change to gain a competitive advantage.

Rule of Thumb 2: IT and Business as Peers
You cannot build a successful SOA model if you cannot forge peer working relationships between the IT and business groups.

Rule of Thumb 3: Incremental Business Services
In an agile business, incremental business services that mirror business process steps become the core deliverables of the IT group.

Rule of Thumb 4: Business-Smart IT Architects
Business-aware IT architects are the bridge between the company's IT and business units.

Rule of Thumb 5: Opportunities for Services
Within a business process, each interaction with an IT asset is a potential location for a service.

---

continues

> **Rule of Thumb 6: Measuring Services**
> A service that mirrors and executes a business process can be used to allocate IT costs and provide IT justification by correlating the IT costs with business process results.
>
> **Rule of Thumb 7: Service-Oriented Means in the Core**
> Companies committed to SOA will find business processes and services at the center of both business design and IT delivery.
>
> **Rule of Thumb 8: Proving Business Value of SOA**
> A company's SOA gives IT a definitive way to prove business value through business results measurements.
>
> **Rule of Thumb 9: Competitive Business Agility**
> When a change in business process no longer requires a change to application programming logic (that is, when you have a successful SOA), your company has attained competitive business agility.

2.5 Summary

As we have shown, the forces of change, enterprise reconstruction, and industry deconstruction have led to a trend toward business componentization and the use of business services. This trend requires organizations to develop agility to change their businesses as needed by their current environment. The implications and benefits of implementing SOAs have led organizations to rethink the business model toward creating reusable components that link business processes to technical services and applications.

The use of SOA is strongly dependent on a true partnership between the IT and business units of an organization in order to achieve business-change agility. As indicated in our checklist, there are seven decision and operational steps toward achieving this agility, finally leading to our rules of thumb in Section 2.4. Without an SOA, the larger concept of building an agile, on-demand enterprise is not feasible. With these business decisions in mind, we will follow with the technical concepts for service-oriented architectures in an on-demand environment that an IT organization needs to understand and take to heart.

2.6 References

Arsanjani, A. *Empowering the business analyst for on demand computing.* IBM Systems Journal, Vol. 44, 1-2005. http://www.research.ibm.com/journal/sj44-1.html.

Bloomberg, J. *Growing an Agile Service-Oriented Architecture.* ZapThink, September 2003.

Bloomberg, J. *When Not to Use an SOA*. ZapThink, April 2005. http://www.zapthink.com/report.html?id=ZAPFLASH-02162004.

Cecere, M. *IT Trends 2004: Organizational Design*. Forrester Research, February 2004.

David, Fred R. *Strategic Managemen— Concepts and Cases, 7*th *Edition*. Prentice-Hall, 1999.

Foster, Richard and Kaplan, Sarah. *Creative Destruction: Why Companies That Are Built to Last Underperform the Market—And How to Successfully Transform Them*, Random House, 2001.

Galbraith, Jay R. *Designing the Global Corporation*. Jossey-Bass, 2000.

Gilpin, M. *Managing the Business Service Model*. Forrester Research, April 2004.

Haeckel, S. H. *Leading on demand businesses—Executives as architects*. IBM Systems Journal, Vol. 42, 3-2003. http://www.research.ibm.com/journal/sj42-3.html.

Kotter, John P. *The Heart of Change*. Havard Business School Press, 2002.

Langel, R. *Business Value of SOA*. IBM Whitepaper, 2004. http://www-306.ibm.com/software/solutions/webservices/eis/businessvaluesoa.html.

Leganza, G. *Managing Emerging Technology: Pearls from the EA Council*. Forrester Research, March 2004. Forrester Oval Program: http://www.forrester.com/Oval/Index.

Marks, Eric A. and Werrell, Mark J. *Executive Guide to Web Services*, Wiley, 2003.

Moore, Geoffrey A. *Inside the Tornado*. Harper Perennial, New York, 1999.

Porter, Michael. *Competitive Advantage: Creating and Sustaining Superior Performance*, Free Press, 1985.

Porter, Michael. *Competitive Strategy: Techniques for Analyzing Industries and Competitors,* Free Press, 1980

Rutledge, K. (ed.). *The Business Case for e-business*. IBM Press, 2005.

Shi, D. and Daniels, R.I. *A survey of manufacturing flexibility: Implications for e-business flexibility*. IBM Systems Journal, Vol. 42, 3-2003. http://www.research.ibm.com/journal/sj42-3.html.

Taylor, B., Stiles, P., and Tampoe, M. "Governance and Performance: The Future for the Board." Strategic Dynamics, Henley Management College, 2001.

Chapter 3

Architecture Elements

> *"Architecture is the learned game, correct and magnificent, of forms assembled in the light."*
>
> —*Le Corbusier*

The main purpose of a service-oriented architecture (SOA) is to offer synergy between the business and IT groups in an organization and to offer the organization greater flexibility, as described in the preceding chapter. This chapter provides more detailed architectural perspectives and models for SOA architects and implementers.

As the title of this chapter implies, architects must examine different elements of an SOA design. The first aspect is the impact of the characteristics of an SOA—the set of implications of service componentization, the reuse of those components from variable requesters, and the capability to compose those services in business processes. The second aspect involves the various architecture domains where services can exist and the functions they provide. The characteristics define how the domains interact with each other.

Figure 3.1 presents a map that includes both aspects of SOA. In this map, the first aspect influences the relationships between the domains, as indicated by the arrows in the diagram. The domains in the rounded rectangles are, of course, the second aspect. These characteristics, which we cover in depth in Section 3.1, include how those relationships are influenced by the following factors detailed in the same section:

- Platform
- Location
- Protocols
- Programming language
- Invocation patterns

- Security
- Service versioning
- Service model
- Information model
- Data format

Enterprise services share some or all of these characteristics that impact what actions the service performs, how it does so, and whom it interacts with. These services can be reclassified in the SOA model and placed into new domains that describe what function they perform in the overall model. An analysis of the preceding list identifies at least four different domains of architecture, along with subdomains that influence where a service can

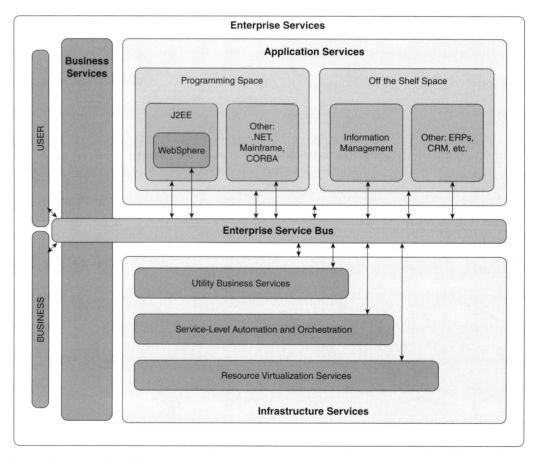

Figure 3.1   The domains of SOA.

exist and the function it performs. These domains and subdomains, discussed later in this chapter, are as follows:

- Infrastructure services domain with subdomains
  - Utility business services
  - Service-level automation and orchestration
  - Resource virtualization
- Middleware domain
- Business services domain
- Application services domain with subdomains
  - Application programming model subdomain
  - Off-the-shelf commercial software subdomain
  - Information management subdomain

It is essential to maintain a separation of concerns and domains. In an enterprise, these domains can have separate implementations using any permutation of packaged applications, custom applications, existing infrastructure, and external or outsourced services.

3.1 Refining SOA Characteristics

Creating reusable service components is just like building the components for a hi-fi stereo system to play music. The music components industry has progressed to a point of near ubiquity. Without knowing the technology inside each component, you can safely buy and plug together a set of components that comes from different technological concepts, manufacturers, resellers, retail outlets, and even regions of the world. To further illustrate this point, you can even take a more modern component such as a Super Audio CD player, plug it into a decades-old amplifier, and still make it work. This type of loose coupling, reusability, and flexibility is made possible by the support for common standards for both signal technical characteristics and content.

Similarly, in an SOA environment, the service component providers might not always know exactly what form the requesters will take at the time a service is created. The requesters, in turn, should not have to care about the technology behind the service implementation.

The degree of flexibility and reusability of the SOA will depend on the enterprise business model and context in use. This will drive the degree of coupling or decoupling that the architecture will need to implement.

The following characteristics address the degrees of flexibility that will affect your architecture decisions and the variability of the system you create.

3.1.1 Platform

The platform used to support a service implementation should not be relevant to consumers. This includes the intermediary layers of the operating system, the communication protocol, and perhaps even application layers. If two systems interact through interoperable protocols, such as SOAP, HTTP, or messaging middleware, each side usually does not need to consider the hardware, operating system, or server platform supporting each. Either side is free to change some or all of these aspects without really affecting the other.

However, if your target architecture for a given business model has the requesters' and providers' platforms under your direct control, you may be able to gain significant advantages in performance and system management by not separating this aspect of the architecture.

3.1.2 Location

Location is usually one of the factors leading to a more loosely coupled architecture, as several instances of the same service may exist in different locations. It is easier to reach service delivery scalability by locating multiple instances of the same service on different nodes. The identity of a service provider can be negotiated through a third-party broker component. The broker might even use geographical location, client identify, membership scheme information, transaction value, or a number of other criteria to match the service requester with a suitable service provider.

As an example, in one of our SOA projects for the defense industry, a device carried by a soldier that invokes a service from a command and control center, such as "identify target as friend or foe," will almost certainly need location independence. Depending on your environment, this aspect might imply that the infrastructure will need to perform service localization and routing appropriately.

3.1.3 Protocols

As with platform considerations, protocol independence is an aspect of SOA that may or may not be necessary depending on the business model and context. As an example, in a retail enterprise, the protocols between corporate and branches are under full control of the enterprise and can thus be unified to a common choice of protocol. Therefore, you can have a preferred binding, such as an EJB binding, for service requests that flow between the branch infrastructure and the corporate infrastructure to improve performance. This does not limit the service exposure that is available using other protocols at the same time, such as SOAP over HTTP.

Communication protocols can be defined by a configuration statement declared in an SOA service interface. In practice, this requires that you create applications using a protocol-independent service API such as JAX-RPC. In this case, the protocol binding in the service interface definition can be changed readily when necessary. For example, you can change the communications protocol from SOAP over HTTP to SOAP over Java Messaging Services (JMS). This does not require changes to the application code, but it will affect the behavior of the service API implementation that will then execute the service interaction through a different protocol.

3.1.4 Programming Language

SOA should be implementation independent, and therefore, it doesn't matter what programming languages are used for implementation. However, experience has shown that there are still some interoperability issues around requesters and producers that use different programming languages. These issues are related to the representation of more complex data types (arrays, null pointers, mainframe data formats, and so on) that are implemented differently on different systems and exhibit different performance behavior. If a high degree of loose coupling is required, then the architecture must plan for a mediation layer that enables proper conversion and that reduces or eliminates language-specific constraints for all possible requesters of a given service.

3.1.5 Invocation Patterns

An invocation pattern is the overall flow of interactions between a requester and a provider. A service might need to be synchronized with another service, or it might need to work asynchronously if the model allows it (that is, sending a service request without waiting for the response, and coming back some time later to gather the response). Support for an asynchronous model has a greater impact on the architecture because it requires the capability to correlate responses that come in at different times, and it also can imply a push or callback pattern that enables the provider to trigger requester activity when the service has completed. We see a growing demand for one-time services (no synchronization and the need for state management). This allows the reuse of services in different contexts. If any response happens, it occurs as a one-time service but with roles inverted between providers and requesters.

3.1.6 Security

The architect will have to consider how to apply the right balance between the reality of business security requirements, and the various security options and their impact on performance, system management, and complexity. Security is discussed in more detail in Chapter 8, "Securing the SOA Environment."

3.1.7 Service Versioning

Service providers might need to take into account greater adaptability in their implementation when they allow differences in the versions of the services that requestors can access. A requestor in this case might need to interface with an earlier version of a service, which implies that the provider will need to keep track of interfaces and the semantics of their implementations between release cycles. This can be done using some form of versioning, and some best practices are available, as in the "Best practices for Web services versioning" article from Kyle Brown and Michael Ellis.

A.3.1

Roughly speaking, there are two types of changes in a Web Services Description Language (WSDL) document that cannot break an existing requestor and several types of changes that can. In accordance with standard industry nomenclature, we will call these backwards-compatible and non-backwards-compatible changes, respectively. The following types of changes are backwards compatible:

- The addition of new service operations to an existing service description using WSDL. If existing requestors are unaware of a new operation, then they will be unaffected by its introduction.
- The addition of new XML schema types within a WSDL service definition document that are not contained within previously existing types. Again, even if a new operation requires a new set of complex data types, as long as those data types are not contained within any previously existing types (which would in turn require modification of the parsing code for those types), then this type of change will not affect an existing requestor.

However, there are a host of other change types that are not backwards compatible, including the following:

- Removing an operation
- Renaming an operation
- Changing the parameters (in data type or order) of an operation
- Changing the structure of a complex data type

For backwards-compatible changes, the WDSL service description can simply be updated in the repository from which it is made available to requestors, and the existing Web service can be updated. We would recommend that every new edition of a service description be stored in a version-control system and that XML comments be used to indicate unique version IDs or a version history. However, this is purely for the convenience of the Web service provider and is not required by the implementers of the Web service requestors.

For non-backwards-compatible changes, you need to take another approach. To solve this problem, begin by using XML namespaces to clearly delineate the versions of a document that are compatible. The mechanism by which this is done depends on whether the SOAP binding uses the literal- or SOAP-encoded style in WSDL. In literal encoding, the namespace is specified in the definition of the messages as part of the XML schema namespace definitions; in SOAP encoding, it can be specified within the SOAP binding element. Regardless of the mechanism chosen, a specific namespace value is sent along with every SOAP message. This allows a Web service implementation to correctly determine what to do with an incoming message, based on the namespace value.

Another version support technique is to use a semantic layer to realize the necessary version adaptation. This technique uses matchmaking to find a "good enough" similarity between the goals of the client requester and the exposed capabilities of the service.

3.1.8 Service Model

Enterprises need a service model that enables requesters to consume services in a way that is independent from services implementations and that allows those implementations to be changed without impacting the requesters. Just as enterprise application integration (EAI) refers to a canonical format for the information (that is, a common format for the information shared across the enterprise), reusability implies a canonical service model that reflects the enterprise view of its business services. The definition of such information and the service model in an SOA should only target the portions of the information and the services that are exposed between the various business domains. Thus, the effort to achieve this model is limited as it must not try to "boil the ocean," but instead focus only on the integration of each service's facade. Controlling the definition of such a model also leads to a specific program management or governance model that is explained in Chapter 4, "SOA Project Planning Aspects."

3.1.9 Information Model

In a service interaction between requestors and providers, there is usually a semantic coupling of business data models between the two sides. The application code for each will need to understand, for example, the information required to describe a "customer," "account," or "order." In the Web services space, there are now matchmaking engines that target semantic adaptation between requesters and providers. The use of such an adaptation might be complicated when there are legal aspects that require the adaptation to be 100% verifiable and traceable, as evident in formally adopted government standards for interaction.

3.1.10 Data Format

In addition to the information model, data formats are also often transformed during an exchange. It is common, for example, to convert formats such as COBOL copybooks into XML formats when enabling new service interfaces to existing operational systems. In addition, different XML schemas might be used by different systems in an SOA to describe the same data models. In either case, the supported format is, or can be, defined in a service interface. Furthermore, you can use middleware transformation capabilities in the service infrastructure to perform the required transformations without affecting application code or behavior.

3.1.11 Applying the SOA Characteristics

We can now apply these characteristics to various aspects of services identified in an SOA. For some scenarios, SOA or other design principles will specify the desired style of interaction; for other situations, several of these characteristics might need to fit an existing scenario. For each aspect, however, a number of different techniques can be applied to implement the desired interaction. To provide some context for how these characteristics come into play in an actual model, we examine the on-demand operating environment (ODOE) later in this chapter.

3.2 Infrastructure Services

As previously stated, SOA is not just a new way of writing code; it affects all elements and services of an enterprise and possibly even beyond to its network of partners. Our domain model for SOA depicts a set of infrastructure services that are the foundation for services operation. As Web service standards define the description, location, invocation, and data transport formats between services, the infrastructure services provide the execution platform and associated utility services. In a way, you can consider this domain as a virtual, distributed, operating system layer for services.

3.2.1 Resource Virtualization Services

The closest to the hardware, especially the network hardware, are the *resource virtualization services*. These are solutions and services that enable a platform-independent environment for the execution of services in a network. Thus, applications as services are no longer strictly bound to a specific predefined operating system or hardware platform. Services are executed in a virtual operating system that manages the available and suitable selection of servers as well the storage systems. As we show in more detail in Section 3.4.6, information integration plays an important role in enterprise and service-oriented solutions. Specific services such as hard disk space or CPU allocation fall into this "resource virtualization" category. For virtual server and storage, the IBM Virtualization Engine is a comprehensive portfolio of systems technologies and tools that can help you aggregate pools of resources to achieve a consolidated view of them throughout your IT environment.

Finally, as long-envisioned, the network of systems itself becomes a computer, the platform for services to run on. The technology that enables the building and management of virtual operation in a network is known as *grid computing*, such as described in the IBM grid computing portal. The grid computing solutions are based on standards defined by the Open Grid Services Architecture (OGSA), standards that help you create computing grids that include heterogeneous sets of hardware virtualized infrastructure components that are used for computing, storing, and accessing of large amounts of data.

In addition to these fundamentals of virtualization, appropriate management services are required to govern the whole system. We won't describe all of the available solutions, but you can refer to relevant literature such as the IBM Redbooks series on grid computing. We do want to point out, however, that these services are gaining importance in the context of SOA.

3.2.2 Service-Level Automation and Orchestration

Just as important are the technologies that facilitate automated management of required service levels and policies in any system running services. Imagine a world in which computers could monitor, analyze, and fix their own problems without much or any human intervention. Making a parallel with the human body, the autonomic nervous system is the part of the nervous system that controls body functions that are not under conscious and direct voluntary control. Computer self-management and self-healing require autonomic computing capabilities across your entire IT infrastructure. Similar to any manufacturing processes, self-managing computing systems can control and orchestrate an increasingly complex and expensive IT environment using appropriate autonomic management systems. This also evolves the role of IT professionals to include expanded responsibility that is no longer focused on basic errors or problems that are handled automatically, but rather to focus on higher levels of operation management such as the overall quality of services delivered.

The specific services that fall under the service-level automation (SLA) and orchestration subdomain are the automated services for problem management and system failure recovery, workload balancing and resource management, and system security services and data provisioning. The provisioning in this context also covers the installation and deployment of services in the system. Products like IBM Tivoli Intelligent Orchestrator provide these services.

All these services contribute to make IT systems resilient, responsive, efficient, and secure. Autonomic computing technologies today are evolving rapidly and enable construction of SOA-based solutions that reflect high service levels.

3.2.3 Utility Business Services

Another class of services that gains importance under SOA is the set of *utility business services* that can be introduced to an enterprise system of services. In an SOA with an enterprise service bus (see Section 3.3) providing central connectivity, you can build specialized utility services in a manner similar to any application service. However, we expose these services as an architectural element of an SOA because they are more closely linked to the operation of the enterprise service bus (ESB).

Among other things, the architecture allows ESB-based services that deal with metering and rating of services in the system, provide billing services based on usage information, or other functions for operating the services as a utility. We expect a specialized market to grow when service providers offer defined business services via the Internet. For this market, we see providers offering brokering and other related services.

3.3 The Enterprise Service Bus (ESB)

To realize the scenario of an automated, self-managed SOA, the ESB is an essential architectural element. As such, it is a core part of the ODOE reference architecture, which is introduced in Section 3.5. Figure 3.2 is a conceptual view of the ESB, representing some service requesters at the top and service providers at the bottom for schematic purposes. In the real world, distributed environment requestors and providers can be located anywhere.

An ESB is a core intermediary, a means to tie services together into componentized, logical sets. These sets reflect the structure of the business and are designed for distributed, widespread use across the enterprise. The logical grouping and design of each service component ensures that there is minimal heterogeneity in the business semantics exposed by the services. Each service forms a facade for the components or other technologies that implement the business logic. The essential infrastructure services that an ESB provides are transport, quality-of-service-based routing, mediation, and gateway services.

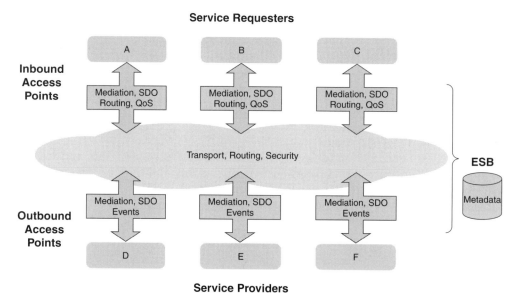

Figure 3.2   The ESB concept.

The ESB is actually an architectural *construct* that can be designed and deployed in a manner that will parallel the business processes environment. The bus can be implemented in various ways, such as with classical messaging, EAI, and brokering technologies or by using platform-specific components such as the service integration buses in J2EE systems (such as WebSphere Application Server). The ESB can also be a combination of both EAI and application server technologies, but the implementation should not affect the overall architecture. The selection between possible implementations will be the result of an initial architecture assessment, including existing IT infrastructure, skills, and processes in the evaluation.

The ESB acts as the intelligent, distributed, transactional, and messaging layer for connecting applications, diverse data, and other services that are commonly distributed throughout an enterprise computing infrastructure. It attenuates its core synchronous and asynchronous messaging backbone with intelligent transformation and routing capabilities, and it ensures that messages are passed reliably. The ESB enables developers to invoke and use business functions in components, regardless of API or protocol, by using them as services defined by a standard interface description based on the Web Services Description Language (WSDL).

WSDL separates the abstract descriptions of service interfaces, the reusable protocol bindings for the service, and the actual deployed endpoints offering the service. It is inherently extensible and offers extensibility elements for ports and bindings, allowing several different protocols to bind to the same service definition, if needed.

Literally, any unit software task can be described in Web Services Description Language (WSDL) directly, regardless of the protocol that is used to expose the service API (for example, Microsoft.Net, remote Enterprise Java Beans [EJB], Common Object Request Broker Architecture [CORBA] based components, applications listening on a Java Messaging Services [JMS] described queue, local entities such as Java bean classes, batch programs, executable files, and so on).

Effectively, the ESB is organically assembled from the different application and data components that provide the infrastructure services, allowing this heterogeneity while still respecting and targeting industry standards that focus on cross-implementation interoperability (from standards organizations such as the Web Services Interoperability Organization [WS-I] or the OASIS consortium that drives the definition and adoption of e-business standards). It consists of attachment points that act as intelligent switches and messaging capabilities that provide the essential distribution capabilities.

3.3.1 Transport

When a service request is processed, the most appropriate transport protocol needs to be selected. As industry standards are mandatory, the essential transports for Web services are SOAP over HTTP, SOAP over HTTPS, and SOAP over JMS. In addition, with its Java 2 Enterprise Edition (J2EE) application server–based nodes, the bus also supports Remote Method Invocation over Internet Inter-ORB Protocol technology (RMI/IIOP) and interoperability with CORBA-based components. Finally, by the use of standard Java 2 Connector Architecture (referred to as J2C or JCA) or other general adapters accessed through JMS, the ESB can connect to nearly all existing applications, even those using IBM's Systems Network Architecture (SNA) protocol or base Transmission Control Protocol/Internet Protocol (TCP/IP) interactions.

3.3.2 Quality-of-Service-Based Routing

Some integration contexts require the selection of the "best" service provider while also routing to locations across several and varied transports. If required, this must occur within the appropriate security context, providing the necessary quality of service (QoS), mapping, and transforming where necessary and invoking auxiliary infrastructure services where needed. The support of quality-of-services features in an ESB in turn enables the support and delivery of services according to defined service-level agreements. These agreements establish the parameters for how the service should be provided over the course of its use; they can include policies on response time, synchronicity, role-based delivery, or other factors defined in the agreement.

QoS plays an important role in a number of scenarios. It is of particular concern in the continuous transmission of high-bandwidth video and multimedia information. Transmitting this kind of content dependably across public networks that use common, best-effort protocols is difficult to maintain. In Web services, QoS can also refer to the quality of the availability, accessibility, integrity, performance, reliability, regulatory, and security capabilities of the service. In the defense industry, the fast delivery of information by selecting the appropriate available route is very important. However, this delivery must use a known, reliable path, both to ensure that communication is achieved and to ensure that no one can intercept or spoof the messages. In other, more batch-oriented contexts, there may not be a requirement for such quality. Optimizing the resources by selecting the most appropriate route is an important element of an on-demand-enabled bus.

3.3.3 Mediation

Mediation in an ESB enables the intelligent processing of service requests and responses, events, and messages. These mediations can be implemented at application service endpoints (either requestor or provider) or can be distributed through the infrastructure of the bus.

Mediation capabilities include the following:

- *Transformations*: XML-to-XML translations, database (DB) lookups, and aggregations.
- *Message validation*: This can consist of verification of any data field or a combination of fields with specific rules.
- *Content or quality service selections*: This requires a service selection based on content or on required quality of service. As an example, a priority customer should probably be routed to a higher throughput server than others of lesser priority.
- *Content-based routing*: As an example, if the service parameters contain some country information, the request can be routed to a provider in that country.
- *Customized logging*: This is a legal requirement that might ask for logging and audit tracks of the services interactions. Mediation is potentially a good place for this purpose.
- *Metering and monitoring*: A bus should have all of the manageability anchor points to enable control of its behavior and of the integrated services.
- *Autonomic behavior*: This is used to react when events are detected—to self-configure, heal, optimize, and so on.
- *Policy management*: This allows a description of all of the behavior rules that are required for the previous items in this list through externalized policies based on XML.

Mediators are intermediary components that operate on logical Web service SOAP message representations between the requestor and the provider. These mediator components can be located close to requestors, providers, or halfway between both requestors and providers as true intermediaries. SOAP messages usually contain a header that has to be processed by the mediation handlers, but mediation can be used for purposes other than just SOAP processing and routing.

You can implement an ESB in many different ways. It is important, however, to reuse whatever standard infrastructure services already exist, ensuring compatibility and reliability. Thus, in a best-practice-based implementation, mediators should use the standard Java Web services SOAP-handling standard: JAX-RPC. This standard provides access to the SOAP headers via the handler API and can be hosted in a J2EE application server infrastructure. Handlers can be easily chained in series and reused across systems. In addition, using embedded mediations, the ESB supports a broad spectrum of ways to hop on and off the bus. The ESB includes business connections that enable external partners in B2B interaction scenarios to participate in the service interaction flows. In this B2B case, it provides the additional mediations and security that external access imposes. Mediation on the protocols that attach to the bus enables the connectivity with existing service-oriented components. These protocols include CORBA, RMI/IIOP, TCP/IP, JCA, native JMS, and other Java protocols.

For example, if an EJB is accessed through a service interface, it can still be invoked via RMI over IIOP at runtime. The same can be achieved for a CORBA component. Protocol mediators enable application integration across different platforms, software models, and messaging standards underpinning the business processes and managed business partner integration without forcing all services to be able to produce and consume SOAP messages.

Mediators can also act on content to provide capabilities such as validating the document against both technical and business requirements, transforming the document into the format required by the recipient, and gathering other information required by the recipient. Most importantly, mediators can handle content-related exceptions originating from invalid content of the payload, ensuring that they are dealt with appropriately and also insulating the recipient from incorrect information.

3.3.4 Web Services Gateway

A *Web services gateway* is an additional component of a bus that provides controlled access to the bus for external partners, hiding details of individual internal services, validating user access, controlling access, and auditing requests. The gateway uses core bus components such as mediation and security to implement its routing and management services.

3.4 SOA Enterprise Software Models

To support all of the characteristics we just described, you need a software model supported by an architectural framework that provides key architecture principles and promotes the integration of new and existing services and business goals.

In this section, we focus on the various models that exist in the SOA space. This includes semantic models that address the business content and dynamics of the interactions, programming models that create or choreograph services, and off-the-shelf integration packages that expose services. We then explore the specific project and method aspects in Chapter 4, "SOA Project Planning Aspects," and Chapter 5, "Aspects of Analysis and Design."

3.4.1 Industry Models

Many industries' communities (some listed in this section) have already initiated their journeys toward SOA and offer modeling or implementation accelerators in the form of information models, services models, or business process models. These initiatives cover one or more SOA aspects such as the data formats, Web services interfaces, business process models, or even business services components with the associated contracts.

The following are some of the major initiatives that have made this level of progress toward an SOA:

- *ebXML*: Specifications and standards from the Organization for the Advancement of Structured Information Standards (OASIS) target the creation of an electronic marketplace in which enterprises can meet and interoperate in their businesses. In a recent move, ebXML has created the Electronic Business SOA Technical Committee.
- *OAGIS*: In the automotive industry, the Open Applications Group Integration Specification (OAGIS) also integrates SOA aspects.
- *NGOSS*: Because of its inherently heterogeneous and multiparty environment, the telecommunication industry has gone a long way in its services definition. The TeleManagement forum standards body has defined contracts in its New Generation of Operation Support Services (NGOSS) specification that are the business services together with business process models and decomposition and the associated information and data model.
- *IFX*: In the banking industry, the IFX Forum addressing public financial services is adding Web services to its existing services and information model.
- *IFW*: Also in the banking industry but targeting all financial domain aspects, IBM has defined a complete Information Framework (IFW) that includes business process and models.

3.4.2 Platform-Independent Realization

The SOA software model implementation must first focus on neutrality by using platform-independent standards. Because such standards address heterogeneous environments, platform-independent modeling, meta-data, and operational standards are necessary. They allow the interchange of software artifacts and facilitate interoperability between tools, applications, middleware, and data stores across platforms.

The Internet is composed of heterogeneous technologies that successfully interoperate through shared protocols. One of the key attributes of Internet standards is that they focus on protocols rather than on specific implementations. The need to implement to a common shared protocol standard prevents individual vendors from imposing their own proprietary standard across the entire Internet. Open-source software development of Internet protocols, for example, plays a crucial role in preserving the interoperability of software vendor products.

In this vein, the Web services family of protocol specifications and standards was created with a multivendor approach to address heterogeneous platforms. The following standards play key roles in Web services: Universal Description, Discovery, and Integration (UDDI); Web Services Description Language (WSDL), Simple Object Access Protocol (SOAP), and Web Services Interoperability profiles (WS-I). There is not one single body that defines a complete platform-independent model, but there are three main organizations that do play an important role: the World Wide Web Consortium (W3C), OASIS, and WS-I.

The Web Services Interoperability Organization (WS-I), in particular, has defined a set of nonproprietary Web services specifications, implementation directives, and common scenarios that focus on promoting platform interoperability in what WS-I has named the Basic Profile. The base standards for interoperability, according to what the WS-I Basic Profile defines, are as follows:

- *XML and XML schemas (XSD):* For defining the model of the information exchanged through the services.
- *HTTP 1.1*: HTTP is the most common application protocol used on the Internet and is also the most commonly used transport for Web services.
- *SOAP 1.1*: Simple Object Access Protocol (SOAP) is a specification for the exchange of structured information in a decentralized, distributed environment.
- *Web Services Description Language (WSDL):* For determining the access and invocation aspects of the services.

Because business processes are essential to the SOA approach, the model must also integrate an additional standard for this aspect: the *Business Process Execution Language (BPEL)*. BPEL is used by business analysts to model the business processes and by programmers to implement the choreography of services.

Finally, a software model must state or include support for aspects that are not covered by the previous interfaces and sequencing standards, such as behavior descriptions of the services. Most of these behavioral (also called non-functional) aspects have not yet been addressed by formal standards, but they still need to be captured using existing tools. As of this writing, there has already been some progression of standards for the meta-data and non-functional aspects, which include the following:

- *WS-Policy* provides a general-purpose model and syntax to describe and communicate the policies of a Web service.
- *WS-Resource* provides a means for expressing the relationship between stateful resources and Web services. This is described by the Web Services Resource Framework.
- *WS-Security* addresses security functions such as integrity and confidentiality. The security is discussed in detail in Chapter 8.
- Other initiatives such as the W3C *Web Services Architecture* working group.

3.4.3 Platform-Specific Realization

An SOA can be realized on any software platform, including J2EE environments, Microsoft .NET, mainframe or existing operational systems with messaging, or even C/C++-based environments. Each of these platforms applies a specific software model to the environment, which also includes the principles of the previously mentioned platform-independent model. We examine the example of the J2EE software platform further in the next section.

Other examples are at slightly higher abstraction levels. For example, the Open Grid Services Architecture (OGSA) defines a computational and data grid system architecture that uses

Web services concepts and technologies and also targets usual operating system–based functions to participate in the architecture as services. In a purely message-based platform, the ESB role can be played by an EAI or message broker that supports services interactions. For example, the IBM WebSphere Business Integration Message Broker uses message processing nodes to implement mediations and can perform all of the functions required for an ESB.

3.4.4 J2EE Realization

We expect that many SOAs will use the J2EE platform. Therefore, there is a need for a complete model with implementation constructs that addresses this platform environment. Such a model has to describe both the business logic and business data aspects of a service. Implementors of this model also need to ensure that their J2EE vendors' implementation respects industry-defined standards, interoperates with the non-J2EE platforms, and supports Java artifacts that are reusable in cross-vendor J2EE implementations.

The model for services components (the business logic implementation) in the J2EE environment is defined by the following standards: *JSR-000921 Implementing Enterprise Web Services 1.1* or the *JSR-000109 Implementing Enterprise Web Services*.

These standards define the model and runtime architecture that deploys and looks up Web services in the J2EE environment, more specifically within Web, EJB, and client application containers. They include the use of JAX-RPC to define the model for mapping WSDL runtime artifacts into Java. More importantly, they also define the notion of a service endpoint interface that defines the object methods for a particular Web service.

A.3.2

In a global SOA approach, these standards have to be complemented with a software model for business data. In Java, there are many ways of representing data, such as `ResultSet` for database queries, DOM or SAX classes for representing XML data, or `Records` in the Java Connector Architecture (JCA or J2C). To simplify the handling of such a variety of representations, a new standard named service data objects (SDO) has been created. It provides a unified way of manipulating all these kinds of data. As stated by *JSR 000235: Service Data Objects*, SDOs define core infrastructure APIs for heterogeneous data access that supports common application design patterns and higher-level tools and frameworks. They provide a common framework for accessing and exchanging data with services.

3.4.5 Services Integration on the WebSphere Application Server

The IBM WebSphere Application Server, starting from version 6.0, provides comprehensive support for SOAs. It offers the following elements:

- *Service integration bus:* This supports applications using message-based exchanges and SOAs. In the WebSphere Application Server environment, the bus is a group of interconnected servers and clusters that have been added as members of the bus. Applications connect to a bus at one of the messaging engines associated with its bus members.
- *Messaging engine:* A component inside one or more servers that manages messaging resources for bus members. Applications are connected to a messaging engine when accessing a service integration bus.

- *Data store:* This consists of the set of tables that a messaging engine uses to store persistent data in a database.
- *Bus destination:* A virtual location within a service integration bus, to which applications can be attached as producers, requestors, or both in order to exchange messages. Applications attach to bus destinations within a service integration bus as producers, requesters, or both to exchange messages.
- *Mediation:* A Java component that processes in-transit messages between the creation of a message by one application and the consumption of a message by another. Mediations allow you to customize the messaging behavior of the bus. They can perform the functions of message format transformation, message routing, message augmentation with various data sources, and distribution to multiple target destinations.
- *Security:* Authenticates the user, authorizes the user, and ensures the confidentiality and integrity of the message in transit, integrating Web services and J2EE security standards.
- *Web services enablement:* You can take an internal service that is available at a service destination and make it available as a Web service, or you can take an external Web service and make it available at a service destination.

An ESB layer might be deployed with multiple service integration topologies, depending on the functional and non-functional requirements. A topology consisting of just a single messaging engine is adequate for some applications. However, there are advantages in deploying more than one messaging engine and then linking them together. This is useful when spreading messaging workload across multiple servers, placing message processing close to the applications that are using it, improving availability in the face of system or link failure, providing improved scalability, or accommodating firewalls or other network restrictions.

A topology can also contain links to WebSphere MQ networks. This allows applications connected to a WebSphere MQ queue manager to send messages to an application attached to a service integration bus and vice versa.

The simplest topology is a bus consisting of a single server (see Figure 3.3). In a single-server bus, there is one messaging engine. All destinations, such as queues and topic spaces, are assigned to this single messaging engine.

You can also have a bus consisting of multiple servers (see Figure 3.4), which provides advantages of scalability, the capability to handle more client connections, and greater message throughput. All of the messaging engines in the bus are implicitly connected through the underlying J2EE infrastructure, and applications can connect to any messaging engine in the bus.

Finally, a topology can consist of a number of interconnected service integration buses, each with its own set of servers (see Figure 3.5). Separate service integration buses might be used for different departments within organizations or perhaps to separate test and production facilities. These buses can be used in their own right, but they can also be connected to allow messaging across the buses.

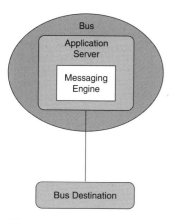

Figure 3.3 A single-bus, single-server topology.

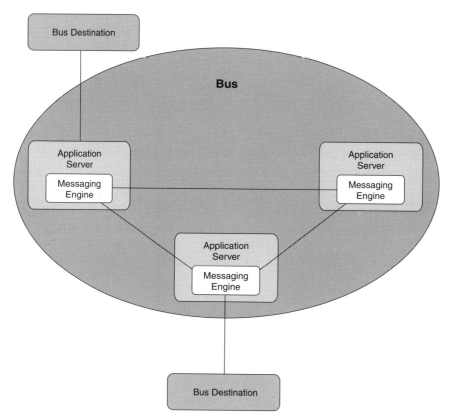

Figure 3.4 Multiple servers in a single bus topology.

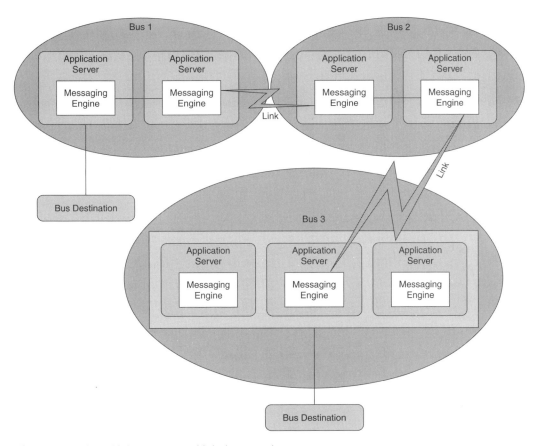

Figure 3.5   A multiple server, multiple-bus topology.

3.4.6 The Information Management Domain

The information management domain focuses on data and information distributed across the SOA as corporate *information assets* and how these assets interact with the rest of the SOA. Without a clear understanding of the intent and value of information management services, one can easily lose the big picture of the types and instances of information that influence business needs and thus make the wrong tradeoffs. A proactive plan to incorporate information management capabilities into a larger SOA picture will prevent gaps in the implementation.

The following sections describe why the information management services model is important to SOA from an architectural point of view. It also attempts to demystify meta-data and demonstrate the importance of integrating meta-data in a common representation. It shows how meta-data management can facilitate information management, and it enables the reuse of many of the same services required by data and content management.

3.4.6.1 Information Management

Information management substantiates SOA, for it deals with one of the most important types of corporate assets: the information assets that are owned by a corporation. Without solid and robust information management, SOA presents fewer opportunities for end-to-end business integration and transformation. It greatly emphasizes *enterprise information integration* (EII), the process of integrating structured and unstructured information sources into a unified information source.

Structured information deals primarily with relational, XML, or tabular data, such as in spreadsheets and databases where the data is ordered and set to specific allowed types. The management of structured information falls under traditional *data management*. Meanwhile, unstructured information includes reports, documents, Web pages, life science data, audio, and video that does not easily conform to an ordered set with strict types. The management of unstructured information is often given a category such as *content management*.

3.4.6.2 Information Management Services

A.3.3

Information management under SOA, particularly EII, provides an abstraction layer between the applications and information sources with the goal of rapidly reducing the total cost of ownership and the complexity of the information and application integration. This is often offered by middleware such as WebSphere Information Integrator that creates the information abstraction layer, insulating application and data layers.

The information abstraction layer is extremely important to SOA because it allows transparency of database vendor products, OS platforms, information location, data format, and the physical data model. You can loosely couple your information sources from your applications in this way. Information management under SOA accesses and aggregates heterogeneous data and content sources (a process known as *federation*) so that they appear to the user as if they were one single database or content source. Because information management under SOA acts as a middleware layer between the applications and data sources, the rules for data connectivity, transformation, and mapping can be centralized and reused by many service requesters.

Moreover, information management under SOA offers extensibility to give applications and users access to information not only within the enterprise but also across enterprises and industries. This complete end-to-end horizontal business and information integration gives business high agility and flexibility.

A.3.4

Finally, to define its services and data representation, information management under SOA uses Web services and other information standards related to data, content, meta-data, meta-model and meta-meta-model. For example, information management uses XML, XML Metadata Interchange (XMI), JSR170, Unicode, Common Warehouse Model (CWM), Web Ontology Language (OWL), Universal Modeling Language (UML), Resource Description Framework (RDF), and Metadata Object Facility (MOF).

3.4.6.3 Reengineering Information Management into Services

Until the rise of information standards such as XML, Unicode, UML, and MOF, most data sources were characterized by their existing proprietary data formats, meta-data and meta-models. It requires an enormous effort to integrate different data sources, typically by building point-to-point data and application integration. A great deal of effort has been put into developing Extract-Transform-Load (ETL) tools. ETL is a common enterprise solution pattern used to extract data from a source, transform it, and load it into a target system.

On the content side, the challenges are equally daunting. Content management solutions came from different historical lineages, and most of them are vertical or departmentally based solutions (document management for the legal department, knowledge management for the IT department, or Web content management for the marketing department). In today's content management market, these solutions are offered in different products from a large number of vendors. Even within a single vendor, the functionalities frequently and heavily overlap across products. This often leads to several coexisting content repositories, each for its corresponding vertical solutions.

However, the lines among these solutions are becoming increasingly blurred, and we are seeing a trend toward convergence in various aspects. Some examples are data and content integration convergence, ETL and federation convergence, knowledge management, and Web content management convergence. SOA helps to move out from the vertical and departmental view by allowing the model to do the following:

- Transform existing information management functions into reusable services
- Integrate large numbers of heterogeneous information sources
- Reduce development costs
- Expand capabilities quickly

Figure 3.6 illustrates the information management stack, a logical view or framework for categorizing information management services based on their value propositions: security, collaboration, availability, management, and information consumption.

As a whole, these services can create a complete information management framework under SOA. Individually, each of these services really deserves a chapter in its own right, but we can offer only a brief overview here. Security is the entry point for applications to access heterogeneous data sources based on *who-can-see-what* policies. Collaboration is indispensable in a team environment, so we need work flow and version control. Federation, ETL, and replication are all aimed at making information available when the user needs it. Because information encapsulates the intelligence and complexity of an organization, (structural and semantic) modeling, (data) profiling, (content) indexing, and quality disciples are utilized to make information more manageable. In addition, the whole purpose is to allow model-based actors to consume information from the top of the stack. Finally, meta-data management connects various service pieces together.

As previously stated, services listed in the information management services domain are typically offered by middleware. Users can always opt to build these services into their applications from scratch; however, the cost and time taken is often prohibiting. The best practice is to understand business requirements, choose a vendor that offers seamless information integration and the most complete information management solution, offer the most standards interfaces, and build a handful of selective services to compensate for the missing pieces or even outsource certain complex services to a third-party information service provider.

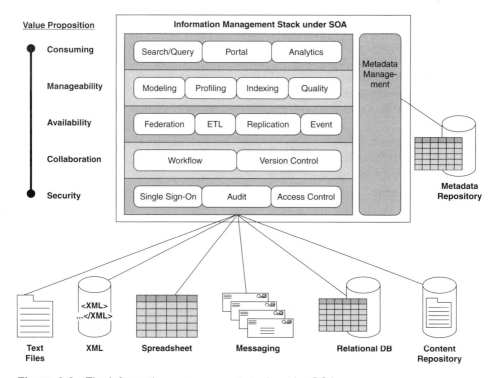

Figure 3.6   The information management stack under SOA.

3.4.6.4 Considerations of Meta-Data Management

When we reengineer meta-data management, XML is usually chosen as the default data format for meta-data because it is the de facto universal data format. Within a single vendor or an organization, the centralized approach to encouraging meta-data asset reuse and reducing development effort and confusion is usually more effective than a decentralized one. The use of standardized meta-data is also helpful.

IBM uses the open-source Eclipse Modeling Framework (EMF) in many of its tools as the common meta-data integration technology. EMF provides meta-data integration for the tools and runtime objects so that all the software developed on top of EMF shares a common understanding of other applications. In an ideal situation, a single meta-data repository will be able to store all meta-data artifacts. Information management services (SSO, ETL, federation, quality, search, versioning, and workflow) can be invoked for data, content, and meta-data management when they are needed. In other words, "write once and use anywhere."

Regarding XML repositories, there are two popular storage mechanisms for storing XML meta-data: a relational database management system (RDBMS) or a native XML database. Both have advantages and disadvantages. Some of the factors that determine which will dominate the future market include performance, flexibility, bandwidth, interoperability, support of user-defined data types, and data quality assurance (for example, cross-schema validation and transformation).

The federation approach is a more practical method for meta-data management across vendors, enterprises, or industries. In this approach, a federated virtual meta-data repository co-locates all application access and heterogeneous meta-data sources behind a single API. Physical meta-data artifacts can be stored either in their original locations or in virtual ones—using a combination of ETL, replication, and caching to improve performance and meta-data availability. Automatic discovery, mapping, and transformation among diverse meta-data sources are critical to improve meta-data manageability.

3.4.6.5 Meta-Data Integration

As previously stated, integrating meta-data can be even more challenging than integrating the actual data and content it represents. This integration is essential to SOA because it decouples the business data models. Meta-data is the "brain" behind information integration. Furthermore, information integration enables business integration; this allows the SOA to expand across departments within an enterprise, all the way to complex cross-enterprise systems. Meta-data integration does the following:

- Provides a single and complete view of customers, partners, and business through data warehouses or federation
- Facilitates business performance management using analytical services
- Enhances business applications with broad information access
- Enables business process transformation with continuous information services

Many factors contribute to the difficulty of meta-data integration:

- Meta-data is pervasive and hard to fully understand.
- Meta-data and meta-models in many products have their own proprietary format, especially on the content management side.
- Adding meta-data to content is typically facilitated by manual workflow. Often, content items lack well-structured meta-data that is useful for enabling integration and search.
- Meta-data integration requires a higher level of automation and orchestration than data and content integration. This requires higher levels of automatic discovery, transformation, mapping, and semantic understanding.
- Vendors might be afraid of losing customers, so they might choose to stick to their proprietary meta-data format.

It takes time and effort to transform to a meta-data standard such as MOF, but this standardization is an important step in the roadmap to SOA and being part of an ODOE.

3.5 The IBM On Demand Operating Environment

The various domains of an IT operating environment have different concerns and requirements. When planning an SOA, the constraints from each domain will lead to different service component requirements. To address this need for an enterprise-wide, service-oriented IT system, IBM defined the on demand operating environment (ODOE) as its reference architecture that supports industry-wide best practices in SOA. As such, it takes a top-down approach to the development of a secure process- and service-oriented enterprise architecture that can be extended beyond a single enterprise into interactions with those of other organizations.

It is important to point out that starting with this high-level view does not mean that you need to rework your entire IT infrastructure. This is an architectural framework that enables you to build and maintain a platform-independent service model that maintains feedback from the many domains and that can be automated, monitored, and audited.

The ODOE encourages compatibility by enabling you to encapsulate the functions of existing operational systems and create a federation of heterogeneous software components. In this case, an existing operational system is anything that does not already have a service-based interface and interacts using well-known service protocols. This environment enables you to compose operational applications from atomic or coarse-grained business services to operate as part of the SOA. The SOA allows these coarse or atomic services to be accessed through various channels such as a visual user interface, through a portal on the Internet, or even through programmatic access using protocols such as Web services.

Web services, as defined by the industry standards and the profiles defined by the WS-I organization, are the basis for enabling these SOAs. Users can easily mix and match functions from heterogeneous environments into a single application built on Web services. You can have a portal that features Web services-based public interfaces that connect to yet another Web services portal to provide the application functionality. These backend services can be aggregated to support a broad spectrum of requirements, from aggregated component construction into groups of services, to transactional management of these service interactions.

Enabling functional access to Web services either through portals or service interfaces is not enough to provide a production-ready SOA. Such a system must also integrate operational aspects such as ensuring and monitoring service levels while using appropriate security protection.

The ODOE provides protection of the internal infrastructure and sensitive data from inadvertent or fraudulent accesses. In some cases, it might also be necessary to protect even the existence of a service from unauthorized access.

The on-demand computing model applies at various levels in the IT stack. At the system level, the components are system objects (computing capacity storage and files). At the application level, the components are dynamically integrated application modules that constitute sophisticated, yet much more flexible, applications. At the business level, the components are business objects, defined for particular vertical industries or, more generally, to apply horizontally across industries. With a basis on industry standards, the on-demand computing model is appropriate not just for intra-enterprise scenarios but also across an industry ecosystem. The use of open standards makes it possible and applicable to the heterogeneous environment to create just such a cross-industry business computing ecosystem. It makes it possible to conceive and implement complete, end-to-end, business-process integration.

As depicted in Figure 3.7, the ODOE architecture defines four top-level domains: Business Services, Application Services, Enterprise Service Bus, and Infrastructure Services. We provide a basic overview of these domains and services, but you can find more details in a separate ODOE architectural overview paper published on IBM developerWorks.

A.3.4

Services in the *Business Services* domain are the exposed part of the business processes and the business logic that is accessed by and provides expected value to the requestor. As previously indicated, the requestor can access these business services through a visual or a programmatic interface. The requestor, in this case, can be a user within the organization (intranet), a user outside the organization's IT infrastructure or outside the organization altogether (extranet), or even a customer or partner completely separate from the organization (Internet).

The *Application Services* domain comprises all of the components that are necessary to build an application. This domain includes components to support user access, business function,

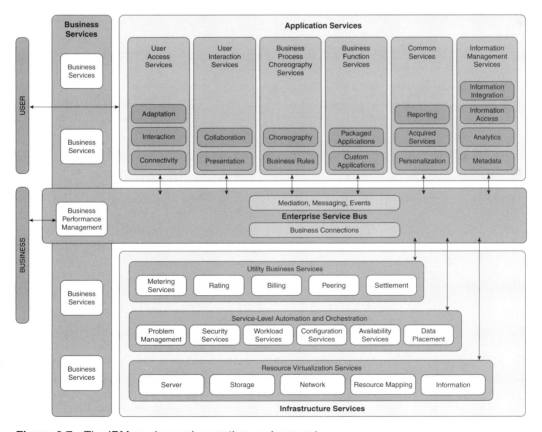

Figure 3.7   The IBM on-demand operating environment.

common services, user interaction, business process choreography, and information management.

The *Business Function Services* components help integrate atomic business functions into business function services, using software packages that adapt enterprise data. The *User Access Services* components support access, sequencing, and presentation of the accessed business function services via the particular channels that the service requestors will use. These channels can either be visual (for humans) or programmatic (for other applications or services). The *User Interaction Services* components provide the additional interaction commonly needed to support a group of requestors.

The *Common Services* components enable personalization of the delivery and individual processing, as well as other utilities such as reporting. The *Business Process Choreography* components enable you to define and execute conditional flows, mainly across logical business function services but also to any other service. Our recommended software model for services choreography uses the industry standard Business Process Execution Language (BPEL) specification.

The *Information Management Services* provide a uniform way of representing, accessing, maintaining, managing, analyzing, and integrating data and content across heterogeneous information sources. They are an essential component of SOA and play a critical role in enabling SOA. There are many functions within information management, such as federation, replication, modeling, search, and analytics. As shown in Section 3.4.6, each of these functions can be provided as reusable and componentized services.

The *Enterprise Service Bus* is an intermediation layer that interconnects all of the services, enabling all of the (loose) coupling characteristics that have been described in other chapters of this book. It is the pivotal architectural concept of the ODOE and deserves to be explored in greater detail, as we showed in Section 3.3.

Finally the *Infrastructure Services* domain, as shown in Section 3.2, is a set of platform-independent services that enables all of the other services domain components to be installed, executed, and controlled on a concrete infrastructure combination of operating systems and network and hardware systems.

3.6 Summary

This chapter first refined the aspect of SOA characteristics such as loose coupling. We then introduced the four main domains of an SOA model. Using the example of the ODOE, we identified each of these domains and layers and their service characteristics. We then focused on the ESB as a pivotal element of the model. We also looked at the programming models that are necessary for the domains that involve programming. Finally, we looked at the domain of information management, which is an essential component. This domain can usually be supported by off-the-shelf software packages or specialized middleware.

Implementing successful SOA will need a selection of methods, models, and a careful analysis of the requirements and its value. This can be done only with structured roadmaps and control of the SOA implementation, which we discuss in the next chapter.

3.7 Links to developerWorks

A.3.1 Brown, K. and Ellis, M. *Best Practices in Web Services Versioning*. IBM developerWorks, January 2004. http://www-128.ibm.com/developerworks/webservices/library/ws-version/.

A.3.2 Beatty, J., et al. *Service Data Objects*. IBM developerWorks, November 2003. http://www-128.ibm.com/developerworks/java/library/j-sdo/index.html.

A.3.3 Selvage, M., Wolfson, D., and Handy-Bosma, J. *Information management in Service-Oriented Architecture, Part 1: Discover the role of information management in SOA*. IBM developerWorks, March 2005. http://www-128.ibm.com/developerworks/webservices/library/ws-soa-ims/.

A.3.4 IBM alphaWorks. *Ontology-Based Web Services for Business Integration*. September 2004. http://www.alphaworks.ibm.com/tech/owsbi.

A.3.5 Schmidt, M.-T. and Kalyana, S. S. *The On Demand operating environment—Architectural Overview*. IBM developerWorks, August 2004. http://www-106.ibm.com/developerworks/ibm/library/i-odoe1.

3.8 References

Bhaskaran, K. and Schmidt, M. T. *WebSphere Business Integration: An architectural overview*. IBM Systems Journal, Vol. 43, 2-2004. http://www.research.ibm.com/journal/sj43-2.html.

Dijkstra, Edsger W. *A Discipline of Programming* (facsimile). Prentice-Hall, 1997.

Dijkstra, E. W. *Go to Statement Considered Harmful* (reprint). ACM Classics of the Month, October 1995, reprint from *Communications of the ACM*, Vol. 11, No. 3, March 1968, pp. 147-148.

Ferreira, L. and Berstis, V. *Fundamentals of Grid Computing*. IBM Redpiece (REDP-3613-00), 2002. http://www.redbooks.ibm.com/abstracts/redp3613.html?Open.

Ferreira, L., et al. *Introduction to Grid Computing with Globus*. (SG24-6895-01), IBM RedBooks, 2003. http://www.redbooks.ibm.com/abstracts/sg246895.html?Open.

Globus.org. *Open Grid Services Architecture*. http://www.globus.org/ogsa/.

Gottschalk, K., et al. *Introduction to Web services architecture*. IBM Systems Journal, Vol. 41, 2-2002. http://www.research.ibm.com/journal/sj41-2.html.

Graham, S., et al. *Building Web Services with Java—Making Sense of XML, SOAP, WSDL, and UDDI, 2nd Edition*. Sams, June 2004.

IBM. *Autonomic Computing Offerings*. http://www-03.ibm.com/autonomic/index.shtml.

IBM. *Virtualization Engine*. http://www-1.ibm.com/servers/eserver/about/virtualization/.

Jacob, B., et al. *Enabling Applications for Grid Computing with Globus*. (SG24-6936-00), IBM RedBooks, 2003. http://www.redbooks.ibm.com/abstracts/sg246936.html?Open.

OASIS. *Web Services Architecture*. http://www.w3.org/TR/ws-arch/.

OASIS. *Web Services Resource Framework*. http://www.oasis-open.org/committees/tc_home. php?wg_abbrev=wsrf.

OASIS. *Web Services Security*. http://www.oasis-open.org/committees/tc_home.php?wg_ abbrev=wss.

W3C. *Web Services*. http://www.w3.org/2002/ws/.

Chapter 4

SOA Project
Planning Aspects

"Adventure is just bad planning."

—*Roald Amundsen*

The architectural consideration of SOA in the preceding chapter offers advice on what directions to choose and how to define the strategic goals for an SOA project. This chapter takes the next step toward execution by focusing on how to plan an SOA project. The topics in this chapter constitute the best practices we have uncovered for forming a project office (see Section 4.1), how to define the phases of SOA adoption, the need for and mechanisms of SOA governance, and finally, the various project roles and how they interact with each other.

This is not intended to be a complete template for a project plan, nor do we intend to show the optimal organizational structure for the parties involved in SOA projects. Based on our vigorous experience with different clients in various industries around the world, we are fully aware that there is no one-size-fits-all solution, nor is there a perfect approach to building an SOA for any scenario. An organization's specific circumstances will dictate its individual needs for project structure and plans. This chapter simply proposes ideas that you can adapt based on your scenario.

The first step is to establish the project office.

4.1 Organizing Your SOA Project Office

As seen in the preceding chapters, SOA implies a greater focus on business value. Business models are described as modular processes. This is achieved by breaking down the business and respective IT systems into components, providing reusability and modularity. Componentization, in this context, applies not just to software systems, but also to the business units across the enterprise and the organization of the enterprise in question. Implementing an SOA project involves not just a consideration of how the project is implemented in an IT infrastructure setting, but in the end, it also results in a business transformation process across the whole enterprise.

To accomplish your project, you first need a roadmap to guide the strategy for your SOA adoption. To build your SOA adoption roadmap, you need to identify who is involved in the SOA project. These individuals should come from the contributing cross-business-unit teams. The actual teams you involve will depend on the level of SOA adoption you choose (see Section 4.2).

Depending on business value analysis and the consequent prioritization of business objectives and services, the team defines "what to do," "how to do it," "who should do it," and "how success is measured." The SOA project team creates the rules, processes, metrics, and organizational structures needed for effective planning, decision-making, steering, and controlling the SOA endeavors. They define the common business service model, the common core processes and business components involved in the SOA project, and the core set of assets that they will use.

Building a suitable team for an SOA project requires a careful avoidance of making radical changes to existing team strategies because such changes can unduly disrupt the culture in the workplace. However, at the same time, the teams need to align with the SOA goals, which usually cut across business units. In addition, the SOA project might need to adopt a management structure—especially at larger IT shops with substantial project goals—to manage the development processes for implementing components or to expose existing applications or legacy functions in terms of the appropriate service granularity.

Achieving the right organizational structure is one of the critical challenges in implementing SOA. At organizations new to SOA, one often encounters strong resistance to change that keeps the focus on short-term successes rather than directing appropriate business transformation to align with the business challenges.

Mature SOA organizations, on the other hand, span business lines and the boundaries of roles while achieving interdisciplinary coordination. However, starting small can help to mitigate risk by allowing you to choose a well-scoped and focused services-integration project that has a modest plan for organizational evolution. A cross-unit, organization structure can address all the aspects of the SOA. Based on our experience, this structure should include the following:

- *SOA business transformation architecture council*: This team is in charge of gathering the business requirements, performing business domain analysis and process engineering analysis, and identifying the necessary business components, services, and process modules. Instead of following a strict top-down approach, the council should use a mixed approach in blending top-down, bottom-up, and goal-based methods to ensure appropriate services identification. In particular, this team ensures that the exposed granularity of the defined services matches the business requirements and specifications—matching business components to IT components as services. More details on granularity issues and associated services layers are described in Chapter 5, "Aspects of Analysis and Design."

- *SOA technical architecture board*: This team ensures the alignment of business and IT, following industry and enterprise standards, and technically ensures that exposed services match the requirements for evolution and reusability as defined in the general guidelines for the enterprise IT development. Its members are well versed in emerging industry trends, state-of-the-art technologies, and standardization efforts. They are responsible for framing the technical enterprise architecture blueprints (the master IT plan for the enterprise), identifying niche architecture patterns, and promoting reusability principles. They work closely with the SOA transformation team.

- *Component design and development centers*: These are the usual IT teams. They provide design and development of the components and processes, along with new skills such as business process modeling (see Chapter 5). This team delivers a solution design outline, high- and low-level design abstractions, service-oriented analysis and design (the essential aspects of which are described in Chapter 5), and various test phases such as unit, integration, system, and acceptance tests.

- *Operations center*: Finally, there is a production team in charge of the services components operational aspects. These aspects include managing quality of service, enforcing business and service-level agreements, managing the security context, charging back services, and assuring revenue. The team is responsible for rolling out the service, performing regular maintenance, and providing overall system management.

This model for organizing teams is derived and distilled from our experience in projects at midsize to larger enterprises. Often, depending on the maturity level of the IT organization, existing installations can be redefined or transformed to support the SOA projects. After these teams have been identified, you can proceed to creating your adoption roadmap.

Based on their definitions and the associated expert knowledge, each team has a certain scope of decision-making. Depending on the size of the enterprise, the scope, the reach of the project, and the institutionalized IT governance structures, the individuals assigned to the teams can vary. Section 4.3 further explains the need for SOA governance.

4.2 SOA Adoption Roadmap

An SOA strategy should not be a big-bang replacement of an existing IT environment; rather, it should be a progressive and evolutionary roadmap. Often an overall replacement is impossible when the majority of people in the IT organization are busy maintaining the running systems. Therefore, the roadmap should reflect an iterative process.

An enterprise has several options for entry points into a service-oriented architecture. These options identify how much the SOA model penetrates into the business and defines levels of adoption. The options are as follows:

- *Initial adoption*: Enterprises that want to reduce risks initially go through a technology validation and a readiness assessment that analyze the technical and business impact in a defined scope. Eventually, the business and technical value realized from this scope can be extrapolated to actual implications for the organization; this usually translates into a deeper commitment to move to SOA. It involves early pilot tests consisting of creating and exposing services from business operations contained in new or existing applications. These tests are used for an early validation of several decision points such as the following:

  - *The capability to transform existing legacy systems.* This might include technical solutions such as messaging, adapters, and connectors, or it might lead to partnership with vendors that can provide products for a service-oriented integration.
  - *The non-functional requirements capabilities* such as performance, security, manageability, and the availability of tooling.
  - *The organizational structure required* to support an evolution of the enterprise, especially one that addresses skills gaps and institutes governance structures.

- *Line-of-business adoption*: At this level, the enterprise will identify a line of business and prioritize processes where the agility and flexibility that SOA offers will increase business value. Of course, the enterprise might have already defined these priorities or have a critical business issue to resolve. In these cases, you still need to assess the SOA applicability to solve the important issue. This involves a broader initial assessment phase and the identification of key metrics and critical success factors.

- *Enterprise adoption*: This level of adoption involves the construction of a business view of a service-oriented enterprise, with a complete prioritization of projects based on business value followed by the architecture and implementation phases. You need to categorize enterprise activities into separate business domains and components that constitute the enterprise. This categorization might already exist within an enterprise or an industry model (for example, the telecommunication eTom model from the TeleManagement forum) that has already-established categories. At this stage, you should establish an SOA governance council with the required empowerment to monitor, define, and authorize changes to services within the enterprise.

- *Enterprise-and-partner-network adoption*: At this level, there is a broad transformation of existing business models or the deployment of new business models involving not only the enterprise, but also its business partners, suppliers, or customers. The enterprise can then select the roles that are appropriate for delivering its value, becoming a service provider, consumer, broker, aggregator, matchmaker, or any combination of those roles.

For each of the prioritized business services and components, the roadmap follows the typical phases of IT project development, with inception, elaboration, implementation, and test and production phases, as typified in the Rational Unified Process™. However, each of these phases includes new activities that relate to the service component identification and realization. Figure 4.1 depicts an overall view of a roadmap, looking at the adoption stages and corresponding activities. This diagram is not exhaustive but gives an indication of potential steps you can follow.

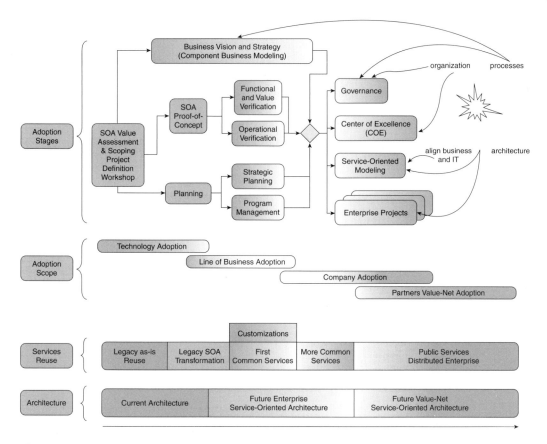

Figure 4.1 A typical service-oriented architecture roadmap.

4.3 The Need for SOA Governance

Enterprises using SOA can adapt to target broader connectivity and increased revenues; on the other hand, doing so requires restructuring applications for greater flexibility and lower costs. This requires the alignment of the business and IT value chain, as described in Chapter 2, "Explaining the Business Value of SOA." With this evolution, the enterprise will also need to adapt the way the business and IT units interlock and define a new way of reflecting business requirements in terms of IT applications. For this reason, organizational governance plays a more prominent role than before. The following sections provide guidance on establishing key governance functions for operating an SOA.

4.3.1 SOA Governance Motivation and Objectives

The business operations and the underlying IT infrastructure in an organization must react very quickly to rapidly respond to new business opportunities. Business units have to prioritize new IT services that have to be designed and managed as part of highly integrated and complex enterprise architecture. To achieve this, we discuss in the following sections a set of key governance functions for a successful SOA roadmap.

Governance provides an overarching structure to prioritize and then support the enterprise business objectives on a strategic, functional, and operational level. The governance model defines "what to do," "how to do it," "who should do it," and "how it should be measured." It defines the rules, processes, metrics, and organizational constructs needed for effective planning, decision-making, steering, and control of the SOA engagement to meet the enterprise business needs and challenging targets. As previously indicated, the SOA project team is responsible for creating this governance model.

The following are key questions that can help define the appropriate governance structure:

- What business change does the enterprise expect from SOA? Is it a better use of its existing infrastructure at lower costs, does it target new business and interaction models, or does it target both?
- Which roles, responsibilities, structures, and procedures exist to allow business prioritization and IT funding, planning, steering, and decision making?
- How can you develop skills and leadership competency?
- Which principles and guidelines are necessary to optimize the alignment of business and IT?
- What is the appropriate way to structure the business-to-IT relationship while keeping consistency and flexibility to allow the organization to quickly adapt to new changes?
- What is the appropriate level of standardization of services, the service definition, and the description?
- How do you control and measure services and service providers? What key business performance indicators do you need to monitor? Who should monitor, define, and authorize changes to existing services?
- How do you decide on a sourcing strategy for services?

We believe that an accepted and formalized governance model is crucial to successfully achieve business objectives, so we will define important governance functions in the following sections. For fast and high-level acceptance, it is essential to start from the existing enterprise structure and adapt it to the SOA roadmap.

To provide architectural governance, you need an organizational structure to help identify all necessary roles and responsibilities. Based on our experience, it is quite useful to establish an SOA *center of excellence (COE)* to control the SOA roadmap and to support large and complex projects. The COE is responsible for keeping the SOA-based implementation aligned with the business requirements on a strategic, tactical, and operational level. It requires authority over technical artifacts such as architecture blueprints, enterprise templates, and design assets.

4.3.2 An SOA Governance Model

In her IBM developerWorks article, Yvonne Balzer describes an SOA governance model on which we based our considerations. SOA governance is an evolution of the ideas of IT governance, introducing a greater business involvement in supporting IT service components. There are different definitions of IT governance, but the IT Governance Institute's definition gives a good general overview:

A.4.1

> ### The IT Governance Institute's Definition of IT Governance
>
> *IT governance is the responsibility of the board of directors and executive management. It is an integral part of enterprise governance and consists of the leadership and organizational structures and processes to ensure that the organization's IT sustains and extends its strategies and objectives.*
>
> *The purpose of IT governance is to direct IT endeavors to ensure that IT performance meets the business objectives so that the following occurs:*
>
> - *IT alignment with the enterprise results in the promised benefits being realized.*
> - *IT enables the enterprise so that opportunities are exploited and benefits are maximized.*
> - *IT resources are used responsibly.*
> - *IT-related risks are managed appropriately.*

SOA governance incorporates the control of the enterprise model as a set of standardized modular business components and processes, and the prioritization of those based on business value. In summary, the SOA governance model is a combination of organizational structure, joint processes, and relationships that are based on accepted ground rules called *governance principles* and the strategic direction.

4.3.3 Strategic Direction and SOA Governance Principles

To sustain the focus on business needs, it is essential to define the strategic direction for developing an SOA. Both business and IT units need a common understanding of the business strategy and objectives. Governance principles and guidelines form the fundamental basis for any decisions. They shape the solution area and define how business and IT units collaborate. Everyone involved should carefully understand and agree upon these principles, from executive management to individual project personnel.

According to E.G. Nadhan in his EDS Solutions Consulting position paper of April 2003, "SOA Implementation Challenges," there are two main governance approaches:

- *Central governance* is optimized for the enterprise. The governance council has representation from each business domain and from technology subject matter experts. The central governance council reviews the addition or removal of services, as well as changes to existing services, before authorizing their implementations.
- *Distributed governance* is optimized for the distributed teams. Each business unit has control over how it provides the services within its own organization. This requires a functional service domain approach. A central committee can provide guidelines and standards.

Each guiding principle should be defined with a rationale explaining the business reasons and implications. The specific principles for architecture design or service definition, for example, can be derived from these guiding principles. In addition, a common understanding of a structured approach from business to IT is fundamental for defining the architecture. You will find different methodic approaches such as process orientation, business functions, or even component modeling like IBM's Component Business Model approach.

4.3.4 Empowerment and Funding

The move to SOA is a paradigm shift driven by the need for more flexible business models, greater integration, and a stronger business and IT alignment. This evolution might face resistance within an organization, which can turn it into just a simpler result of implementing Web services on a small scale rather than a move toward the benefits of a true SOA. In truth, a successful SOA project can happen only with the strong support of senior executives, identified funding, and proper empowerment of the SOA governance body.

One of the pitfalls is the institution of a rubber-stamp governance body or one that has a mere consultative role and cannot enforce its recommendations. At the end of the day, the governance body needs to have proper practical control of project funding.

> **Rule of Thumb**
>
> The governance body needs to have proper practical control of project funding.

4.3.5 Managing the Risk of an SOA Roadmap

When embarking on an SOA roadmap, the first action of the governance body should be to develop an initial *readiness and risk assessment*. The governance body should then periodically update this assessment during the development lifecycle. Figure 4.2, an

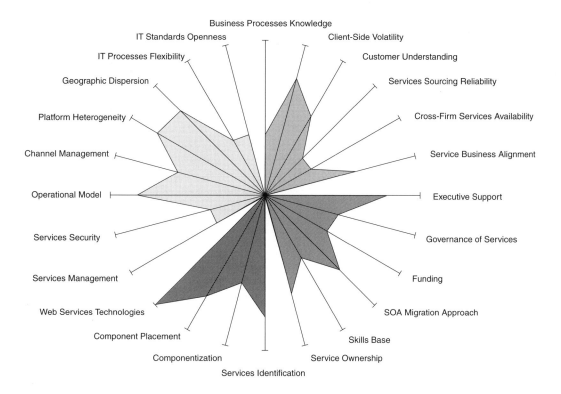

Figure 4.2 An SOA readiness and risk factor assessment.[1]

example of this assessment, shows important aspects and criteria that need to be taken into account. The scale values and the specific criteria can be chosen based on the situation of the individual project. The goal of this assessment is to identify the business, organizational, and technical gaps and roadblocks between the current state of the enterprise and a future service-oriented business model.

This kind of assessment should balance the vision of the SOA-based solutions with the delivery capabilities of the IT department and should help establish specific a business case for the SOA for the organization. It includes both an evaluation of business readiness and one of IT readiness. It requires customer and partner understanding and determines if changes to the client's or partner's needs can be mapped to existing products or applications in a service-oriented fashion.

---

1. This was adopted from IBM internal SOA assessment practice and was modified by editors.

The assessment then suggests possible action plans, with focus on improving the less mature aspects of the enterprise relative to the SOA. As before, these improvements to develop the SOA should be executed in well-planned, incremental projects.

4.3.6 SOA Governance Processes

Governance processes are those needed for strategic business and IT planning and steering—for example, strategy development, IT technical planning, portfolio management, sourcing, innovation management, and architecture management. Any IT organization also needs processes that provide control. Depending on the size of the organization, these processes should be implemented at the appropriate level matching the size, from individuals to teams to departments or even larger. The following types of processes are essential for successful SOA adoption.

A business component identification and prioritization process:

- Defines a structured approach to model, identify, and prioritize business processes and services components.
- Provides formal definition of the business goals and key performance indicators that can be delivered by the architecture and implementation.

A business exception fallback process:

- Business process models can rarely be exhaustive. No one can preview each and every possibility that can happen in an enterprise. Therefore, there must be rules for exception handling that are set up and agreed to.
- This ensures that the concrete SOA solution architecture has to incorporate entry points that enable certain users or processes to bypass the normal, formalized processes and process exceptions. In a way, this gives another degree of flexibility for ad-hoc business process changes.

An architecture review and approval process:

- Defines a structured approach to review and approve changes to the existing SOA and to make decisions in accordance with the governance guidelines.
- Formal design and service evaluation reviews are key control points of SOA development for the installed governance units.

An architecture exception and appeals process:

- Provides means to appeal architectural decisions.
- Allows exceptions to the SOA architecture to meet unique business needs.

An architecture vitality process:

- Ensures that the SOA is maintained and communicated as new services are incorporated into the architecture.
- Variances to the architecture are documented and communicated.

An architecture communication process:

- Ensures that the SOA is available to all who need access.
- Promotes the understanding of the importance of the SOA.

Having outlined the process we now describe how to launch a governance model in practice.

4.3.7 Launching the Governance Model

The process we use to develop a governance model is a three-phased approach (see Figure 4.3). This *governance launch* model was adopted from Yvonne Balzer's developerWorks article "Improve your SOA project plans" and enhanced by the authors. The approach is based on time-constrained SOA engagements. The key to success is to begin to establish the governance functions from day one. To speed up this operation, you can launch the governance model in the following three steps:

A.4.1

Step 1: Operationalize

- Set the governance core functions in place, integrated with the enterprise's business operations.
- Perform the initial SOA assessment.
- Learn and adjust by doing by experiences and available assets, delivering quick results.
- This phase will need experienced practitioners.
- Define the next steps.

Step 2: Professionalize (Automate)

- Build up the necessary structures, processes, methods, and tools.
- Adapt experiences from the operational step.
- Initialize the service-oriented modeling and architecture practice.
- Gather experienced architects and method practitioners.

Step 3: Stabilize

- Teach and train the personnel to run the operation.
- Change from operations mode to coaching mode.
- Need to nurture coaching expertise.

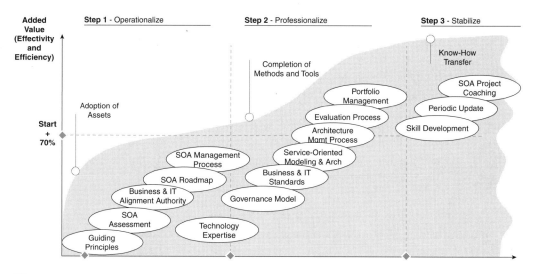

Figure 4.3 Launching the governance model.

4.3.8 Hints and Tips for Success

Even with strong governance, in the real world there are many roadblocks that prevent this type of evolution; thus, it is essential to build on solid ground. The following are some practical lessons we have learned from engagements:

- Set up rules and roles (discussed in Section 4.5) to organize and project-manage the SOA endeavor.
- Communicate regularly. SOA also involves corporate cultural change; therefore, to hurdle barriers, communication is critical, especially between lines of business and technology teams.
- Document each decision, constraint, and assumption to ensure transparency in decision-making and departmental buy-in.
- Define key deliverables and necessary toolsets or templates. These deliverables need to be readable by a variety of parties in the enterprise.
- Set up pragmatic tools for lifecycle management and versioning. Particularly see the discussion on long-lived business processes in Section 4.4.
- Assign a weight factor to each decision and then document and communicate those decisions and their weights.
- Continue to keep a strong sponsorship by all stakeholders and the buy-in of decision-makers.

4.4 SOA Technical Governance

With SOA, you can expect that business process cycles will be different from vendor product cycles. As a result, it is inevitable that, in the case of long-running or long-lived processes, you will need to support scenarios in which different versions of a business process exist concurrently on a changing infrastructure. Managing this challenge has implications throughout the project development lifecycle, not just for the runtime but also for the tools and methods used to define business processes within an enterprise.

You can manage the challenge of the dichotomy between business process cycles and product cycle by doing the following:

- Reducing the impact of changes by modularization
- Achieving middleware independence by defining the explicit process state
- Monitoring and handling business exceptions

Each of these topics is discussed in the following sections.

4.4.1 Reducing Impact by Modularization

Just as services can have different levels of granularity and permutations in the enterprise, processes also can have such granularity. This granularity appears when processes are designed as a composition of individual process modules. Each module offers a service interface and manages its own particular state internally. It then becomes much easier to change parts of the processes by developing new process modules that are selected from existing services using policies.

4.4.2 Achieving Middleware Independence with Explicit Process State

Current business process middleware engines maintain their process state internally. This dependency ties the process instances to the particular middleware engine, sometimes even to a particular version of the middleware. To avoid this, business process designers should elevate the explicit state beyond the engine level at each process step that leads to a waiting state until an external event arrives.

Thus, there is a need to be able to maintain and communicate state as distributed across the SOA. One particular programming model support for capturing these state descriptions is the set of specifications included in the WS-Resource Framework (as published on IBM developerWorks). These specifications allow the programmer to declare and implement the association between a Web service (a process module) and one or more identified, data-typed state components called *WS-Resources*.

A.4.2

4.4.3 Business Exceptions Monitoring and Handling

Even if the enterprise has spent a significant amount of time and effort to understand and model its business processes, undoubtedly unplanned business exceptions can still occur.

A fully automated, services-oriented infrastructure that is capable of supporting any such exceptions to the business processes is unrealistic. This means that all business processes and their supporting infrastructure should be designed to allow manual recovery and control. Furthermore, for each business or technical domain, the organization should identify individuals that can handle such exceptions and act on the infrastructure. In most process and services identification modeling activities, the focus is on delivering mainstream models and a few variations. The business analysts must look at making the processes more granular so that unexpected variations and exceptions will be easier to handle in the operational environment.

4.5 SOA Project Roles

The notion of handling exceptions in a manual fashion brings to light the key significance of people involved in SOA projects and the roles they might play. SOA projects involve many familiar project roles: project manager, business analyst, architect, developer, security specialist, and system and database administrator. However, these roles were created for different purposes and might have different inherent meanings based on the organization's viewpoint. To appropriately structure an SOA project, you need to consider that these roles might need to evolve to match the componentization and decomposition of the applications into services. In addition, implementing an SOA might also call for some additional roles.

In the following sections, we explain the functions of roles, and then we discuss roles versus skills in a project, followed by the phases in the project where these roles might apply. We then describe how these roles can be extended under SOA, as well as the new roles that follow. Finally, we examine some of the interactions among the various roles in SOA projects.

4.5.1 The Function of Roles

There is no single, global, standard definition of all IT jobs, not to mention SOA projects. Many jobs require certifications, a defined knowledge base, or cognitive tests; however, these certifications cannot always truly prove a candidate's applied knowledge, skill transfer, and creativity aspects. Because the team size, the workload, the types of work, and the subjects needed to solve IT problems vary greatly across companies, industries, and geographies, flexible teams with some specialist members are necessary. To coordinate such teams, the leaders (the architects and project managers) have to demonstrate the aforementioned capabilities beyond mere subject knowledge.

In this book, we use the notion of roles because doing so brings some order to the chaos. Roles are related to project phases and define an abstraction layer separate from actual job descriptions and assigned human resources. All project team members take on one or more roles.

Roles are a common concept in project management and design methodologies. The role concept establishes a commonly understood vocabulary, which has proven to be a powerful instrument at project-initiation time. A role does not imply that a specific individual person must execute the tasks that are associated with the role; instead, it implies an identity (an individual, a team, an organization, and so on) that fulfills that part of the process.

4.5.2 Roles and Skills

Identifying the roles involved in your project will certainly help, but finding the right people with appropriate skills is crucial. Services typically are technologically lightweight and simple; this is part of their power. With this technology, islands of heterogeneous systems can be more easily opened up for collaboration. However, along with these new possibilities come new sources of errors. SOA projects may be a new kind of project for your organization, but chances are they will not be a simpler kind of project.

An SOA project team setup should reflect these specific issues with the inclusion of appropriate skill levels and talents. We highly recommend a mix of practitioners who have experience with different platforms, different technical problems, and different skill domains. This is especially important for the SOA architect. If such a person is not available to the team, it would be feasible to have additional (part-time) co-architects to fill the gaps.

4.5.3 Project Phases

Development projects have different phases, requiring different skills and collaborations throughout the lifecycle, and SOA projects are no different. Independent of your organization's choice of the individual methodology used (waterfall approach or others), most projects will generally include the following development phases:

- Requirements engineering
- Business domain analysis
- Solution architecture outline
- High- and low-level design
- Analysis and design (today mainly OOAD and DB design)
- Various test phases (such as unit, integration, system, and acceptance tests)
- Going live
- Maintenance
- Management

Aspects such as service modeling (for example, using a coarse- or fine-grained interface), choice of SOAP engine (IBM WebSphere SOAP, Apache Axis, or Apache SOAP 2.3), and organizing interoperability tests are primarily examples of Web service–specific considerations. The nature of these issues varies. For example, service modeling prerequisites a different skill and mindset than interoperability testing.

4.5.4 Examining and Adapting Roles

The following sections look into a model that shows how existing roles work in SOA development projects. For presentation purposes, we divided the roles in our model into two categories—existing roles and new roles—followed by a discussion on the integration of both categories.

Because SOA projects are just another type of development project, it is not surprising that we find a lot of well-known roles that we can define as a category of *existing roles*. However, some of the existing roles receive additional SOA-related responsibilities. From our SOA project experiences, we saw the need to establish new roles, which are listed as the *new roles* section. Please keep in mind that these are general descriptions of roles rather than detailed job descriptions.

4.5.5 A Look at Existing Roles

Let's start with the six roles you may have seen (or participated as) on different technical projects: the project manager, the business analyst, the architect, the developer, the security specialist, and the system and database administrator. Note that this list is certainly nonexclusive, and it is not always applicable to every organization. Therefore, we have limited the list to the most prevalent roles that will later apply to SOA projects.

4.5.5.1 The IT Project Manager

The project manager has the overall management and leadership responsibility for the project team. He or she defines and tracks project plans and determines the work breakdown structure. For an SOA project, certain additional skills and knowledge are needed to best perform this role, as described in Section 4.5.5.11, "The SOA Project Manager."

4.5.5.2 The Business Analyst

The business analyst harvests the functional requirements of business users and provides domain knowledge to the team. He or she must understand the business language and have industry- and domain-specific skills. In an SOA approach, the business analyst should use a *component business modeling* approach, a technique for modeling an enterprise as disjunctive components in order to identify opportunities for innovation or improvement.

4.5.5.3 The Architect

This is the technical leader of the project. The architect's task is to develop the logical and physical layout (structure) of the overall solution and its components.

4.5.5.4 The Developer

The developer creates and tests the software implementation. In SOA, the role is not significantly different, with the exception of the code written in SOA projects, which is written as services. This turns the developer into a *service developer*.

4.5.5.5 The Security Specialist

The security specialist is responsible for the definition of security guidelines (policies) and the implementation of security means adhering to these guidelines. The domain for this role is described in Chapter 8, "Securing the SOA Environment."

4.5.5.6 The System and Database Administrator

This role performs the installation and provides ongoing maintenance on the technical infrastructure: the hardware, operating and database systems, and middleware. Certain aspects of information integration under SOA were described in Chapter 3, "Architecture Elements." This role typically falls into the domain of the classic database administrator.

4.5.5.7 The Service Deployer

The service deployer takes the development artifacts and installs them in the target runtime environment, generates stubs and skeletons for the target environment from WSDL and installs them together with the service implementations, and provides JAX-RPC (Java API for XML-based remote procedure calls) mapping and handler configuration through services-specific deployment descriptors.

4.5.5.8 The Service Integration Tester

The service integration tester is responsible for the various standard test stages such as integration, load, and acceptance tests. He or she also defines test cases for services interoperability and conformance tests. This role is aligned to the architect and to the governance bodies, as previously described. It is the quality assurance role.

4.5.5.9 The Toolsmith

The role of toolsmith is responsible for designing and implementing the project-specific scripts, generators, and other utilities needed by various aspects of the SOA. The degree of standardization in the Web services world now makes it possible, for example, to develop custom WSDL-, JAX-RPC-, or JSR-109-aware tools.

4.5.5.10 The Knowledge Transfer Facilitator

This role provides access to subject matter experts and technical instructors who bring in extended knowledge regarding SOA, on-demand, and in most cases, Web services concepts and implementation assets. By relating the use cases created during requirements gathering to the functions of this role, this role can easily be taken by so-called *customer-proxies* that represent individual service requests within the SOA.

4.5.5.11 The SOA Project Manager

This role is an evolution of the classic project manager. The SOA project manager not only needs to plan for much shorter delivery cycles, but he or she must also establish new acceptance models. The project manager has to work with service providers to establish the appropriate service-level agreements and resource usage. This role becomes more important with increased use of aggregated services (those that are composed of other services).

4.5.5.12 The SOA System Administrator

In this role, in addition to managing and monitoring the platform infrastructure, the system administrator also manages the business and service-level agreements within the SOA.

4.5.6 A Look at New Roles

In addition to the revised roles, there are other roles involved with SOA projects: the SOA architect, the service modeler or designer, the process flow designer, the service developer, the integration specialist, the interoperability tester, the UDDI administrator, the UDDI designer, and finally, the services governor.

4.5.6.1 The SOA Architect

The architect role evolves into an *SOA architect*, a mediator between business and technology. More than a structural architect, as in the role of a classic software architect, the SOA architect acts more like a city planner, with a higher-level view. This person plays a dynamic business-to-IT adaptation role to transform the ideas and concepts of business operations into terms and concepts available in the IT infrastructure. In this role, the SOA architect is responsible for the end-to-end service requestor and provider design and takes care of inquiring about and stating the non-functional service requirements.

4.5.6.2 The Service Modeler or Designer

A service modeler applies data and function modeling techniques to define the service interface contracts, including the schemas for messages during an exchange. The service modeler works with the SOA architect to create these contracts.

4.5.6.3 The Process Flow Designer

In place of an integration specialist, this role investigates the explicit, declarative, service orchestration (aggregation, composition) possibilities. It concentrates on the technical process flows that support given business processes. It is an optional role in most cases.

4.5.6.4 The Service Developer

The service developer is typically an enterprise developer, expert in programming models such as J2EE and familiar with Web services concepts and XML. The role develops service interfaces and implementations on the provider side and service invocation code on the requestor side of service interactions. The *service developer* is probably the best-equipped role today. An SOA development environment focuses on providing tool-based support for designing and deploying service-based components.

It is the role of the SOA architect to ensure that the SOA developers are not overemphasizing the use of technology. It often becomes easy to expose any piece of logic as a service but at the cost of ignoring best practices for defining the granularity of these services, thus impacting overall performance and manageability. For example, you can easily turn a useful, simple, calculation function into a service so that it can be called from numerous other services.

A service developer using WS-* and J2EE standards-based tooling might also have some subroles:

- *Web Services designer and programmer*, with implementation skills in J2EE, C++, or .NET
- *Legacy integration and adaptation designer*, with services-enabled adaptation skills

4.5.6.5 The Integration Specialist

Integration specialists are mediators and users of both the service modeler's and the process flow designer's work. They typically have a broad-based technical knowledge in the integration field because they will need some understanding of SOA systems, enterprise integration means, business processes, and applications coded in Java or other languages. Tools like WebSphere Business Integration Workbench™ allow the person in this role to compose complex systems of available services.

4.5.6.6 The Interoperability Tester

The interoperability tester verifies that any developed requestor and provider implementations will interoperate seamlessly. Another primary activity is to ensure Web Services Interoperability (WS-I) conformance and industry standard conformance.

4.5.6.7 The UDDI Administrator

The UDDI administrator defines how a generic UDDI data model can be customized and populated with services. This is, in most cases, an optional role. It also depends on whether UDDI is chosen as the standard or there is an alternate proprietary data model in the organization. In this case, there might be another similar role, often part of the IT governance body, that acts as administrator.

4.5.6.8 The UDDI Designer

There might be the need for a *UDDI designer* who is responsible for planning, designing, and building the UDDI registry where services are published and announced for the various levels of the SOA.

4.5.6.9 The Services Governor

This is an important new role that has the cross-enterprise responsibility, on the SOA governance team, to validate and select the business services most appropriate for the given enterprise and then identify who owns them. This role can be played by either SOA architects or business analysts when working in the SOA governance team.

4.5.7 Integrating Existing and New Roles

These new roles originate from existing ones (for example, SOA architect and service developer). However, we believe that for the new roles, the introduction of new names for these roles is justified. Each of the roles addresses a different aspect of the project as a whole. Earlier we stated that one person typically wears several hats, in other words acts in more than one role. However, a project's risk decreases if different people with broad and diverse skills are on board. There are situations in which only such a purposeful cooperation of different individuals can unveil the crucial issues of the project and lead to a sound solution.

On the other hand, the communication overhead increases with each new team member. There is no single or simple answer to the roles-to-people mapping challenge. There are many different opinions and controversies regarding how it should be approached. As previously mentioned, the assignment of individuals to these various roles depends on the situation, the skills and experiences available, and the scope of the project.

Rather than entering a debate about what is the optimal formation, consider the following scenario: A fictitious company in the insurance industry has decided to build a new set of mid-office business applications for risk and policy management, and the set has to interface with two different backend systems. Both backend systems have been built as J2EE applications: one uses EJBs and the other uses only servlets, JSPs, and JDBC to connect to its customer and contract databases.

During the initial stages of the development project, the roles defined in the example are assigned to team members. In addition to the Web services–specific activities, the standard project tasks and roles are also identified and assigned. To illustrate how a team setup can look, Table 4.1 shows an example of selected new roles, their tasks, prerequisite skills, and supporting tools. Additionally, we list the other roles on the team that collaborate with each selected role.

Because the definition of roles depends on the concrete project situation, assignments to the actual people cannot be prescribed in a standardized way; they have to be defined and assigned per the needs of the situation. Assignments can be used by the project manager in cooperation with the SOA architect to create the work breakdown for the project at hand. Further corporate guidelines, restrictions, and best practices are influencing the final project setup and management.

A.4.3

In addition to the previously mentioned roles at the SOA level, there is a complementary list of roles specific to Web services in the developerWorks article, "Web Services project roles," by Olaf Zimmermann and Frank Mueller (2004).

4.6 Summary

After the SOA governance model has been launched, it sets the stage for the services modeling and architecting phase, which also includes the design of the necessary supporting IT infrastructure. This step requires the use of a formalized method. The next chapter covers the best practices and the modeling and architecture method we have captured from many of our SOA projects.

Table 4.1 The Responsibility of Selected New SOA Roles

Project Role	Performed Tasks	Collaborates With	Prerequisite Skills	Supporting Tools
SOA architect	Solution outline, requirements analysis, architectural decisions, component modeling, operational modeling, communicating business issues and components to services	Any other team member plus line-of-business (LoB) representatives	General IT architectures, J2EE technology, XML, XML schema Web services and SOA concepts, platforms, best practices, business knowledge	UML editors, office suites
Service modeler	Interface contract design, WSDL editing (top-down, bottom-up, meet-in-the-middle)	Business analyst, SOA architect, service developer	WSDL XML schema and namespaces J2EE technology	WSDL editors, Java-to-WSDL generators
Process flow designer	Business process modeling, assembly of atomic services into chains (processes)	Service modeler, business analyst, SOA architect, LoB representatives	BPEL4WS, WSDL	Graphical flow modeling tools, BPEL4WS generators, corresponding runtime support
Service developer	Service provider coding, service requestor coding, provide SOAP header handlers if needed, code documentation	Service provider coding, service requestor coding, provide SOAP header handlers if needed, code documentation	J2EE, XML, SOAP, WSDL	Web services wizards in IDEs, WSDL-to-Java generators
Interoperability tester	WSDL inspection, SOAP envelope tracing, conformance testing, troubleshooting	Service developers (requestor and provider side)	SOAP, WSDL, WS-I profiles	TCP/IP tunnels and monitors, WSI test tools

4.7 Links to developerWorks

A.4.1 Balzer, Y. *Improve your SOA project plans*. IBM developerWorks, July 2004. http://www-106.ibm.com/developerworks/webservices/library/ws-improvesoa/.

A.4.2 IBM. *The WS-Resource Framework*. IBM developerWorks, March 2005. http://www-128.ibm.com/developerworks/webservices/library/ws-resource/ws-wsrfpaper.html.

A.4.3 Zimmermann, O. and Mueller, F. *Web services project roles*. IBM developerWorks, June 2004. http://www-106.ibm.com/developerworks/webservices/library/ws-roles/.

4.8 References

Belbin, R. Meredith *Management Teams, 2nd Edition*. Elsevier Books, 2004.

Belbin, R. Meredith *Managing without Power*. Butterworth-Heinemann, 2001.

Bieberstein, N. *Application Development as an Engineering Discipline: Revolution or Evolution?* IBM Systems Journal, Vol. 36, 1-1997.

Hess, H. M. *Aligning technology and business: Applying patterns for legacy transformation*. IBM Systems Journal, Vol. 44, 1-2005. http://www.research.ibm.com/journal/sj44-1.html.

IT Governance Institute. *IT Governance definition*. http://www.itgi.org/template_ITGI.cfm?Section=Purpose&Template=/ContentManagement/HTMLDisplay.cfm&ContentID=14697.

MacMillan, K. and Downing, S. *Governance and Performance Goodwill Hunting in Strategy Dynamics*, Henley Management College, 2001.

Meredith, Jack R. and Mantel Jr., Samuel J. *Project Management—A Managerial Approach, 3rd Edition*. John Wiley & Sons, 1995.

Nadhan, E.D. *Service Oriented Architecture Implementation Challenges*. EDS Solutions Consulting, position paper, April 2003. http://www.eds.com/services/innovation/downloads/so_architecture.pdf.

Telemanagement Forum. *Homepage*. http://www.tmforum.org.

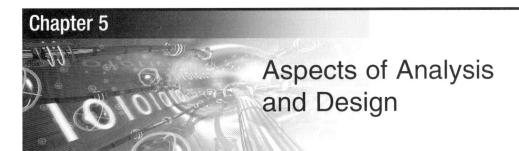

Chapter 5

Aspects of Analysis and Design

"Every bright thing has been thought of before. One must just try to think of it again."

—*Johann Wolfgang von Goethe*

SOA has been developed and implemented in many ways by enterprises during the last decade using custom approaches for analysis and design. The increasing focus within the IT industry on widespread deployment of SOA is bringing greater attention to the practicalities of introducing specific service-oriented analysis and design methodologies and technologies.

In this chapter, we will explore some of the analysis and design considerations that apply to the development of service-oriented systems—those based on open-standard concepts and technologies as well as industry-tempered methods and well-tried software engineering principles.

Chapter 4, "SOA Project Planning Aspects," discussed the considerations for establishing SOA projects, and the roles needed as services are developed and deployed. In Chapter 6, "Enterprise Solution Assets," and Chapter 7, "Determining Non-Functional Requirements," we will continue to explore the SOA compass headings, with discussion focused on reusable architectural patterns, non-functional requirements, and qualities of service.

5.1 Service-Oriented Analysis and Design

The IT industry has been innovating techniques and methodologies for developing reliable, efficient enterprise software for the last four decades. Several models for construction of such software have evolved. Simple procedures, structured programming, data-flow programming, message-oriented programming, and object-oriented programming are just a few of those that are still in widespread use today.

Although these paradigms introduced new concepts and principles, each was built on the approaches that preceded it. For example, modularity is one of the engineering qualities associated with structured programming, and information hiding (encapsulation) is one of the qualities associated with object-based programming. In keeping with this evolution in thinking about software construction, there has been an evolution in techniques and tools for analysis and design and an evolution in runtime execution technologies.

The good news is that, throughout this lengthy period of evolution, a number of sound principles, acceptable constraints, and best practices have been learned within the IT industry and embodied in modern software. This evolving framework for architectural design carries forward as new models emerge.

A.5.1

Service-oriented, event-driven programming is the latest in a long succession of ideas to emerge. It incorporates many of the advantages of earlier models, builds on valuable lessons learned in previous eras, and introduces valuable new concepts, patterns, and practices.

The question is, what must we consider in order to analyze domain requirements and identify the best candidates for implementation as software services, and what must we consider when designing services that fulfill those requirements in the best way possible? The answer is that many well-established and familiar considerations still apply, but interestingly, SOA introduces some new ones that we will focus on in this chapter.

5.1.1 On Modeling

It is especially interesting to note that, independent of the industry focus on SOA, there has been an increase in focus on modeling. The OMG has published industry standards for model-driven architecture (MDA) and the Unified Modeling Language (UML) for use in development methodologies for commercial and other types of software. Others have proposed standards and technologies for business process modeling (BPM).

What used to be called "analysis and design" in previous technological eras is now often called "modeling." This development suggests a new level of formality and rigor in theoretical foundations and recognizes that there might be a continuum of definition, refinement, and transformation activities for analyzing requirements, developing architecture and design, and generating software code for target execution platforms. Some would argue with the suggestion of rigor, but there is no doubt that modeling is here to stay as a powerful technique for developing SOA solutions.

5.1.2 Layers of Abstraction

Much has been written about the value of abstraction and layering as techniques for thinking about software in an enterprise. They help organize thoughts, discussion, and documentation and provide focus at the most appropriate level of detail (see Figure 5.1).

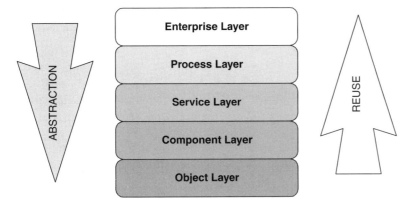

Figure 5.1 SOA layers of abstraction.

Each layer in a typical SOA is characterized by a number of important categories of artifacts, each with its own set of properties and relationships.

The Enterprise layer, for example, is characterized by a business model that describes the business that an enterprise is engaged in, whereas the Process layer is characterized by descriptions of business processes that together fulfill the business model.

Changes to the business model at the Enterprise layer raise requirements for change at the Process layer and a probable cascade of requirements in lower layers. Analysis of these requirements at each layer results in a number of architectural and design decisions that must be logged for traceability and allowed to evolve over time in accordance with best practices. Chapter 6 provides guidance for capturing these architectural decisions so that they are reusable across enterprise projects.

5.1.2.1 Enterprise Layer

A number of existing architectural frameworks (for example, the Zachman framework) and methodologies can be applied at the Enterprise layer, and SOA introduces a small number of new artifacts and new architectural considerations.

However, the business model that describes the way an enterprise operates in a particular industry will most likely identify criteria by which business processes are judged to be either core competencies (and therefore essential to competitive advantage and implemented under tight control) or supporting competencies (and therefore possibly delegated to industry partners). Refer to Chapter 2, "Explaining the Business Value of SOA," for our earlier discussion on the business model.

Although these criteria are not new to enterprises at the highest level, they are becoming more relevant as SOA enables partnerships to be established at the Process and Service layers and enhances enterprise responsiveness in the on-demand era.

5.1.2.2 Process Layer

A number of existing, well-known frameworks and methodologies also operate at the Process layer. They do so by identifying and characterizing business processes that are incorporated into the enterprise business model. Each process is unique in its handling of one major functional area of the business and might be characterized by decomposition into subprocesses as required to achieve its goals.

A.5.2

Subprocesses might be further decomposed to expose dependencies on services. It is usual to find that the collection of subprocesses needed to implement a given business process at the highest level is unique within an enterprise context, but this might not be true in enterprises that have grown by acquisition, where duplicated processes are often found. Top-down analysis techniques, such as BPM and Component Business Modeling (see the CBM discussion later in this chapter), can be useful for populating this layer.

The Process layer is emphasized in SOA, as some processes can be modeled and later implemented as services. Unfortunately, this presents a gray area in the use of terminology between "process" and "service." What is a process, and what is a service? In our experience, one distinguishing characteristic between these concepts can be found in intended usage. Processes are defined once and used ideally within a single context. Services, on the other hand, are defined once and reused many times over within diverse contexts such as different business processes, corporate divisions, and lines of business.

5.1.2.3 Service Layer

Abstraction at the Service layer is characterized by a number of services that carry out individual business functions. In an SOA, this layer often provides a conceptual bridge between the higher-level Enterprise and Process layers and the lower-level Component and Object layers. Some business analysts use this layer to identify critical functions that are needed to run the business, whereas IT specialists use this layer to identify and expose technical functions that match business analysts' requirements. These critical functions are often regarded as integration points within the enterprise application domain.

A.5.3

Each service within this layer can be decomposed into a flow of simpler services that in turn are implemented using a number of components. For example, a billing service might be introduced at this layer that is dependent on customer information and order-processing services. These, in turn, are mapped in the next layer to component implementations such as CICS transactions and AS/400 programs. IBM Patterns for e-Business can be used to identify a number of different possible technical mappings at this layer.

5.1.2.4 Component Layer

Abstraction at the Component layer in an SOA identifies and characterizes a potentially large number of components that might be composed as service implementations at some future time. Bottom-up analysis of existing application systems will often reveal components that could be considered as candidates for reuse in this way. Unfortunately, some components, such as customer inquiry, are often implemented many times over in existing application packages and are deployed redundantly in operational systems. Selection of just one of those implementations for exposure as a service becomes an important activity (see 5.2.4. "Realization of Services" later in this chapter).

Components identified at this layer are the building blocks for services in an SOA. Although some components will be designed specifically to satisfy the requirement for a new service, most will be adapted and composed from existing systems in a successful SOA deployment. A number of different techniques and technologies will have been used to implement components in those existing systems.

5.1.2.5 Object Layer

Abstraction at the Object layer identifies a wide range of business objects, their attributes, and behaviors needed for each of the business functions required in an SOA. Well-established analysis and design techniques (Yourdon and Coad) can be used at this layer to identify and characterize object classes, inheritance of properties and behaviors, and the important relationships between them. These are used to implement components at the higher layer.

It is interesting to note that although SOA does not introduce any new artifacts in the Object layer, it does apparently reuse the concept of "services" taken from object methods. However, this overlap in terminology can be deceiving. One of several activities introduced by OOAD was to identify and characterize services by their functional interfaces. Some services were identified as internal or private to a domain of interest, whereas others were public and designed for external use. In many respects, a similar activity was also important to earlier structured programming methods. Analysis and design for services in an SOA builds on previous learning in OOAD but goes further by characterizing certain functional interfaces as suitable for publication and invocation at the higher service layer (not just within the object layer as "public" methods).

In a modern SOA, services are often implemented using objects. When this is true, there is a choice to be made: whether to invoke a service using open-standard—Service layer—mechanisms or to use Component or Object layer mechanisms such as object language method invocation. The decision should be made on the merits of the service as a reusable component in the SOA at large and on the motivation for decoupling of components in such an SOA tempered by performance and other non-functional requirements.

5.1.3 Reuse

Because each of the abstraction layers is populated in an SOA, it is easy to see that the number of artifacts increases dramatically as decomposition progresses top-down from enterprise models to business processes to services to components and objects. In a typical enterprise scenario, there might be a great deal of undesirable redundancy at each of these layers, such as multiple business processes for supply chain, redundant services for credit checking, duplicate components for inventory, and many, many different objects representing customers.

The goal for every SOA is to maximize reuse at each of these layers by refactoring redundant capabilities, exposing and promoting common functionality, and composing new business-relevant functions as reusable services. This can only be achieved by introducing strong SOA governance focused on measures that relate reuse to reduced IT costs and time-to-market for competitive advantage.

5.1.4 Service Encapsulation

Abstraction is one of the principal techniques used by SOA modelers to bring focus to the most significant characteristics in a system and to manage complexity. Service encapsulation (information hiding) is perhaps the next most important. Yet the principle is simple enough.

Every service in an SOA must have an interface that is accessible to a wide range of service consumers and that encapsulates or hides the details of implementations made available by service providers (see Figure 5.2). Several aspects are important here. First, any consumer of a service must not be aware of or sensitive to service provider implementation details. This allows for different implementations to satisfy consumer requests and flexibility to be built into the SOA for evolution over time. Second, any provider of a service must not be aware of or sensitive to service consumer implementation details. This loose coupling between consumers and providers allows for new types of consumer to be introduced at a later time without the need for reimplementation of service providers.

Modeling for a service interface therefore should be neutral to implementation dependencies such as platform, operating system, programming language, provider location, or timing considerations. In addition, the description of information flow across the service interface should be as stable (that is, nonvolatile) and as constrained as possible to improve longevity and reuse for services in an SOA. This will be discussed later in this chapter.

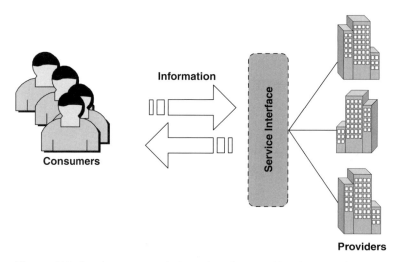

Figure 5.2 Service encapsulation—interface and implementations.

5.1.5 Loose-Coupling

The lack of dependencies between service providers and consumers is very important for the health and success of an SOA. This is often discussed in terms of the loose-coupling within an SOA (see Figure 5.3 for seven useful dimensions of coupling). Note that these dimensions are listed in a memorable sequence, but no particular significance is attached to the relative positioning or distance from either provider or consumer. Elements of coupling from these dimensions are found to be additive in SOA scenarios.

The first dimension is concerned with location. Service consumers should not be dependent on any knowledge of where a service provider is located or on any form of nonstandard addressing. A configurable or dynamic service discovery component can be used to provide the necessary decoupling, and this, in turn, can be deployed as a gateway or ESB in an SOA solution.

The second dimension is concerned with coupling introduced by service consumer and provider implementations based on specific platform technologies. This form of coupling can be removed by using open-standard technologies (hosted by both consumer and provider platforms), providing they have been proven to be interoperable. A common example is the use of TCP/IP, XML, SOAP, and WSDL technologies to decouple .NET consumers from J2EE providers.

The language dimension is concerned with a form of coupling introduced by dependencies on specific language technologies. For example, the use of serialized Java object streams in service messages might be a highly effective mechanism for certain (Java language) consumers and providers, but it might limit the amount of reuse that is achievable as an SOA solution evolves. The use of open-standard formats and protocols from within languages of choice is probably the best way to avoid this coupling.

The contract dimension is concerned with the most desirable form of coupling between consumers and providers. The contract is implemented as a service interface with operations and policies that must be known to both consumers and providers. The strength of

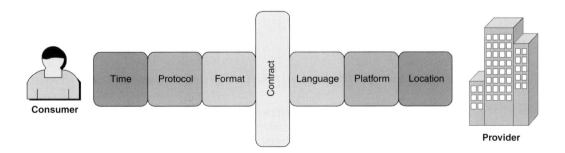

Figure 5.3 Dimensions of coupling in SOA.

this coupling might be measured in terms of the breadth of dependency on the operations, information types, and policies (for example, the number of operations, types, and policies used). Note that this coupling is between consumers and the service contract. Any number of possible providers can satisfy the contract and deliver the service to consumers.

The format dimension is concerned with coupling introduced by specific message formats used in SOA solutions. Proprietary or custom formats might be used for many reasons, but they introduce dependencies that will become an obstacle to flexibility and growth in the future. Open-standard formats, such as SOAP XML, provide the best insurance against this form of coupling, but adaptors, gateways, or an ESB can be used to provide format transformations to remove this coupling.

The protocol dimension is concerned with coupling introduced by specific protocols used in SOA solutions. Proprietary or custom protocols can be introduced for networking, federated single sign-on, transactionality, and other capabilities, but they impose dependencies that might become an obstacle to future flexibility and growth. Open-standard protocols, such as SOAP HTTP and the Web services standards, provide the best insurance against this form of coupling, but configurable dynamic binding mechanisms built into SOA infrastructure can be a reliable way to insulate consumer and provider business logic from this coupling.

The time dimension is concerned with coupling introduced by the assumption that service consumers and providers are available at the same time or, more generally, at a specific time. Although some service requests must be satisfied within a constrained time period, most requests can be designed to operate "as soon as possible." The use of asynchronous service invocation mechanisms may provide the most generally applicable decoupling solution. However, no open standard has yet been agreed upon to provide such a mechanism in a general way. SOA infrastructures such as gateways and ESB can provide at least a partial solution in the interim.

The dimensions of coupling listed are not the only sources of dependency that should be considered. Neither are they ranked in order in Figure 5.3. In nearly all SOA projects, some of these forms of coupling will be found, and SOA architects should be careful to remove as many as possible. Designing for use of open-standard technologies and infrastructure patterns such as the ESB is the principle strategy for implementing the loose-coupling needed for a successful SOA. See also Chapter 3, "Architecture Elements," and Chapter 7, "Determining Non-Functional Requirements."

5.1.6 Strong Cohesion

Another important consideration when modeling services is cohesion between the operations in a service contract. Strong cohesion is an indication that a service contract contains operations that are closely related by shared reference to information about specific objects (usually business objects) and their properties and relationships. Some of the dimensions of cohesion that are considered most relevant to SOA modeling are shown in Figure 5.4.

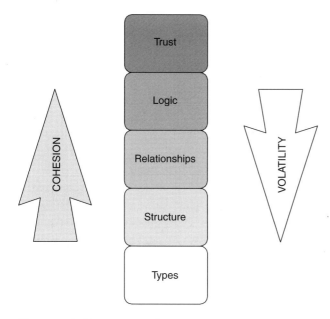

Figure 5.4 Dimensions of cohesion in SOA.

A service interface is only weakly cohesive when information required by the operations is not of the same type or is possibly untyped. Most modern SOA interfaces are described in terms of XML data types, according to preferred WSDL practices, but it is only when operations share the use of specific information types that the interface become weakly cohesive. The more complex the (business object) types that are shared, the greater the cohesion in this respect.

When structure between information elements is shared in the operations of a service interface, some additional cohesion results. Structure often implies certain relationships between elements of information in the operations that must be understood by both service consumers and providers bound by the service contract.

Cohesion in a service interface becomes even stronger when relationships between information elements are made explicit (for example, by using standard resource definition framework [RDF] technologies) and are shared by operations. Such relationships begin to expose the semantics—that is, the intended meaning—of the information that flows when the service operations are invoked. Operations that do not share this meaning probably do not belong to the same service interface.

At higher levels of cohesion, the operations of a service interface must be based on shared logic and rules of trust. At present, these aspects cannot be expressed explicitly in a standards-based service description, but the implementation of the operations will be based on inferences that can be made about the information flowing and rules that govern the level of trust assumed when handling that information.

The most cohesive interfaces will be the most resilient to change over time and the most reused in an SOA.

5.1.7 Service Granularity

Much has been written about the granularity of services. Should services be coarse grained or fine grained, high level or low level, business or technical? Our experience tells us that the answer to this question is in the balance between two fundamental, competing motivations in analysis and design for SOA solutions.

First, there is a top-down motivation to identify services that can be directly related to delivery of business value. These are often called business services and are named using verbs (like `fulfillOrder`) taken from the business community's vocabulary. Second, there is a bottom-up motivation to identify and promote services that encapsulate the most highly reusable business logic and rules. These are often called technical services and are named using verbs (like `getOrderInfo`) taken from the IT community's vocabulary.

In practice, a spectrum of service granularities results in an SOA solution from these motivations. Analysis of a dependency graph between services in the SOA will often show that coarse-grained (highly valued) services have relatively few invokers but a much larger dependency on fine-grained services that are invoked. Fine-grained (highly reused) services, on the other hand, have a relatively large number of invokers but almost no dependency on services that are invoked. It becomes a matter of judgment as to where the line between coarse-grained and fine-grained services is drawn. It is also often predicted that coarse-grained service descriptions will specify larger amounts of information in their operational boundaries, whereas fine-grained service descriptions will specify smaller amounts. This proves to be an unreliable measure of granularity, but it is useful as a factor in SOA network capacity planning.

5.1.8 Well-Designed Services

We are often asked what makes a well-designed service. The answer is always that a well-designed service is one that satisfies all of its functional and non-functional requirements. But this answer is perhaps not as helpful as it might be. It urges you to spend time ensuring that requirements are well analyzed, design is well focused, and development well executed.

A better service is one that satisfies a wide range of consumer requirements with a stable and well-published description. The combination of best practices for loose-coupling and strong cohesion (see Figure 5.5) defines many of the important aspects of well-designed and deployed services in the face of wide-ranging and possibly unpredictable future requirements. One of the best-known maxims from the world of distributed applications is that no matter how hard you try to capture known requirements accurately, there will always be users (consumers) who will find new ways to reuse your service. This is particularly true of distributed systems built using highly reusable services.

Conclusion: *Perhaps the best service is one that already exists and can be reused in creative ways rather than being designed and developed afresh from requirements.*

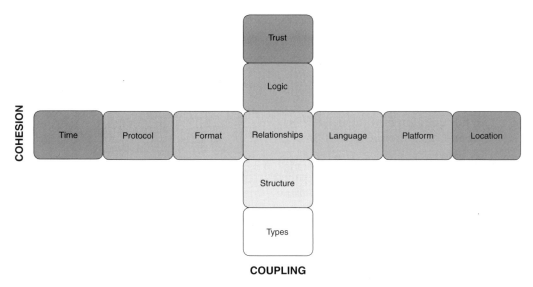

Figure 5.5 Combined coupling and cohesion in SOA.

5.2 Service-Oriented Analysis and Design—Activities

Analysis and design is based on good decision-making according to the best principles, acceptable constraints, and best practices. Service modeling based on good abstraction into layers, information hiding, loose-coupling, and strong cohesion can yield good services. However, just as *modeling* has changed the focus of analysis and design, so have *activities* come to the fore in any discussion about development methodology. Activities are the building blocks for the methods used when constructing software, whether they are sequential (waterfall), iterative (spiral), or extreme (agile).

A number of activities have been identified as essential to any method used for architecting and building an SOA. The activities are specific to services and do not replace any of the more traditional activities for developing objects and other application components. This section discusses some aspects of the most-often-used, service-specific activities.

5.2.1 Identifying Services

Perhaps the most obvious activity is identifying services. This can be done using input analysis, top-down domain decomposition, bottom-up existing systems synthesis, and meet-in-the middle techniques. Input analysis involves reviewing business models and existing system documentation for the business process in focus. The following are questions that arise frequently in this phase:

- Are the business drivers and goals for the SOA project articulated and quantifiable in terms of key business performance indicators?
- Have the business processes to be realized been named and described at a level of detail that is sufficient for architectural decision-making at the IT level?
- Have the existing and future non-functional requirements been documented with any unresolved pain points?

If the input from business modeling and the existing system documentation is not sufficient, it must be possible to schedule additional analysis activities as there is no point in proceeding with the modeling without a solid baseline.

5.2.1.1 Top-Down Analysis

Top-down business analysis techniques, such as IBM Component Business Modeling (CBM), may be the best starting point for identifying services. Using such techniques, it is possible to map major business functionality against industry templates in order to identify a "heat map" of core business processes that are candidates for SOA transformation or re-engineering. Once the candidate business processes have been identified, they may be modeled to capture requirements.

A.5.4

Existing object-oriented analysis and design techniques can then be applied to identify and define services required. However, a higher viewpoint needs to be taken in most situations because a process-wide object-oriented analysis might lead to a large, unmanageable object model. SOA does not dictate a particular decomposition style, and alternative methods have described the use of different styles. For example, the IBM service-oriented modeling and architecture (SOMA) method starts with a functional decomposition step for this activity.

Traditional business process modeling and other forms of direct requirement analysis—for example, using stakeholder interviews—are also an appropriate way of identifying an initial set of candidate services. Any existing technical use-case models coming from non-SOA projects should also be consulted if they relate to the business process in focus.

5.2.1.2 Building a Taxonomy

As top-down decomposition of business processes proceeds, we recommend that you build a vocabulary of terminology used by both the business and technical communities. It is likely that some of the terminology will be peculiar to the industry that the enterprise operates in (for example, ACORD), and some will come from the culture that is peculiar to organizational units within the enterprise. Some relationships between terms used might also be discovered and should be recorded for later use.

The motivation for building such a taxonomy of terms has several aspects. First, it might be possible to establish a vocabulary that becomes standard for enterprise discussion and documentation as SOA projects are completed over time. Second, the abstractions that are captured during analysis should be expressed in the terms that are documented in the taxonomy—this will facilitate reuse of services over time. Third, the taxonomy will provide the basis for categorization and refinement of services as the SOA deployment evolves. A successful taxonomy will provide a communications bridge between business and IT communities as it becomes more widely accepted.

5.2.1.3 Bottom-Up Synthesis

SOA implementation rarely starts on a green field and almost always involves integrating existing systems. This integration can be done by decomposing relevant existing systems into business process flows, business rules, and potentially reusable components. In accordance with the SOA reference architecture, business process flows and rules are factored into a separate Process layer, and components remain at the Component layer (see Chapter 3).

By decomposing existing systems in this way, it might be possible to synthesize a set of candidate services from the components identified and synthesize others by adapting the business process flows that have been discovered at the higher layer of abstraction. It should be noted that process flows can be realized as services and services realized as process flows as modeling activities conclude (see Section 5.2.4, "Realization of Services").

5.2.2 Categorization of Services

Once an initial list of candidate services has been compiled using both top-down and bottom-up techniques, the list must be refined in an iterative and incremental fashion. Services have different uses and purposes and reside in different layers of SOA reference architecture. For example, application utility services such as `authenticateUser` or `logActivity` can be distinguished from business function services such as `manageInventory` or `planCapacity` in a manufacturing context. During the categorization step, the candidate services are assigned to a number of recognizable types such as the following:

- Categorization by role in the business model, such as `processService`, `businessFunctionService`, `businessRuleValidationService`, `applicationUtilityService`, `infrastructureService`
- Categorization by type of consumer, such as `customerService`, `partnerService`, `internalService`
- Categorization by implementation strategy, such as `externalService`, `composedService`, `adaptedService`

Furthermore, certain services can be composed (orchestrated or choreographed) into higher level processes. This composition step is important in SOA and is facilitated by process modeling languages such as Business Process Execution Language (BPEL). As SOA projects categorize new services, the lists developed should be hardened into a catalog or directory of services that are included in the SOA. This catalog will serve as the repository for metadata about reusable services. Indeed, categorization of services should be based on the characteristics captured in the enterprise services taxonomy and reflected in that metadata.

5.2.3 Specification of Services

A formal interface contract defining the necessary preconditions, postconditions, and invariants, as well as the invocation syntax for services, is a very important design consideration for SOA. Service consumers and providers must have a common understanding of the request and response information types and structure to be exchanged when service operations are invoked. However, the semantics must also be addressed if strongly cohesive interfaces are to be specified. Business-level domain modeling can be part of the answer, especially if combined with a meaningful taxonomy for that domain. In many cases, that taxonomy will include industry-specific terms (such as those defined in Insurance Application Architecture [IAA] for the insurance industry) as well as those that are enterprise specific.

A.5.5

In addition to syntax and semantics, non-functional *qualities of service* (QoS) must also be modeled. In Web services–based SOA implementations, the formal interface contracts must cover more than just the WSDL information elements. RDF can be used to model semantics when inserted as annotations for the WSDL syntactic types. Non-functional requirements may be modeled in the future using constructs from the proposed WS-Policy specification framework (WS-Policy).

5.2.4 Realization of Services

Once services have been identified and specified, they must be realized for deployment in an SOA. The first objective at this stage is *to avoid having to develop new services where others can be reused*. Even if a service is not currently available in the most appropriate form, it might be possible to realize the service by composing existing reusable components. Many projects expose reusable components by performing bottom-up analysis of existing systems. These components are candidates for the implementation of services.

A number of issues must be addressed when abstract service definitions are mapped to IT components and are deployed into a runtime environment:

- Whether or not to realize as a service. If a positive decision is made, should the service be realized by an IT component or by a human worker?
- Implementation technology and target runtime of choice. For example BPEL, J2EE, or other.
- A choice of architecture alternatives for service implementation, including advice about transaction management (for example, one- or two-phase commit, business activity compensation).
- Deployment considerations including ESB mapping, QoS, non-functional requirements, security settings, and others.
- Runtime aspects such as management. How can a service be designed to be manageable?

Several reasons for not implementing a service may exist: The human being is a better (or the only available) transaction coordinator, service realization is too expensive, the existing systems components are not yet SOA ready, or other nontechnical circumstances (politics) prevent service realization.

For example, the state management and workflow engine (with sound compensation capabilities) most frequently used today in enterprise applications is the human worker. This is not necessarily the best solution, but sometimes reality constrains design, and the introduction of an automated process layer must be a conscious architectural decision and not implemented simply because SOA and process choreography are in vogue.

Often you make the simplifying assumption that a subsystem has a one-to-one correspondence with enterprise components. Restructuring of components occurs when you use patterns to construct enterprise-level components with a combination of mediators, facades, rule objects, configurable profiles, and factories.

During the realization step, the need for adaptation also has to be investigated based on the results from earlier analysis. For example, there are several scenarios requiring introduction of adapter services (see Chapter 3):

- Better quality of service is required (perhaps a caching adapter).
- Only batch interface available, but real-time access is required.
- Protocol conversion or data transformation is required.

Allocation of components and services to layers in the SOA is also an important task that requires the documentation and resolution of key architectural decisions that relate not only to the application architecture but also to the technical operational architecture designed and used to support the SOA realization at runtime.

5.3 Summary

Techniques for analysis and design have evolved dramatically in the last four decades. Recent developments have focused on modeling and the use of metadata as the basis for methods and tools that cater to a wide range of activities, from business process modeling to automated generation of executable software. In this chapter, we have discussed service analysis and design (modeling) with emphasis on the most important considerations: encapsulation of service functionality, loose-coupling for service providers and consumers, and strong cohesion for SOA longevity. In the next chapter, we will discuss appropriate ways to capture decision-making patterns as templates for use across enterprise SOA projects.

5.4 Links to developerWorks

A.5.1 Zimmermann, O., Krogdahl, P., and Gee, C. *Elements of Service-Oriented Analysis and Design.* IBM developerWorks, June 2004. http://www.ibm.com/developerworks/webservices/library/ws-soad1/.

A.5.2 Beck, K., Joseph, J., and Goldszmidt, G. *BPM: Learn Business Process Modeling for the Analyst.* IBM developerWorks, February 2005. http://www-128.ibm.com/developerworks/webservices/library/ws-bpm4analyst.

A.5.3 IBM. *Patterns for e-Business.* IBM developerWorks, 2004. http://www.ibm.com/developerworks/patterns/.

A.5.4 Arsanjani, A. *Service-Oriented Modeling and Architecture—How to Identify, Specify, and Realize Services for Your SOA.* IBM developerWorks, November 2004. http://www-128.ibm.com/developerworks/webservices/library/ws-soa-design1/.

A.5.5 IBM, Microsoft, BEA, and SAP, *WSPF: Web Services Policy Framework*. Standard specification proposal, IBM developerWorks, July 2003. http://www.ibm.com/developerworks/webservices/library/ws-polfram/summary.html.

5.5 References

Bennett, K., et al. *Service-Based Software: The Future for Flexible Software*. Paper submitted at Asia-Pacific Software Engineering Conference, 5-8 December 2000, Singapore. http://www.service-oriented.com/publications/APSEC2000.pdf.

Bhattacharya, K., et al. *A model-driven approach to industrializing discovery processes in pharmaceutical research*. IBM Systems Journal, Vol. 44, 1-2005. http://www.research.ibm.com/journal/sj44-1.html.

Booch, Grady. *Object-Oriented Analysis and Design with Applications, 2nd Edition*. Addison-Wesley Professional, 1993.

Fowler, Martin. *UML Distilled: A Brief Guide to the Standard Object Modeling Language, 3rd Edition*. Addison-Wesley Professional, 2003.

Grossman, B. and Naumann, J. *ACORD & XBRL US—XML Standards and the Insurance Value Chain*. Acord.org, May 2004. http://www.acord.org/news/pdf/ACORD_XBRL.pdf.

IBM. *IBM Service-Oriented Modeling and Architecture*. IBM Business Consulting Services, white paper, 2004. http://www.ibm.com/services/us/bcs/pdf/g510-5060-ibm-service-oriented-modeling-arch.pdf.

IBM, IAA. *Insurance Application Architecture, 2nd Revised Edition*. 2004. http://www.ibm.com/industries/financialservices/doc/content/bin/fss_iaa_gim_06-29-04.pdf.

Jacobson, Ivar. *Object-Oriented Software Engineering: A Use Case Driven Approach, 2nd Edition*. Addison-Wesley Professional, 2005.

Jacobson, Ivar, Ericsson, Maria, and Jacobson, Agneta. *The Object Advantage: Business Process Reengineering with Object Technology*. Addison-Wesley Object Technology Series, 1994.

Jacobson, Ivar and Ng, Pan-Wei. *Aspect-Oriented Software Development with Use Cases*. Addison-Wesley Object Technology Series, 2004.

Kloppmann, M., et al. *Business process choreography in WebSphere: Combining the power of BPEL and J2EE*. IBM Systems Journal, Vol. 43, 2-2004. http://www.research.ibm.com/journal/sj43-2.html.

Koehler, J., et al. *Declarative techniques for model-driven business process integration*. IBM Systems Journal, Vol. 44, 1-2005. http://www.research.ibm.com/journal/sj44-1.html.

Latimore, D. and Robinson, R. *Component Business Modeling: A Private Banking Example*. IBM Business Consulting Services white paper, 2004. http://www.ibm.com/industries/financialservices/doc/content/news/newsletter/1061213103.html.

Mellor, Stephen J., et al. *MDA Distilled*. Addison-Wesley Object Technology Series, 2004.

OASIS, BPEL: *Web Services Business Process Execution Language*. http://www.oasis-open.org/committees/tc_home.php?wg_abbrev=wsbpel.

OMG, MDA: *Model Driven Architecture*. MDA Guide 1.0.1, 2005. http://www.omg.org/mda/.

OMG, UML: *Unified Modeling Language*. Standard Specification. http://www.uml.org/.

Shlaer, S. and Mellor, S.J. *Object Lifecycles—Modeling the World in States*. Yourdon Press, 1992.

Stevens, W. *Software Design—Concepts and Methods*. Prentice-Hall, 1991.

W3C, RDF: *Resource Definition Framework*. http://www.w3c.org/RDF/.

W3C, WSDL: *Web Services Description Language Version 2.0*. Standard Specifications, May 2005. http://www.w3.org/TR/wsdl20/.

Yourdon, Edward and Coad, Peter. *Object-Oriented Analysis*. Englewood Cliffs, N.J.: Prentice-Hall, 1991.

Zachman, J.A. *A Framework for Information Systems Architecture*. IBM Systems Journal, Vol. 26, 3-1987. http://www.software.org/pub/architecture/zachman.asp.

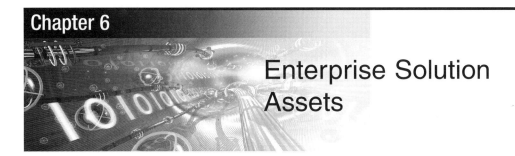

Chapter 6

Enterprise Solution Assets

"Great things are not done by impulse, but by a series of small things brought together."

—*Vincent van Gogh*

Enterprise architects and consultants are faced with some serious challenges when formulating an IT solution. First of all, large-scale enterprise solutions are never easy to construct. They usually involve bringing congruency to a collection of heterogeneous legacy systems; breaking down silos of processing centers; migrating applications from niche, unviable products and homegrown platforms; and replacing ad-hoc enterprise plumbing that currently holds up a shaky infrastructure—this, by itself, is a Herculean task. Add to this the new demands for enhanced, non-functional requirements and qualities of service that CIOs traditionally expect when embracing emerging technologies, and you have opened a Pandora's Box that contains all the deferred wish lists of the past. You will have to accommodate the wish list requests in the proposed solution.

The lack of well-established, industry-tempered, reusable assets, such as templates, patterns, best practices, and road maps, further exacerbates the architect's dilemma. This is largely due to the pace at which enterprise technology progresses today. New specifications bloom with a rapid regularity (along with a slew of acronyms and buzzwords), and vendors rush to incorporate and provide support for them, churning out frequent product releases to keep pace. Hence, it is difficult to formalize, create, and maintain *truly* reusable assets because the underlying technologies and the product mappings keep shifting. Therefore, the assets become obsolete at the same pace with which technologies emerge. Additionally, there are organizational barriers in creating and maintaining assets because of the early investment to initiate an asset repository and because the return on investment is realized gradually. IT decision-makers are also concerned with whether asset creation and reuse would slow the usual IT development processes and the shelf life of any assets that are created.

This chapter describes how to identify and create architectural assets that are reusable across enterprise projects. These assets can be used for accelerating solution transition, articulating best practices, and capturing architectural decisions.

6.1 Architect's Perspective

Before describing enterprise solution assets (ESAs), it is important to understand the broad issues that an enterprise architect faces in any reasonably sized project. These issues range from selecting the appropriate architectural methodology to effectively mapping software products to the solution.

6.1.1 Selecting the Architectural Methodology

The first thing an architect attempts to identify is a coherent methodology and a set of techniques to apply to the project. Some of the choices available are model-driven architecture (MDA), component business modeling (CBM), and Rational Unified Process (RUP). Chapter 5, "Aspects of Analysis and Design," covered these architectural facets in detail, so they are not discussed in detail here.

6.1.2 Formalizing Architectural Decisions

After analyzing the solution requirements, an architect can then look further to derive architectural artifacts, which can be used to create high-level solution components. He can then place them in a solution context. During this process, several alternatives are placed on the architectural palette, such as technology choices, application patterns, and vendor choices. Based on these alternatives, the architect has to make certain choices to meet the functional and non-functional characteristics of the eventual solution. Some of these architectural decisions are often encountered and "rediscovered" across other intra-enterprise projects. Being able to capture and formalize these architectural decisions would provide a key reusable asset for future projects. This is especially true for SOA projects because defining common, shared services is a critical success factor.

Currently, there are no formalized methods to capture this architectural decision framework. *Design patterns* (such as Gang-of-Four patterns) primarily provide guidance only for design decisions. They provide low-level, object-oriented patterns that are targeted and applicable for the solution design and construction phase. However, design patterns have been available for a while, and their structure is well understood by architects. The ESA concept will reuse the nomenclature and structure of design patterns (with certain modifications) to preserve syntactic and semantic concepts so that they can be easily understood; it will then extend these concepts to formalize architectural decisions.

6.1.3 Identifying Architectural Best Practices

Because SOA best practices are still maturing, an architect usually spends a lot of time searching for existing best practices. These can then be evaluated for applicability to the enterprise solution at hand. Compounding this is the fact that these best practices apply at various layers: low-level technology (such as J2EE) practices, service-orientation procedures, industry vertical standards, business domain–specific scenarios, and others.

The following are some of the formalized options for such best practices currently available:

- J2EE patterns and blueprints have been extensively used for adopting architectural practices that leverage a Java-based middleware platform to implement solutions.
- IBM patterns for e-business provide a group of reusable assets to create e-business applications. They provide platform-agnostic guidance to create effective enterprise solutions quickly. The patterns are classified into the following:
  - *Business patterns* that are used to create simple end-to-end scenarios involving interaction among users, business processes, and data. They are the fundamental building blocks of most e-business solutions.
  - *Integration patterns* connect Business patterns to provide advanced functionality and create more complex applications.
  - *Composite patterns* combine Business and Integration patterns to provide commonly used high-level architecture scenarios.
  - *Application patterns* provide a conceptual layout describing how the application components and data within a Business or Integration pattern interact.
  - *Runtime patterns* define the logical middleware structure that supports an Application pattern. Runtime patterns depict the major middleware nodes, their roles, and the interfaces between these nodes.

These patterns provide useful direction in articulating the high-level architecture, but they do not currently provide reusable implementation code assets that can be leveraged for accelerating solution realization. The ESA content can make references to these architectural patterns and exploit their concepts.

6.1.4 Performing the Product and Package Mappings

While mapping the solution context to concrete vendor products and packages, an architect might find a number of identifiable gaps. Usually the product or package feature sets do not meet the precise requirements of the solution. As recourse, depending on the project schedule, the gap tends to be filled in an ad-hoc fashion. Sometimes these methods and the resultant interim "gap" solution tend to be the weakest link in the overall solution. Providing a well-engineered solution to fill gaps has key benefits: A well-engineered solution is reusable and prevents the proliferation of custom code to solve similar gaps in other enterprise projects.

A variety of mechanisms are available to create reusable code assets. Most prominent among them is the reusable asset specification (RAS). RAS is an industry-tempered specification that details the structure, content, and descriptions of reusable software assets. For the ESA code assets to have greater reuse potential, the code assets will be RAS compliant, especially since recent development tooling (such as the Rational Studio suite) and accelerators incorporate RAS support.

6.2 Enterprise Solution Assets Explained

An *enterprise solution asset* (ESA) is defined to assist the architect in creating reusable assets to primarily address the issues of architectural decisions and vendor product gaps, as described in Section 6.1. An ESA describes common problems and difficulties that occur frequently in architecting and designing enterprise solutions, and it proposes solutions to address them. As these assets are created, they will be classified and housed within a catalog.

As described in Section 6.1.2, the layout of an ESA closely resembles that of design patterns *only* to exploit its structural familiarity. In general, an ESA has the following essential elements:

- An enterprise solution asset *name* is a handle to uniquely describe an enterprise problem and is used as an index into the ESA catalog. It also contains a one-line statement to describe the intent of the asset.
- The *problem synopsis* captures the essence of the problem and describes where to apply the asset.
- The *context* describes the problem in terms of a concrete example and lays out the situation in which the asset might be leveraged.
- *Forces* summarize the architectural decisions and design considerations that led to the solution presented within the asset.
- The *solution* is the core of the asset, and it describes a general-purpose solution to the problem that the asset addresses. The solution section can also include technical specifications such as diagrams describing the solution model (for example, UML class diagrams, sequence diagrams, component diagrams, and so on) and descriptions of the participating components in the solution.
- The *consequences* lay out the implications—the pros and cons—of using the asset. They also propose architectural alternatives.

The solution section of an ESA also has accompanying executables and the associated usage documentation that are compiled as an RSA-compliant package. The ESAs described later in this chapter are derived from IBM engagement experiences with real-world SOA projects. They have been generalized and abstracted from the engagement specificities. These primarily provide ESA samples to help create your own ESAs.

6.3 A Catalog of Enterprise Solution Assets

We recommend that from the onset of an SOA project, you create an ESA catalog to publish the assets so that they are visible across the enterprise. Incorporating a taxonomy to classify the growing list of ESAs would be beneficial and would help promote the reusability of the ESA across other enterprise projects. This book is not intended to be an extensive ESA reference; however, to explain the concept, we describe the following ESAs:

- *Multitiered disconnected operation* allows an enterprise application to operate in the event of failures such as network outages and unreliable data availability. This is described in Section 6.6.
- The *request response template* provides an infrastructure facility for client components to control how data is requested. This allows a client to request only a data subset returned by the service. This minimizes data flow during a service request and also helps isolate the client from service version changes and enhancements. This is described in Section 6.7.

The IBM service engagement teams are gathering potential assets in ongoing customer projects. As the list of assets grows, they will be classified into various taxonomies such as problem domains and industry segments. These assets will be part of the IBM SOA integration framework. However, this chapter's primary intent is to provide guidance to create your own ESA and ESA catalog.

6.4 How Does an ESA Solve Enterprise Problems?

An ESA provides some key facets in solving enterprise architecture problems. An architect equipped with an ESA catalog is able to use formalized architectural decisions and well-engineered solutions. The key ESA benefits and value proposition are as follows:

- *Productivity*: By providing well-documented assets contained in an ESA catalog, an architect is able to use these assets to address the core solution requirements, reduce the project delivery timeline, and arrive at robust and resilient solutions.
- *Consistency and standardization*: By generalizing the specific problem or gap scenario from a particular project scenario, the ESA allows applicability to other enterprise projects. It also enables architects to consistently apply a standardized asset to solve similar problems within and across various industries.
- *Risk mitigation*: By leveraging the ESA, the architect is able to provide robust solutions for product and technology gaps identified during a project engagement. This reduces the risk of ad-hoc architectural decisions and solution weaknesses.
- *Maintainability*: An ESA will be well maintained in its lifecycle with controlled changes and relevant updates. This facilitates the delivery of further ESA enhancements and potential defect resolution in a quality-controlled environment.
- *Knowledge and intellectual capital sharing*: As the ESA catalog grows and evolves, it serves as an essential artifact that enables effective awareness and guidance on key enterprise architectural issues.

6.5 Selecting an Enterprise Solution Asset

Finding the correct asset to solve your enterprise architecture problem is difficult, especially if the catalog of ESAs is new and unfamiliar. The following list provides guidelines and advice for identifying the relevant assets that might be applicable to your situation:

- Scan the ESA name and intent area to narrow down your choices and read the context to ensure applicability to your problem.
- Study the assets applicable to your industry segment based on the catalog classification that is available.
- Check the ESA catalog regularly because more assets are introduced as the catalog is formalized.

6.6 Using an Enterprise Solution Asset

After you have identified the ESA that you need, you can leverage it for your enterprise architecture by following these steps:

- Read the asset for an overview, paying attention to the forces, context, and the consequence sections to ensure that the asset is applicable for the situation.
- Step through the solution in detail and understand the core components used in the solution, paying particular attention to the potential solution variations.
- Peruse through the technical documentation and code that accompany the asset.

6.7 Multitiered Disconnected Operation

Multitier disconnected operation allows an enterprise application to operate in the event of unreliable data availability due to failures such as network outages.

6.7.1 Problem Synopsis

Enterprises use applications or suites of applications requiring data that spans multiple infrastructure tiers. Although increasingly reliable, the networks connecting these tiers are never 100% reliable. In addition, there are cases when, even if connected, the data might not be available to the tier that requires it.

A fundamental problem facing enterprises is the capability to allow such multitier applications to continue functioning during events such as network failures. This asset enables a multitier application to operate in an environment without reliable data availability. Solutions that require multitier operation can leverage this asset.

6.7.2 Context

Scenarios from customers in the retail industry exemplify the need for multitier disconnected operation. Figure 6.1 shows a sample multitier retail enterprise. There is a point of sale (POS) application that must run at the POS terminals in a store (terminal tier), on the store server (store tier), and at the retail headquarters (considered here as the enterprise tier).

Figure 6.1 shows three databases with different characteristics. `Pricing` represents a read-only database (containing static lookup data) that must be available to all tiers. This is because a POS terminal must know the price of items sold, even if the terminal is disconnected from the store server. The store server acts as a POS application as well, in case all terminals are down. The light gray arrows in Figure 6.1 indicate that the pricing database is created at the enterprise and copied to the store server; the store server then cascades the data to the individual terminals.

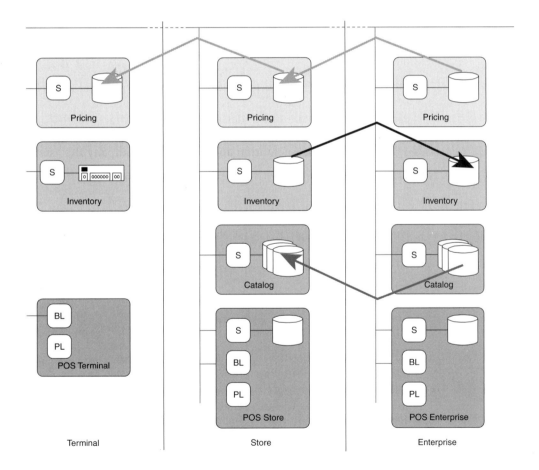

Figure 6.1 Multitier context for the retail industry.

The `Catalog` database represents another read-only database. It differs from the `Pricing` database because it does not need to be present at the terminals; the POS application can function without access to that data. The catalog is copied from the enterprise to the store level, which is indicated by the dark gray arrow in Figure 6.1.

The `Inventory` database represents a transactional database that must be available and updated at all tiers. The POS terminal needs to modify the inventory kept at the store server as items are sold or returned. Because it never reads from the inventory, the updates to the database must be reliable, even in the event of disconnected operation. The black arrow in Figure 6.1 indicates that the store inventory is created and then copied to the enterprise.

6.7.3 Forces

The retail example shows that different databases demand different treatment within the same enterprise and sometimes even the same application. Thus, the asset must support disconnected operation in a flexible way. Furthermore, a goal of the asset is to maximally leverage middleware infrastructure in an SOA roadmap–based solution. Thus, the solution relies on the following:

- Projection of a subset of enterprise data to appropriate levels in the hierarchy.
- Advanced database replication technology to maintain consistency of the data across multiple tiers.
- Enhanced services access infrastructure.

6.7.4 Solution

Because the solution is presented in terms of an SOA, we need to characterize a service. Figure 6.2 shows the requestor and provider in a classic SOA model. In this case, the provider of the service wraps a database.

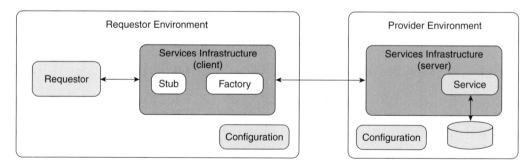

Figure 6.2 Service definition in a classic SOA model.

In this classic SOA, to access the database, the requestor must do the following:

- The requestor calls the factory provided by the requestor's infrastructure to get a client stub. (This is enabled by the client configuration.)
- The requestor calls the stub to send a request (read/write) to the service provider.
- The provider's infrastructure (using the server configuration) invokes the service to access the database and produce a result.
- The provider's infrastructure returns the result to the requestor's stub.
- The stub returns the result to the requestor.

Figure 6.3 outlines the basic enhancements that enable disconnected operation in a multitier environment:

- The database of interest is duplicated in the requestor's environment.
- The provider's infrastructure includes database replication technology to replicate data from the database master to the replicas that reside on the requestors; likewise, the requestor's infrastructure includes database replication technology.
- The requestor's environment duplicates the service provider's infrastructure to enable the service wrapping the database to run in the requestor's environment.
- The requestor's infrastructure supports enhanced stub generation by the factory.
- The configuration spans the tiers to configure the cross-tier replication and smart behavior of the enhanced requestor infrastructure.

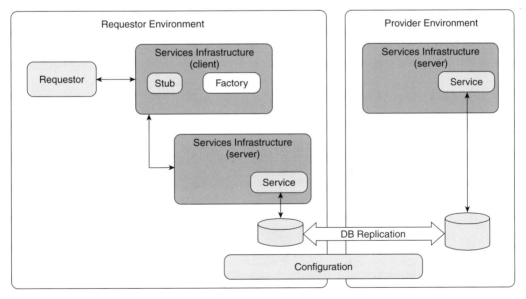

Figure 6.3 Disconnectable (disconnected) service definition.

In the enhanced version of the SOA architecture for disconnected operation, the stub can transparently access either the local or remote version of the service without any explicit requestor action. The database replication ensures that the same data, within the bounds of the replication schedule, is available to both the local and remote service. In theory, this makes access to the local data as good as access to the remote data.

The following additional terms are needed to further characterize this asset:

- The *owner* is the logical master of the database wrapped by a service, due to physical or logical considerations. For example, in the retail scenario, the store owns the inventory for that store, and the enterprise owns the pricing. Note that the owner is potentially different than the database *master*.
- *Local* refers to the local copy of the owner's database or the service representation and implementation at the requestor.
- *Staleness* refers to a measure of how inaccurate or incorrect data might be based on age. For example, data replicated 10 minutes ago is better than data from an hour ago. Staleness can be made available from the enhanced services infrastructure, but the impact of staleness is left to business logic.
- A *read-only service* provides business function based on largely static data; examples from the retail environment are pricing and tax tables. The typical implementation would be as follows:
  - Deploy an instance of a service at all applicable tiers.
  - Read from a local or remote replica—performance is a consideration here—with failover.
  - Write to the owner with a possible local copy.
  - Update the subset of data replicated from the owner to the appropriate tiers.
- A *transactional service* updates shared data while maintaining data integrity. This implies reliable updates via queued writes from the service requestor (using message-oriented middleware). Examples from the retail environment are inventory and postsales tender. The typical implementation would do the following:
  - Deploy an instance of the service at all applicable tiers.
  - Read from the local replica, recognizing the possibility of staleness.
  - Write to local replica or write to owner (or both) via a *reliable* mechanism.
  - Update the appropriate subset of data replicated from the owner to the appropriate tiers.

There are three different solution variations in the asset: a simple service, a smart stub, and a smart service.

The simple service solution shown in Figure 6.4 has the following general characteristics:

- The service is usually deployed at all levels, and the access is always to the local service. You access the service using standard mechanisms.
- It relies on cross-tier database replication to maintain data consistency. Replication is from the owner to replicas. (The configuration determines the database master-slave relationship.)

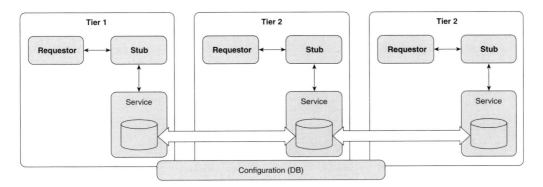

Figure 6.4 Simple service solution.

The simple service solution is especially good for read-only services on largely static data that must be available on multiple tiers even when disconnected.

The smart stub solution shown in Figure 6.5 has the following general characteristics:

- The service can be deployed at all levels. For example, it can be deployed as a smart stub configured to cascade access, as an access service using intelligent on-demand services infrastructure, and as an intelligent stub that accesses local or remote services according to configuration and conditions, which permits failover.
- The variation also relies on cross-tier database replication to maintain data consistency.

The smart stub solution is good for when a simple service solution is not adequate, for example when it might make sense to access data on another tier, if it is available, or to back off to a local copy, if it is unavailable.

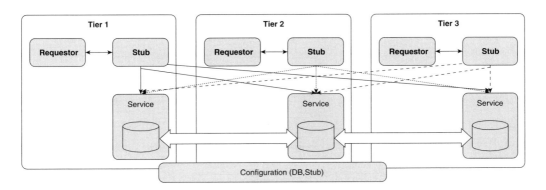

Figure 6.5 Smart stub solution.

The first two scenarios don't require any custom business logic, nor do they allow for a lot of dynamic modification. The smart service scenario, shown in Figure 6.6, recognizes that custom logic might be necessary. The scenario has the following general characteristics:

- Service implementation logic determines the access pattern and conditions.
- The smart service solution may depend on cross-tier database replication.

The smart service solution is good for where infrastructure support is not adequate to achieve the desired flexibility. For example, the smart service in tier 1 in Figure 6.6 might decide, based on current conditions that include time of day, connectivity, customer, and other factors, to access the local service, the tier 2 or tier 3 services, or even all three services for whatever reasons. The three scenario variations have advantages and disadvantages, as shown in Table 6.1.

Table 6.1 Comparing the Solutions

Solution Variation	Advantages	Disadvantages
Simple service	No custom service "routing" configuration Simple database replication mechanism is sufficient	Least flexible
Smart stub	Increased flexibility Maximal leverage of infrastructure but still no custom business logic	Requires a more sophisticated database replication mechanism
Smart service	Most flexibility	Custom "smart service" must be implemented and maintained

It should be noted that any given enterprise architecture can choose to use only one or all three solution variations for different aspects mandated by the requirements.

6.7.5 Consequences

This ESA enables the maximal use of middleware infrastructure to lessen the burden of operation in a potentially disconnected environment. An architect can use tested, supported, and continually improved middleware to reduce the time spent on a custom solution for disconnected operation and to increase the time spent on application logic. Tools that support the asset can further reduce the effort it takes to create custom configurations and

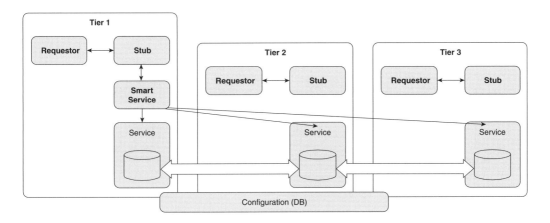

Figure 6.6 Smart service solution.

deploy the configured solution. This can lead to cost savings, simplified management, or faster deployment.

There is no such thing as a free lunch, as the saying goes; everything has consequences. Disconnected operation carries an overhead to support the operation of the service provider infrastructure within the requestor environment, necessitating deployment and runtime resources to support that infrastructure. Similarly, database replication carries some additional burden, namely the deployment and runtime resources to support the database and its replication; this is a factor in any tier that owns a database or needs disconnected access to a database. These additional aspects can drag in more complex versions of companion products, such as WebSphere Business Integration—Server Foundation (WBI-SF) deployment versus Network Deployment and so on. All these extras can increase cost and management complexity.

6.8 Request Response Template

The *request response template* ESA is useful for decoupling the message schemas of a service requestor from their service provider.

6.8.1 Problem Synopsis

Web service interfaces are tightly coupled contracts with usage patterns mandated by the service provider. The asset decouples client usage of a Web service from the contract specified by a service provider.

6.8.2 Context

The following are some common problems due to the tightly coupled nature of service requesters and providers:

- Tightly prescribed interfaces implicitly determine the usage patterns for a service. Service providers build their own efficiency compromises into their interfaces, and clients are forced to accept them.
- Clients need more control over the data and service models for service responses.
- Clients want to circumvent large response message payloads associated with coarse-grain services.
- Service providers need to evolve the interfaces they provide without breaking existing clients.
- Clients would rather program toward abstract data and service models rather than directly to WSDL-specified interfaces.

Web service providers have a common problem when dealing with multiple clients: WSDL prescribes an exact interface for data types, messages, and operations that implicitly restrict clients to a usage pattern that is not necessarily appropriate. Service providers must choose the WSDL they expose, even though clients are the only ones who know the most efficient interface for their usage patterns. The result is an unattractive choice for a service provider: It must provide multiple interfaces for multiple clients (which are hard to develop and to maintain), or it must provide a single, one-size-fits-all, compromise interface. However, that compromise can be difficult to realize because service and data models might provide more or even less information than a client actually needs; the provider is left with another choice as to how to avoid message bloat (too much data) or overly chatty interactions (not enough data). Whether producing multiple interfaces or compromise models, the provider still might have imperfect information about the needs of its clients, forcing it to make an educated guess about the operations and data models it should expose.

6.8.3 Forces

These are the main forces in designing this asset:

- To build on existing Web service standards, enhance the existing specification, and do not reinvent the wheel.
- To use existing, well-known modeling tools that can define abstract interfaces (UML, for example).
- To increase flexibility, granularity, and maintainability of an application's Web service interfaces.
- To customize service results and optimize the data flow between the client and server.
- To allow consumers and providers to develop against abstract data and service models rather than directly against prescribed interfaces.

6.8.4 Solution

The solution to this is to use the request response template ESA tools and patterns to define abstract data and service models and let the client determine which parts of the data and service model should be used on a per-request basis. This is shown in Figure 6.7. Rather than prescribe an interface, a service provider defines an object graph of the information it is willing to provide. From this model, XML schemas are generated that follow the structure of the object graph, and they are included with the deployed service's WSDL file. Then, at request time, clients invoke a Web service operation and include a partially filled version of the request XSD that defines for the server exactly what data the client would like returned. The server then fills in a response accordingly and returns it. The sequence diagram is shown in Figure 6.8.

This ESA requires that the service provider include special libraries in its deployed service to process Web service response template requests, though the requirement does not preclude the provider from offering other, non-template-based Web services in the same application. Also, although client-side libraries are available to facilitate the use of templates, they are not required. Web service template–based requests can be sent manually because they obey existing Web services standards.

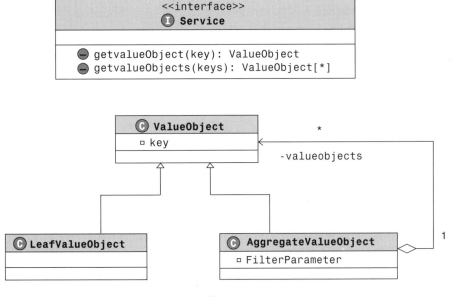

Figure 6.7 Response template class diagram.

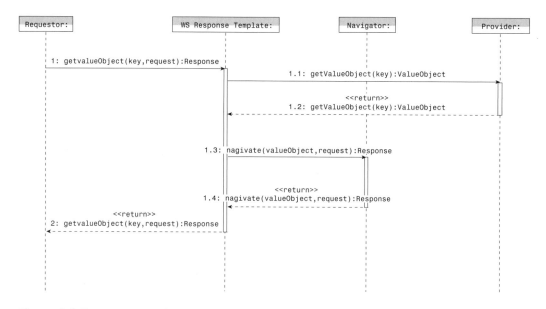

Figure 6.8 Response template sequence diagram.

6.8.4.1 Participants

These are the primary actors within the solution:

- *Information model/service graph.* The object model and service model that define what information a Web service will provide (and the operations that can request it).
- *Request template XSD.* Lays out the possible formats of a request template by defining the structure of the information model.
- *Request template.* XML that follows the request template XSD but without data. It defines an object graph for the response that is a subset of the information model.
- *Response template XSD.* Defines the possible formats of a response template. Similar to the request template XSD, but it allows collections of data.
- *Response template.* The "filled in" data according to the response template XSD.
- *The client.* The Web service client.
- *The client framework.* Tooling supplied to the client. It includes mechanisms for sending requests with templates and for generating request templates from an XML file.
- *The navigator.* The WS response templates engine deployed inside the Web service code parses the incoming request template and creates a response template as a result, pulling information from the Web service's result object graph.

A.6.1

6.8.5 Consequences

The following are some of the consequences of using this ESA:

- *Extra overhead:* Web services template (WST) based solutions do have some extra overhead. Requests transmit more data than a typical Web services solution because additional information is required to prune and filter the resulting object graphs and because each item desired in the response must be specified. In addition, extra code is executed on both the client and the server to process a WST request. This overhead is not excessive, but WS response templates are obviously not as effective in all cases.

- *Customized result:* Clients of a Web service template–based service can adjust the results they receive from service invocation. Unwanted data will not be sent by the server, nor will any placeholder data be received on the client side (not even with nil or empty values).

- *Optimized data flow:* The service invocation consists of a data exchange between two parts (traditionally two computers). The Web services templates solution must minimize the data flow between those two parts. This is partially expressed by the previous requirement (customer result); attention must also be paid to the expression of the data flow in order to minimize the weight of this. For example, when using XML, pay attention to namespace declarations, element prefixes, and hierarchical structure of the data flow.

- *Optimization of the service implementation:* The Web services templates solution will allow the service provider developer to optimize the process by only invoking methods or retrieving data that will be needed to construct the result as defined by the client.

- *Web services templates designed in conformity with the Web services standards:*
  - Web services templates must be implemented using the SOAP communication protocol. We will use a JAX-RPC-compliant engine as the platform of choice for the service implementation (server side). Whereas this implementation exists primarily for HTTP transport protocol, this does not mean that the Web services templates must only be bound to a specific transport protocol (but can be used with others such as JMS).
  - Services will be defined using WSDL and XML schema to define the formats of the exchanged objects.
  - The operations have a document style and a literal usage (document/literal) for WS-I compliance.

- *Parameterized navigation path:* The navigation path against an information model hierarchy can define extra parameters to filter a particular relationship. Also, this parameterized path can be repeated in the same service invocation to extend the potential of the service (especially for the parameterized path). Note: This does not mean that the Web service operation can be invoked multiple times in the same call. It means only that the returned object graph can be controlled to a greater degree than in normal Web services design patterns.

- *Level of granularity for services:* The Web services template solution will reduce the granularity of Web services. Service providers, rather than defining different services for different client use cases, now define a single, more abstract service, which clients adjust to their individual needs.
- *UML as a possible way to describe service:* UML notation (used in this document) is a possible way to express the information model. Although UML is not a requirement for modeling services and data objects (users can directly code their own WSDL and XSD according to WST specifications), there is significant tooling available to convert UML into proper WSDL, XSD, and skeleton WST implementations that would otherwise have to be built from scratch.
- *Easier maintenance and compatibility:* Service providers can extend their existing Web services template services without impact to existing clients. By extension, we mean adding a new property in a data structure. In that case, the existing clients don't require this property in the request, so they won't get it in the response from the new implementation. Only clients who require this new property (especially new clients) will get it in the result.

6.9 Summary

Enterprise solution assets are primarily intended to formalize architectural decisions and create reusable solution artifacts that can be leveraged across enterprise projects. It is recommended that project managers and architects accommodate the ESA tasks as part of project schedules. Managing and maintaining the ESA catalog should be placed under the SOA governance principles. As ESA catalogs mature with the addition of new ESA assets, it will also provide the capability to share ESAs across enterprises.

 ## 6.10 Links to developerWorks

A.6.1 IBM alphaWorks. *Web Services Response Templates.* http://www.alphaworks.ibm.com/tech/wsrt/.

6.11 References

Adams, J., et al. *Patterns for e-business—A Strategy for Reuse.* IBM Press, 2001.

Gamma, Erich, et al. *Design Patterns, 1st Edition.* Addison-Wesley Professional, 1995.

Kruchten, P. *The Rational Unified Process: An Introduction, 3rd Edition.* Addison-Wesley Professional, 2003.

OMG (Object Management Group). *Model Driven Architecture.* http://www.omg.org/mda/.

OMG (Object Management Group). *Reusable Asset Specification.* http://www.omg.org/cgi-bin/doc?ptc/2004-06-06.

OMG (Object Management Group), UML: *Unified Modeling Language.* http://www.uml.org/.

Sun Developer Network. *J2EE Patterns.* http://java.sun.com/blueprints/patterns/index.html.

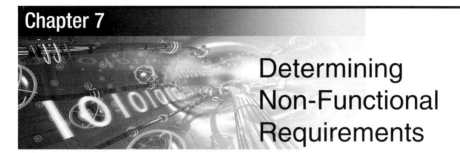

Chapter 7

Determining Non-Functional Requirements

"There are two kinds of truths: those of reasoning and those of fact. The truths of reasoning are necessary and their opposite is impossible; the truths of fact are contingent and their opposite is possible."

—Gottfried Wilhelm Leibnitz

The non-functional requirements (NFRs) of a service-oriented business system address those aspects of the system that do not directly affect the functionality of the system but can still have a profound effect on how the business system is accepted by both service consumers and those responsible for supporting the system. The non-functional aspects of SOAs cover a broad range of topics, each of which can have a significant impact on the architecture. These topics can be classified into four major categories:

- Business constraints
- Technology constraints
- Runtime qualities
- Nonruntime qualities

In the context of SOAs, each of these categories has additional implications for target systems. The runtime qualities, for example, include those often specified in service-level agreements (SLA). This chapter examines each aspect in greater detail.

7.1 Business Constraints

Business constraints are non-functional requirements that can have a significant impact on the overall design or deployment of an SOA. These constraints include operating ranges, regulatory constraints, legal constraints, or standards established in specific industries.

7.1.1 Operating Ranges

Public services can be accessed from anywhere in the world, and this might imply that availability for such services is almost continuous (24 hours a day, 365 days a year). Enterprise services in an intranet that spans geographic regions may share this requirement. The enterprise service bus (ESB), an important component in any SOA, meets such requirements. The ESB can dynamically route service requests and responses to maximize availability of critical services based on applicable policies.

7.1.2 Legal Constraints

Legal and regulatory constraints are often forgotten when defining SOAs, but they can have significant impact on system design. For example, the law in Luxembourg requires that information about a banking customer be encrypted while it is in transit between service endpoints with no possible breaches by decryption. This implies that service consumer programs running on PCs of banks must encrypt information that cannot be exposed by intermediate application servers that would have to decrypt the information to process it. It also implies end-to-end certificate management through software installation on the bank PC machines.

Confidentiality and the need for encryption are not the only constraints of this kind. In certain countries, there are stringent laws regarding data privacy. SOA deployments in these countries must make provisions for an appropriate data-privacy-handling mechanism that includes solutions such as digital signing to ensure that data is not exposed. Another legal constraint that might arise in cross-border scenarios involves regulations and contracts that must apply when consumers and providers are located in different countries. For this reason, many public service providers install networking entry points in each of the countries they operate in, with provisioning cycles that include the contractual aspects that are specific to the country.

7.1.3 Industry Business Standards

Some industries have started to characterize the significance of SOAs within their domain. These industry-specific standards must be identified in advance of widespread SOA adoption because they influence many aspects of the architecture. For example, the Telecommunications Industry Telemanagement Forum (www.tmforum.org) has defined NGOSS contracts that are truly service models for operational support services. Some governments, such as New Zealand's, have already published standards on the Web for service delivery architectures that are for vendors who want to use their IT infrastructure. These provide a framework for delivery of a wide range of e-government services to citizens of that country.

7.2 Technology Constraints

Technology constraints are based on choices, decisions, and commitments to specific technologies in current and continued use in the enterprise infrastructure. These decisions and commitments to buy and use certain technologies can originate from business choices and relationships or from recommendations from IT technical teams. For example, choice of particular application packages, decisions to use OEM hardware platforms, and commitments to use industry-specific standards can impose constraints on future development of SOAs. The difference between these business-originated technology constraints and the business constraints defined earlier is that the former involves the use of *specific products and technologies*, whereas the latter involves the need for *specific features in the implementation* (which might be independent of the product or technology used to implement the features).

The business reasons for choosing technologies—and thus creating a technology constraint—can originate from the following:

- *Business commitments to use a particular technology* to support various internal departments, external suppliers, partners, or governmental organizations that dictate the need.
- *Mergers and acquisitions* that introduce additional technical infrastructures (from the acquired or other organization) that you might need to continue operating and supporting while attempting to integrate into your own organization's infrastructure.
- *Budget limitations* that restrict teams from acquiring or implementing new technology.

Technical teams within an organization might also make commitments to use a particular technology based on their evaluation and research. These technology-originated constraints might reflect technical choices that are based on the following:

- Adoption of existing or new technology standards (as opposed to business standards)
- A need to continue supporting an existing base of products (usually too tightly coupled to replace or upgrade quickly or easily)
- A need to continue supporting *a* technical design
- A lack of available technical knowledge or expertise to change the existing system or adopt a new one

Whether the technology choices are made for business or technical reasons, they can still result in the same types of technology constraints that impact the non-functional requirements of your architecture. These technology constraints include the following:

- Operating environment constraints that restrict changes to the infrastructure (hardware or software)
- Technical design/model constraints that restrict the technical teams to using or supporting an existing model or design and the data contained in those models and designs.
- Access constraints that restrict changes to interfaces and access mechanisms
- Expertise constraints that restrict changes to the infrastructure due to a lack of expertise

7.2.1 Operating Environment Constraints

Most existing IT systems, such as corporate order-processing systems, have not been designed with service-oriented flexibility and loose-coupling objectives in mind. These systems constitute core assets that companies rely on to run their businesses, supporting mission-critical processes that must be protected from disruption. These considerations make it difficult to change existing applications to expose service interfaces, yet rewriting these applications is generally too costly, time-consuming, or risky to be a practical proposition. For example, some governments now require that Linux be installed as the operating system for their new servers, whereas a large portion of their existing business logic still runs in COBOL on mainframe computers.

Therefore, sound technical migration strategies must include comprehensive plans for managing and reusing existing applications, data, and skills. The most important goal for this migration is to enable access to these applications through open and standard interfaces such as Web services, enabling them to be integrated in new enterprise-level, service-oriented architectures. Two possible styles of migration to a service-oriented architecture include adaptation and innovation.

Adaptation, the first style of service-oriented transformation, focuses on extending existing applications beyond their original design to create integrated solutions that yield significantly greater business value and process flexibility. Applications can be turned into reusable services accessed by a new set of users or reused from new front-end business functions. The underlying principle—that you can reuse existing applications with little or no change—means this is a lower-risk approach than a replacement strategy.

Innovation, the second style of service-oriented transformation, involves some reengineering of the original application. Undoubtedly, this method requires higher investment of resources and time, but it delivers the capability to create components from existing applications, which are fully flexible and configurable for use in new applications. This reuse of business logic is called *componentization* and might result in significant cost savings over time when compared to developing new application code.

Often a key concept of the adaptation style is that you can reuse applications through programmatic interfaces that allow the application to be invoked locally or remotely, either through a standardized application programming interface (API) or through a standardized network protocol.

For example, IBM CICS and IBM IMS™ are two of the most widely used and popular mainframe transaction managers in the world, used by many of the world's largest companies for their business transactions. Like IMS, CICS was introduced in the early days of the mainframe platforms. It has been evolving at the same pace as technology, running on centralized mainframes, distributed client-server architectures, and more recently on service-oriented architectures. This has allowed enterprise users to continue to access their applications as components through Web services technology.

Mainframe application services will probably be made accessible to several types of service-oriented clients, and therefore a range of synchronous and asynchronous access options is needed and can be provided by such mainframe transaction servers.

7.2.2 Technical Model Constraints

The data or information model used by an organization before introducing an SOA or in transition can have limited flexibility. It can also be difficult to change certain information models such as the user identity model. This is turn can have an impact on the non-functional characteristics of the SOA.

7.2.3 Access Constraints

Due to commitments to a particular technology, an organization might be forced to use specific interfaces or access mechanisms when interacting between elements of the infrastructure. This is most often true when off-the-shelf application packages have been deployed or production systems acquired from a third party that is no longer available to make changes. Non-functional runtime qualities, such as performance, might become dependent on external interfaces that your organization does not have the capability to change.

7.2.4 Expertise Constraints

Expertise constraints limit an organization from improving or changing the technical environment and non-functional requirements. The skills and education needed for technology are constantly in flux, and often the technical staff might need new training or you might need to bring in outside consultants to provide the expertise. This expertise can be used to examine the existing system to determine the non-functional characteristics and limitations, as well as to indicate how to improve the system.

7.3 Runtime Qualities

Runtime qualities explore all of the system aspects that are directly involved with system dynamics such as performance, scalability, transactional integrity, security, and fault tolerance. In SOA systems, runtime qualities are directly addressed by service-level agreements. SLAs are often based on end-to-end measurements—from consumer to provider involving all intermediary components. Consumers usually do not care how the internal systems perform within service provider boundaries and are more concerned with the performance of services in relation to the delivered quality at the endpoints.

7.3.1 Performance NFRs

Customers expect perceived service performance to be expressed as a combination of both response time and throughput. The choice of technical architecture components will have serious impact on the overall delivery capability within an SOA. For example, loose-coupling and interoperability often require the use of service messages based on the SOAP wire format on the HTTP protocol. A SOAP message can easily be many times larger than a traditional binary message. This results in greater bandwidth requirements. In addition, applications need to parse the content of service messages, converted from their portable, on-the-wire format into a format that can be more easily processed by endpoint programs. Some of the emerging Web services standards, such as Web Services Security, present further processing and size issues. Performance in SOAs is impacted by decisions made about the following:

- Service granularity and placement
- Binding choices
- Message parsing and data volume
- Security models
- Network bandwidth

These considerations are mainly focused on the protocol needed for service invocation, the amount of information that flows across a service interface, and the need for security-related networking interactions.

7.3.1.1 The Impact of Service Granularity and Placement on Performance

The granularity of exposed business services needs to be carefully designed. Services that are too fine grained lead to a greater number of interactions between endpoints; on the other hand, services that are too coarse grained can lead to unnecessarily large information exchanges. (Refer to Chapter 5, "Aspects of Analysis and Design," for the discussion about granularity.) Poor interface design can stem from designing interfaces that do too little with each message (sometimes called "chatty" interfaces). One reason for chatty interface design is that the message content model does not lend itself to complex, multipart messages. This is common in remote procedure call–based distribution models. The best practice to avoid these chatty interfaces is to have a rather coarse-grained interface with an information model that can dynamically adapt to the consumer's needs.

Mainframe systems often require the breakdown of service requests into sequences of lower-level service requests, or non-service–based interface requests into existing transaction systems (such as the previously mentioned CICS or IMS examples). You can achieve this breakdown using middleware components such as MQ Integrator Agent for CICS™, WebSphere MQ Integrator™ flows, or WebSphere Application Server™ using micro-flows. Mainframe transaction managers seek to minimize flows that are highly optimized for traditional styles of access, such as 3270-Terminal access over a systems network architecture (SNA) network. However, most services-oriented solutions require additional elements (such as connectors, adapters, encrypted data flows, or new data stream architectures) that are less optimized, and impose an apparent overhead on the execution of the target business service.

7.3.1.2 The Impact of Binding Choices on Performance

The use of WSDL for service descriptions allows services to be invoked through interfaces bound using a number of different protocols (such as SOAP/HTTP or RMI/IIOP). To allow tighter and faster interactions, the use of multiple service bindings with faster protocols (RMI/IIOP, for example) is an option that improves system performance. An ESB access point can select the appropriate binding based on predefined binding optimization policies.

7.3.1.3 The Impact on Parsing and Data Volume on Performance

Compared to binary messaging, the widespread adoption of XML for encoding message contents can add considerable processing overhead to application systems. You can reduce processing cost by not attempting to parse or reparse XML at every node. The use of a Web services gateway that relies only on partial parsing of XML messages can provide significant performance improvements.

Another aspect of improving parsing is to consider using a service as the control flow that carries a reference to a separate and optimized data flow. This becomes particularly true in large data batch scenarios. For example, in the oil industry, reservoir simulation computation can result in several gigabytes of data. Business processes in these types of scenarios can still use a service-oriented approach for the control flow of the process; however, they should separately pass references to the resulting data stored in a common location rather than transferring the data each time. Failure to do so would probably result in unacceptable service performance.

7.3.1.4 The Impact of Security on Performance

You should select appropriate security architectures to match your business requirements, but avoid unnecessary overhead. Just as for Web applications, the combination of HTTP over SSL/TLS can be used to secure communication pipes and provide some degree of protection within an SOA. The addition of signature and payload encryption might not be necessary for all services deployed within an SOA or for every service interaction. For more details on security, see Chapter 8, "Securing the SOA Environment."

7.3.1.5 The Impact of Network Bandwidth on Performance

Even if the application performance, system performance, processor usage, or system processing latency at a provider are carefully controlled, the network and processing nodes between consumer and provider endpoints can still severely impact the level of service. Organizations that need to ensure that specified SLAs can be met appropriately should use networks with guaranteed performance characteristics as an option to minimize risk. Some ISPs are now providing such network capability with guaranteed bandwidth and propagation delays, albeit at a higher cost.

7.3.2 Scalability NFRs

Scalability can become a serious problem in service-oriented systems. By definition, it is difficult to predict over a long term the number of consumers a publicly exposed service will have. Publicly exposed services can also lead to undesirable accesses, which can be intentional or accidental but nonetheless still be potentially adverse to controlled scalability of the system. Controlling scalability requires the following:

- *Capacity planning*: This is particularly relevant to internal use of services within an enterprise. The capacity can be deduced in many cases from existing transaction measurements, with quite good accuracy. Capacity planning for SOA needs to include the additional processing power required by the new flexibility layers.
- *Provisioning*: Most enterprises that expose public services to partners also define a provisioning process that enables them to evaluate the number and type of additional resources required to deliver the service to comply with a given SLA.
- *Upstream filtering*: To prevent undesirable accesses that can overwhelm provider systems, access should be filtered as early as possible. Filtering components are available on the market, and they are sometimes delivered by Web services management software extensions.
- *Policy-based routing*: For service requests that are allowed to proceed after any filtering, there can be different SLAs applied per server group, thereby enabling better scalability control. These agreements can range from best-effort delivery to guaranteed response time. As for upstream filtering, this capability is sometimes delivered by Web services management software extensions.

In addition, when integrating with mainframe systems, the access option should support business goals and qualities-of-service requirements. The access option should also facilitate infrastructure workload management capabilities.

7.3.3 Transactional Integrity NFRs

Transactional integrity refers to the support for local atomic transactions (using the one-phase or two-phase commitment protocol) in any given access mechanism, enabling a group of updates performed by the server applications to be processed as a single unit of work. It also refers to support for global transactions (two-phase commit), enabling an external server to coordinate updates performed by transaction managers with updates to local resources held by that server.

Loose coupling, in many cases, implies the potential loss of controlling atomic transaction from the consumer side. All of the integrated services are usually part of a business transaction, and the undo operation (rather than rollback) is processed via compensation techniques that perform the opposite logical action. However, the application design should ensure that it enables such atomic transaction capability in conjunction with granularity concerns of service interfaces. This is accomplished either by using application server transactional composition techniques or by using mainframe transaction decomposition software that provides this support.

7.3.4 Security NFRs

The most common security requirement is to authenticate end users and middle-tier servers. In many SOAs, simple user ID and password authentication is still widely used, although X.501 client certificates, Kerberos tickets, and other schemes are becoming more popular. Whichever technique is adopted, a user's credentials must eventually be mapped to an external security manager–enabled user ID to support authorization and accounting requirements that normally apply to existing operational applications. For more information on security issues, see Chapter 8.

7.4 Nonruntime Qualities

The non-functional requirements discussed so far have related to decisions made about the runtime components of an SOA. *Nonruntime qualities* explore all of the system aspects that are related to a system's lifecycle and that control aspects such as manageability, version management, and disaster recovery.

7.4.1 Manageability NFRs

As we progress toward delivering true SOAs, what becomes distinctly evident is the critical need for managing agents that operate deep within the operating environment, in conjunction with high-level controlling layers. A single *management dashboard* is often required to satisfy this need, and for this to work well, it must be part of a larger *services management* environment, not just a slightly modified environment for gateways and exchange management.

7.4.1.1 The Requirements for Services Management

To understand the overall effort and scope of requirements needed for services management, it is important to achieve a common baseline of IT functionality that the services management system needs to provide. This is not simply an issue of capturing SOAP fault alerts in a monitoring console, but rather a need to encompass a broad range of interoperable and loosely coupled services within a SOA framework. A proposed starter set of these functions should include the following:

- *Security management*: This includes the capability to manage individuals and roles for authentication ("Who are you?") as well as authorization ("Are you allowed to perform this function?"). As part of an overall policy management capability, authentication and authorization services need to be managed under broad security policies as they exist for an enterprise.
- *Catalog support*: The capability to catalog services with associated deployment metadata requires management of catalogs as components in a federated network of repositories. This includes authorization and authentication ("Can a requesting service 'see' all services available in a catalog?") so that entitlement to access is appropriately managed.

- *Provisioning*: This includes the capability to provision a service as well as provision additional capacity for a service (if a service is under duress). Capacity management should be included as part of the provisioning process.
- *Configuration and versioning*: Another essential function in services management is the capability to configure services as part of a policy. That configuration can be static or dynamic, depending on the terms and conditions of the contract for which the service is being exploited. Versioning is vital to ensure that the exploitation of services happens in accordance with prerequisite and co-requisite dependencies (such as between the calling service or program and the receiving service).
- *Monitoring*: The foundation of management, this includes the capability to manage service capacity thresholds, faults, errors, and otherwise predictable and unpredictable conditions in which valid processing did not occur.
- *Performance and SLA monitoring*: This is the capability to monitor service throughput metrics and capacity, as well as work with an intermediary such as a metering service to aggregate performance data and create input for SLA reporting.

Further details on the topic of services management systems are covered in Chapter 9, "Managing the SOA Environment."

7.4.2 Version Management NFRs

There are many solutions to managing service versioning issues. Service interfaces can be made flexible enough to allow flexible evolution without the requirement for strict version management. The available solutions are already in production with banking IT providers that can decouple client-platform development cycles from their execution lifecycle.

A.7.1

An alternative approach is to use dynamic adaptation layers that play the matchmaker role at runtime. These layers work by interpreting the semantics of client requests and performing corresponding service requests to compose the response expected by the client. This matchmaking capability is illustrated by the Ontology-based Web Services for Business Integration tool.

7.4.3 Disaster-Recovery NFRs

SOAs, through their capability to deliver the same service in a rather ubiquitous manner, can facilitate a de facto disaster-recovery capability. However, service interfaces are only the façade to concrete implementation; the infrastructure executing the services must still be designed for disaster recovery. For example, the data processing and storage centers still require appropriate redundancy. All routing policies and security infrastructure must be capable of remote recovery, including long-running business process data. In particular, when using BPEL choreography for long-running processes based on services, particular attention must be paid to the execution infrastructure so that the process fallback capability and transactional compensation are supported by the appropriate middleware.

7.5 Summary

In this chapter, we identified some of the non-functional requirements that SOA systems must satisfy. These requirements were categorized according to their source and significance as business constraints, technology constraints, runtime qualities, and nonruntime qualities. The intent was to illustrate some of the requirements found in typical SOA projects rather than to provide an exhaustive list.

Which of many non-functional requirements will dominate the architecture of your next SOA project is impossible to predict. Within a particular enterprise, it might be that industry standards and partner systems dominate the requirements. The most likely scenario, from our experience, is that existing systems and the technology choices made in previous years will dominate the non-functional requirements that must be accommodated.

7.6 Links to developerWorks

A.7.1 IBM alphaWorks. *The Ontology-based Web Services for Business Integration.* http://www.alphaworks.ibm.com/tech/owsbi.

7.7 References

Appleby, K., et al. *Policy-based automated provisioning.* IBM Systems Journal, Vol. 43, 1-2004. http://www.research.ibm.com/journal/sj43-1.html.

Buco, M. J., et al. *Utility computing SLA management based upon business objectives.* IBM Systems Journal, Vol. 43, 1-2004. http://www.research.ibm.com/journal/sj43-1.html.

Dan, A., et al. *Web services on demand: WSLA-driven automated management.* IBM Systems Journal, Vol. 43, 1-2004. http://www.research.ibm.com/journal/sj43-1.html.

Kreizman, G. and Fraga, E. *E-Governmment Architecture: Development and Governance.* (TG-14-6799), New Zealand State Services Commission, October 2001. http://www.e-government. govt.nz/docs/service%2Darch%2D200303/.

New Zealand Government Initiative. *A Service Delivery Architecture,* New Zealand State Services Commission. http://www.e-government.govt.nz/docs/service-arch-200303/chapter3.html.

Telemanagement Forum. *Catalyst Spotlight: Model Driven Architecture for NGOSS.* TeleManagement Forum, March 2005. http://www.tmforum.org/browse.asp?catID=1118&sNode=1118&Exp=Y&linkID=30310.

Chapter 8

Securing the SOA Environment

"Let every eye negotiate for itself and trust no agent."

—*William Shakespeare*

Security in a service-oriented architecture is a process of identifying areas of risk within an architectural model and providing trusted practices and countermeasures to mitigate those risks. As an integral component of an SOA solution, we need to understand the business-level concepts of risk and trust to explore what security services are required. Most enterprises already have security solutions that largely rely on established security controls, such as firewalls and virtual private networks (VPNs), to provide perimeter protection. As deployments of SOA solutions become more widespread, the process of securing the enterprise must become a fundamental part of an SOA development process. In addition, as an enterprise moves toward implementing SOA patterns, concrete implementations will require a move from the reliance on perimeter controls to a more granular view of security services and security architecture.

This chapter covers security in SOA in terms of understanding security concepts, the available standards and technologies in the industry, and how to structure your own SOA security model. It then examines SOA security in the context of a multi-organization environment, including federated security. Finally, this chapter presents an overview of relevant products for SOA security.

8.1 Architectural Considerations for an SOA Security Model

When evaluating existing deployments, you will need to understand any new risks and countermeasures that the SOA development model introduces. You should look at where security is implemented in an enterprise, either embedded in applications or as IT processes, and then evaluate how you can implement new security services to provide support to both application and enterprise SOA components.

From a security perspective, you will generally need to authorize any changes in software within an enterprise. This requirement can be met by a range of solutions, from clear business practices that identify the people in the organization that are responsible for managing software installation, to providing automated tracking of software patches applied to systems through an asset management process. The critical thing is to start capturing the business requirements for securing the change management process. These requirements fall into the following areas:

- Messaging characteristics—The capability to interact without depending on a particular messaging format, protocol, or interaction model allows a wider reach of integration capabilities.
- Transport protocol independence.
- Data format independence.

The requirements for transport and data independence usually imply that the organization needs a security model that can ensure the security of multiple, varied protocols. In an initial assessment for an SOA project, it is important to understand what security mechanisms currently exist and identify the enterprise-wide solutions versus the tactical solutions. The following are things to consider:

- Multiple interaction models such as synchronous and asynchronous models
- Message semantic independence, along with the role of tooling and runtime environments in providing semantic support
- Programming language independence
- Business model independence in the form of canonical format support, industry-based message exchange formats, and others
- Independence from business process standards such as RosettaNet, OAGIS, and so on

Each interaction model generally has its own mechanism to secure message exchanges. Depending on the number of standards that an enterprise must support, there might be a security requirement to support multiple mechanisms and to translate from one security domain to another. These mechanisms include the following:

- Support for various integration styles that provide architectural flexibility
- Unified user experience to provide a consolidated and singular interaction mechanism for users
- Application connectivity that addresses the communications layer that underlies all of the architecture
- Process integration for choreographing applications and services
- Information integration that federates and moves the enterprise data
- The build-to-integrate method, which builds and deploys new applications and services

The more complex an environment becomes, the greater the need for a systematic method that will reduce the complexity. Most common security errors in enterprises today are related to IT decision-makers who do not understand the risk or the security solution. The primary goal should be to provide solutions that support the secure deployment of complex applications on heterogeneous systems.

The complexity of the security model can transcend the needs of a single organization's environment. When introducing an SOA or a Web services environment within an enterprise, security requirements might extend the concept of the environment to include virtual organizations that allow intra-enterprise as well as cross-enterprise business transactions. In some deployment topologies, transport layer security techniques (point-to-point security) might be sufficient to meet the business requirements to protect messages in transit. However, in other inter-enterprise scenarios, end-to-end security might be required to provide data integrity and data confidentiality of messages in transit. The scenarios must also support authentication and authorization across trust domains. In some environments, authorization policies include not only who is allowed to access a resource but the purpose for which it is intended. Privacy controls and annotations are a way to express this additional characteristic of authorization.

The next section introduces the elements of security and how these concepts apply to SOA.

8.2 Concepts and Elements of Security

The basic elements of security include the concepts of integrity, confidentiality, identity and authentication, message authentication, session management, authorization, privacy, non-repudiation, and cryptography. These concepts directly impact the architectural and design plans for SOA security.

8.2.1 Integrity

Integrity of information refers to the state of a piece of information such that it is not altered in an unauthorized or unexpected manner. Maintaining the integrity of messages during an exchange between message partners allows all parties to have some level of assurance that the message has not been tampered with in transit. Integrity protection means that if a malicious user were to intercept and change the message content, it would be detected.

8.2.2 Confidentiality

Confidentiality of information refers to the state of such information with respect to any unauthorized or unexpected disclosure of that information. Integrity and confidentiality can apply to data or information at rest or to messages in transit. Confidentiality of messages allows partners to have some level of assurance that their messages have not been read by outside parties while in transit when it is important that sensitive details of a message not be revealed to outside parties.

Transient message confidentiality protection means that during the message transmission, its contents are undisclosed to malicious interceptors. *Persistent message confidentiality* mechanisms ensure that even after transmission of a message, the confidentiality of the message data (for example, credit card numbers, social security numbers, and so on) is maintained. If messages are logged, for instance, persistent confidentiality ensures that if someone were to access a log on a server, he or she would not be able to read the contents of the message.

Confidentiality and integrity also apply to information that is resident. For example, persistent data integrity applies to information such as persistent data or code, whereby signing techniques are used to ensure that the information is not altered. In general, you will need integrity and confidentiality techniques wherever you need to ensure that the state of information is not adulterated or introspected while in transit or in storage.

8.2.3 Identity and Authentication

Authentication is the process of validating a claimed identity. The authentication process evaluates a public piece of information (such as a username) and a private piece of information (such as a password, in theory known only to the user) to determine its validity compared to what the system knows. This private information is often referred to as an *authentication credential*. Authentication credentials might be based on something that is known (such as a password), something that is possessed (such as a private key maintained on a hardware token such as a portable USB storage device or *fob*), or an idempotent object that never changes (such as a fingerprint for a physical user).

After authenticated, systems and applications typically establish the privileges of the authenticated entity. These privileges, sometimes referred to as *authorization credentials*, are used to determine what this entity is allowed to do within an enterprise (also see Section 8.2.6). Thus, within the context of an authenticated secure session, the system can enforce authorized requests by the authenticated entity, and in some cases, it can also keep a record of everything the authenticated user attempts to do (for instance, an audit trail of his or her activities).

Consider, for example, an application used as part of an order-fulfillment process. This application might need to leverage other applications such as shipping schedules or updating stock levels. Access to shipping schedules might be restricted so that schedules for the next 24 hours can be viewed by the warehouse manager, but beyond that, schedules should be viewable only by order-entry clerks. Likewise, all updates to stock levels will be audited so that fraudulent activities can be monitored and stopped. In either case, having an authenticated identity, a set of authorization credentials, and an established trust relationship between the parties allows the appropriate actions to be permitted or denied, and it allows you to log requests (permit and deny) for audit purposes.

8.2.4 Message Authentication

One interesting side effect of confidentiality and integrity techniques is that when applied to messages (rather than processes or applications), they can be used to also provide message authentication. Message authentication ensures that a message is from the claimed party and is a result of previously agreed upon cryptographic techniques used to provide integrity and confidentiality. It is important that message authentication or data origin assurances also allow the receiver to identify the message sender.

8.2.5 Session Management

A *session* is the context shared between two parties engaged in a long-running exchange of messages. Instead of having to prove their identities to each other for every message exchange, the parties establish a session context that is bound to the authenticated identities of the parties in question. *Session management* refers to the management of this session context, including the creation and deletion of this session context.

Securing a session involves authenticating each party, establishing the appropriate *tokens* that can be used to secure the exchange of multiple requests and responses (transactions) in the context of this entity, and then terminating the exchange and cleaning up any relevant information that was cached during the session. Maintaining secure session state means that multiple request and response messages can be linked together as part of a larger, multimessage transaction.

Managing session state is essential, from both a security and a performance point of view. One of the fundamental issues in providing security is ensuring that users take advantage of the security offered to them. User inconvenience often results in the first security challenge: If users must provide their authentication credentials (such as a username and password) for every single request, they often find ways to shortcut the security mechanisms in place.

Mechanisms such as WS-SecureConversation and single sign-on can help reduce the number of individual authentications required but still provide the protection necessary to meet the business requirements.

8.2.6 Authorization

Authorization is the process of making a decision about the actions that an entity is able to perform and then enforcing the appropriate decision to allow or disallow actions. At its simplest, authorizing a request addresses the issue of "Can X do Y?" or "Can user X access resource Y?" In more advanced scenarios, this decision process can include an evaluation of the conditions under which a request is being made: "Can user X access resource Y at time of day Z?" Or similarly, "Can user X access resource Y given restrictions Z?" Access decision enforcement is the process of ensuring that access is granted or denied according to the result of this decision.

A simple example of an authorization decision is the answer to "Can Sue transfer money between account A and account B?" There are, of course, more complicated decisions than "Can X do Y with Z?" Often the answer to a question requires additional information. For example, the answer to this question of Sue transferring money can be further qualified by the authentication type the system uses to establish the session, the time of day, the exact nature of "Y," and its effect on "Z." For example, if "Y" is "transfer $10,000 from account

A to account B" where "Z" is account A, but account A has a balance of only $4.21, then clearly, the response to this question is "No."

Granularity of authorization is an important issue to understand in a service-oriented architectural pattern. Following the secure-the-perimeter paradigm, the system should handle initial authorization as close to the edge of the domain and as far from the actual request invocation as possible. The strategy is to provide circles of control. It is useful to take a layered approach to authorization in that it has the effect of removing unauthorized requests at lower processing layers. This means that the requests that are presented to the higher processing layers have a high ratio of authorized-to-unauthorized requests—this is good in terms of performance and security.

Consider the layering of access control decisions, given Sue's requests to transfer money:

- "Can Sue transfer money?"—Yes
- "Can Sue transfer money between accounts A and B?"—Yes
- "Can Sue transfer $10,000 between accounts A and B?"—Yes/May
- "Can Sue transfer $10,000 between accounts A and B given that account A has a balance of $4.21?"—No

You can break down or layer the decision "Can Sue transfer money from account A to account B" to allow the access control request to become further refined the closer the request gets to the data in question.

In general, the system can make an initial decision about authorizing a given request based on the authenticated identity. For example, Jane is not an authenticated user, and so her requests are stopped at the edge of the network. You can then refine those decisions as the request moves further into the enterprise network.

In the *mediation layer*, where requests are brokered, proxied, and routed through the enterprise, the system can apply the next level of decision-making: "Can Mark apply for a new trading account?" No, because his account has been suspended for six months due to improper usage; Mark is restricted to only viewing a report. At the application layer, the system makes the final decision on "Can Sue transfer $10,000 between account A (balance = $4.21) and account B (balance = $2,124.25)?"

When exposing resources and services to business partners, it is possible to implement filtering of authorization at both sides of an exchange. Thus, a business partner might be responsible for ensuring that only requests that it is willing to honor are allowed to be issued to the service provider. So if a business partner is not willing to honor an order for 10,000 widgets at $1.25 each, the business partner should not authorize this request nor build it, and thus the service provider should never receive this request.

This is not to say that the service provider is now exempt from making and enforcing authorization decisions. Instead, the requests that the business partner receives have already been authorized, and the level of decision required by the service provider moves to the level of "Is this business partner allowed to make these requests?" and "Can I fulfill these requests?"

8.2.7 Privacy

Privacy of data, a dimension of authorization, involves mechanisms for confidentiality. This is an additional attribute that can be defined for data elements included within a message itself. In the previous example, for an order of 10,000 widgets at $1.00 per widget, the price of the good itself might need to be private (for example, it might be confidential). Therefore, the system needs proper encryption to protect this data from unauthorized viewing in addition to any previous message-level confidentiality. Within the enterprise, after the system removes the message-layer confidentiality mechanism, it might still need to protect the price of these widgets (that is, $1.00 per). This allows someone at the receiver side to possibly determine that an order for widgets was placed—if they have access to the message after message confidentiality was reversed or decrypted—but not the cost per widget.

Privacy concerns apply to this type of information within a message (for example, competitive information), but they also apply to personal information, which is also known as *personally identifiable information* (PII). PII includes information such as social security number, address, age, or even soft drink preference, and this data might have different requirements for privacy protection.

8.2.8 Non-Repudiation

Legal situations in business often need evidence that a particular event has occurred under a set of conditions. As businesses rely more often on computer systems to provide business services, the systems will likely receive challenges to provide evidence to support to legal challenges. One aspect of distributing authorization decisions across trusted partner relationships is that the business services need to have evidence of non-repudiation.

Non-repudiation refers to the inability of a party to repudiate (deny) a message or request. For example, if a company places an order for 10,000 widgets, non-repudiation ensures that the company cannot at a later time claim to have not placed such an order. Although true non-repudiation is extremely difficult to achieve, systems can now use digital signatures in some circumstances to provide a form of non-repudiation that's sufficient for online transactions.

Digital signatures, issued by the requestor in a message, provide a measure of assurance that the signor (requestor) has approved the request. This relies on several assumptions:

- The signed information includes a timestamp and the identity of the requestor.
- The private (signature) key is assumed to be known only to the signor, indicating that only he is able to generate this digital signature. The system might need separate levels of supporting evidence to assert that the requestor is, in fact, the only entity that has knowledge of this signing key.
- The system assumes that the requestor is following good practices by signing only information of which he has knowledge and responsibility. Thus, a requestor cannot come back at a later date and claim that although he signed a message, he did not read or understand the contents of the message.

Business policies around non-repudiation play an increasingly important role within a transactional environment and may enable the establishment of trust relationships so that electronic systems can make authorization decisions throughout a requestor-provider environment.

8.2.9 Cryptography

Techniques for protecting the integrity and confidentiality of electronic information are based on cryptography. This is a complex mathematical subject, but there are many good references for cryptography and cryptographic techniques. Briefly, *encryption* is the process of converting information from one format to another using a mathematic transformation. This transformation takes as an input a *key* and the message to be transformed and produces an output. *Decryption* is the process of reversing this transformation using the transformed output message and another key to recover the original message.

In general, encryption is based on either symmetric or asymmetric keys. *Symmetric key systems* use the same key for both the encryption and decryption functions. Symmetric key systems lead to what is called a *shared key system*, in which the symmetry is known to both parties and thus must be kept secret from any other parties. An *asymmetric key system* uses one key value to transform the message and a related but different key to recover the message. A subset of asymmetric key systems are those in which one of these keys must be kept secret, but the other can be made public—hence, a *public key system*.

Public key infrastructure techniques are based on asymmetric keys. In this approach, a user keeps secret a private key while making available to partners a public key. Information that is encrypted with this private key can be decrypted with the public key and vice versa. The issuance, registration, and distribution of the key pairs become an important component in their use and are often the most difficult part of this technology to deploy. A public half of the key pair is placed in a certificate, thus creating a binding of the user's public key to his identity. This allows the user to assert his identity through the use of the private key and allow a public key holder to validate this assertion.

Public key infrastructure (PKI) techniques are useful because they allow partners to establish a trust infrastructure by allowing each partner to focus on managing his or her own (private) keys, while being able to exchange the corresponding public key certificates with those partners with whom they wish to establish trust. This is, in general, a more tractable approach to managing a broad trust relationship with a lot of partners. This type of mechanism offers many advantages, but it does require that partners regularly check that their certificates are still valid. An enterprise needs proper business policies to govern the validation time period.

Both shared key and public key systems are used for the encryption of data. Encryption provides protection against the disclosure of information: If information is encrypted, then this information will be disclosed only to those parties able to decrypt the information—that is, those parties that have access to a shared key in a shared key environment or those that have a public key in a PKI environment.

From a performance point of view, the challenge with a public-private key pair approach is that operations on the public key side are significantly more expensive in terms of processing power than those on the private key side. With a symmetric key system, the cost of encryption and decryption is usually much smaller. Despite the processing cost of the public key–based system, it is operationally cheaper than managing numerous shared keys in the alternative. Nevertheless, when encrypting large volumes of data, shared key techniques are preferred to reduce access time.

Public key infrastructure techniques have been used largely for the purposes of providing data integrity and data origin authentication. In addition, PKI techniques are used for providing and managing digital signatures. In a digital signature scenario, you usually do not encrypt large amounts of data. Instead, a hash function is used to generate a unique, fixed-size representation of the message. This *hash* value is then encrypted and sent with the message. This overall process is referred to as *digital signing*, and the encrypted hash value is a *digital signature. Signature validation* compares the decrypted signature (the original hash value) and the result from performing the same hash function a second time on the original message. If the two results are identical, then it is an authentic signature. The cost of this combination of hash function and cryptography is such that it is a preferred alternative to encrypting an entire message when only integrity protection is required.

Digital signatures provide proof against the alteration of information (that is, they maintain integrity). When information within a signed message is modified, the signature of the information will no longer be valid (since the hash values will be different). An invalid signature, in turn, implies the message integrity loss.

8.2.10 Trust

For two partners to secure communications between themselves, they must exchange security credentials either directly or indirectly. However, each needs to determine what level of confidence it has in the credentials asserted by the other party. This level of confidence is defined as *trust*.

Trust is another element of authorization, but it works on a larger scale between groups of entities (such as users, systems, applications, processes, and so on). It is a required element of interorganizational message interactions, but it can also apply inside the model of a single organization (between departments or network domains, for example). Using trust, you can define authorization policies across the entire group of entities as they relate to their interactions with other groups.

A *trust domain* defines the nature and identity of entities that it contains. It is possible to have different domains across the same set of entities based on how these entities are viewed or mixed together in the domain. For example, a single database can belong to two different trust domains, depending on which other domain (containing applications for specific purposes) is allowed to access the database. These domains can also contain other domains;

for example, the trust domain for an entire corporation can contain all the trust domains of its individual departments.

8.2.11 Federation

A higher abstraction beyond establishing trust across domains is the consideration of how services across multiple owners can be integrated together. The common mechanism to build this level of abstraction is federating multiple systems together. In a *federation* of services, there can be multiple owners of all the services involved, but the model allows them to establish trust across the federation, provide user single sign-on (and single sign-off), and provide distributed attribute management. Federations are particularly useful in SOAs that extend beyond a single organization. It builds a virtual common security model by relating the individual models of each organization to a common reference model.

8.3 Implementation Requirements for SOA Security

The elements of security have different dynamics and impact on the architecture of an organization. Approaching security requirements from a service-oriented architectural perspective raises some new requirements on these elements. These requirements address how to coordinate security mechanisms across business partners and trust boundaries and are defined in terms of policies in the following aspects:

- When establishing trust between partners, the accurate definition of security policies covering transport, message, and data protection, including the security tokens in a request, will be essential (see Sections 8.3.1 through 8.3.6). In addition to having each policy, it is important to communicate these policies.
- After a business has its own policies defined, it will need to manage and coordinate any changes of security information (signing or encryption keys) across partners (see Sections 8.3.7 and 8.4).

8.3.1 Managing Security Policies

In advance of interacting with a business partner's SOA resources, you will need to determine appropriate security policies such as requirements for transport and message layer protection as well as data level protection. These policies can provide a component of an overall assurance strategy, leveraged by the individual businesses. They provide confidence that the SOA will allow only authorized, trusted business partners—with known, defined, legal liability relationships—to participate in cross-business transactions. In addition, you might need to implement such policies and monitor these implementations for business agreement or legal compliance.

8.3.2 Defining Transport Security Policies

Transport layer security refers to the type of protection offered in the actual delivery protocols involved in the interaction, such as using secure sockets layer (SSL) over Internet transactions. SSL is used to provide a confidential (encrypted) channel between two endpoints.[1] The result of this encryption is that the contents of any message flowing over this channel are not discernable to any observing, outside party. This encryption is based on keys stored within digital SSL certificates. These are long-term keys bound to an entity during initial SSL session establishment. Both parties use a common new encryption key that is possibly previously unknown for the purposes of encrypting all of the messages on the wire.

One side benefit is that SSL certificates, while defining a cryptographic key, also contain a binding of this key to a given entity. This enables software to use SSL certificates to also determine data origin authentication—if I am able to encrypt something for you to decrypt using the SSL certificate's key, and if I can determine that it is a valid certificate issued by someone I trust, then we both have established some level of trust.

After the SSL channel is terminated at the SSL endpoint, the messages are available in cleartext for anyone to see (and alter). In scenarios in which you need to terminate an SSL channel and forward the message to its intended destination service without using SSL (with intermediaries or gateways, for example), you can open a potential vulnerability into the system. This then leads us to a new requirement: message layer security.

8.3.3 Defining Message Layer Security Policies

Message layer security allows the system to protect the message body itself (transmitted in the HTTP message body, for example) in terms of integrity and confidentiality; this is on top of any protection applied at the transport level. Because this is applied to the message body, the protection is provided end to end. Furthermore, transport layer security might change depending on the network boundaries that the message traverses (different levels of security over the many individual networks constituting the Internet). End-to-end protection implies that the contents of the message cannot be read or modified at any point other than the required endpoint. In some cases, you need to protect both the message body and the message headers.

In general, both message layer and transport layer security are applied to messages within an SOA environment as follows:

- *(Transport layer) security:* All encrypted messages passed between two entities cannot be read or altered by any third party able to observe these messages in transit. Transport layer security can also be used to authenticate the entity presenting the request (which might not be the entity making the request but simply represent the SSL endpoint at the entity's network edge).
- *(Message layer) privacy and confidentiality:* This is the encryption of a message body so that the message itself is not readable even if and when transport layer security

---

1.   One quick note: Because this information is encrypted and not readable, a form of integrity protection is implied. This follows from the fact that it is extremely difficult (practically as well as mathematically) to modify a message (violating its integrity) without being able to read it. So in a scenario in which it is not easy to decrypt/re-encrypt a message, integrity protection can be said to follow.

is not applied. In general, implementations to date have not leveraged end-to-end message layer confidentiality, preferring to rely on the combination of transport layer security and message layer integrity.

- *(Message layer) integrity:* This is the signing of information in a message that you must guarantee is original and not tampered with. Note that this signing of information also provides some evidence of origin authentication. We can determine the identity of the entity associated with the key used to sign the information

8.3.4 Defining Data Protection Policies

You can achieve data protection by applying encryption mechanisms to the data-level elements within a message. Although not widely adopted, the notion of data element confidentiality is recognized as critical in many SOA environments (especially those that will be applied within financial and health sector environments). Data element confidentiality enables individual data elements to be encrypted as opposed to encrypting an entire message. This element-level confidentiality allows protection of sensitive information (such as patient medical information) while still allowing the exposure of other elements in a message for other purposes (such as coarse-grained authorization, routing, and so on).

8.3.5 Defining Security Token Policies

At some level, cooperating business partners will determine the types of security tokens they can issue, manage, and exchange with each other. These tokens are used to assert information about requestors of business processes. As such, different scenarios require different tokens with various characteristics where appropriate. Some typical token types and their typical scenarios are as follows:

- *Username token:* An identity assertion token that includes a password (usually in digest form). In general, Web browsers and servers use this token in an HTTP environment in which the intelligent browser collects a username and password that is then validated by the service provider. A special form of a username token is an IDAssertion. This is a username token without a password, generally used within a trusted environment in which the security token is used to communicate or assert an already authenticated identity.
- *X.509 certificate:* This certificate is typically used to identify a requestor that has signed part or all of a message. Typically the certificate provides a "two-for-one" approach for identifying the requestor based on information already included in the request by the requestor.
- *SAML assertion:* A SAML assertion can provide a means of asserting an identity or providing attributes for a claimed identity. A SAML assertion is typically used in a passive client scenario (for single sign-on, as described later in this chapter) or in an active client scenario when additional information about a requestor is required (such as attributes describing the user's roles, groups, privileges, and so on).

- *Kerberos token:* Kerberos tokens are based on an authentication mechanism designed at MIT and since adopted by both DCE and Microsoft as a means of asserting an identity.

8.3.6 Defining Cryptographic Key Policies

An SOA environment requires that partners establish key management policies when used for signing or encrypting information. This is both a technical consideration—technically, one should never use the same key pairs for both signing and encryption—and a legal liability consideration. SSL certificates are easy to come by; businesses running large volumes of high-dollar transactions will almost certainly require more assurance of their business partner's identity than a free or self-generated SSL certificate.

8.3.7 Coordinating Policies Between Business Partners

Establishing common policies for transport layer security across the enterprise (business) is a well-understood exercise today. Almost all businesses using the Internet have SSL certificates. Businesses have a well-established understanding of managing such certificates and SSL sessions with the help of IETF-defined standards.

Other aspects of security policies are less understood. As business processes become service oriented, you cannot assume that messages will be bound to just the well-known HTTP transport layer. When considering Web services requests, we need to leverage well-defined message structures based on XML and SOAP and their respective security mechanisms. XML Encryption, XML Digital Signature, and the WS-Security roadmap describe the mechanisms necessary for any security strategy for services-oriented architectures. Therefore, to understand how you can define and relate policies to transactions that span between organizations, it is necessary to look at the mechanisms and protocols that allow this.

8.4 Standards and Mechanisms for SOA Security

This section introduces and describes the different security mechanisms available in the industry that can be used to address security requirements within a service-oriented architecture, both within a single organization and across multiple organizational boundaries. We will focus primarily on how this technology is implemented in the Web services (WS-*) security family of specifications.

The basis of security in Web services is in the WS-Security Roadmap published by IBM and Microsoft to describe the components necessary to address a secure Web services solution. This roadmap defines security elements as composable units that can be applied only when necessary to solve a particular problem. Thus, a security solution does not need the drag of additional functionality and components that are not required. We will describe how the parts of this roadmap fit together to help fulfill the security requirements previously described.

A.8.1

8.4.1 The Basic Security Standard: WS-Security

A.8.2

WS-Security refers to two distinct efforts: the initial WS-Security specification (published by IBM, Microsoft, and VeriSign) and the full WS-Security roadmap containing several defined specifications (including the WS-Security specification itself). This subsection focuses on the basic WS-Security specification.

A.8.3

The WS-Security specification was originally published in April 2002 by IBM, Microsoft, and VeriSign and subsequently was submitted to the OASIS Web Services Security Technical Committee (WSS-TC) created for it. The effort through the OASIS process led to an OASIS standard in March 2004 known as Web Services Security.

As described in the OASIS document, the specification provides three main mechanisms: sending security tokens as part of a message, message integrity, and message confidentiality. These mechanisms by themselves do not provide a complete security solution for Web services. Instead, this specification is a building block for other Web service extensions and higher-level, application-specific protocols to accommodate a wide variety of security models and technologies.

WS-Security enables you to apply XML security techniques (described in the following sections) to authenticate and secure message exchanges between a Web service requestor and a Web service provider. It uses signatures and encryption placed on a message and security tokens bound to the messages.

8.4.1.1 WS-Security Tokens

The WS-Security specification is agnostic to the type of token that is actually included within a message. WS-Security uses an XML approach to defining tokens that enables extensibility and supports multiple security tokens. This enables services to communicate in a secure manner and exchange security information across different implementations.

The Web Services Security: SOAP Message Security (WSS-SMS) specification defines three classes of token: username, binary, and XML. The *username token* is a simple representation of a username and optional password that represents the binding of commonly presented user authentication credentials into a simple XML-based token. The *binary token* format provides a means of representing binary-formatted information such as Kerberos tickets, X.509 certificates, and other non-XML-formatted (or -formattable) security tokens. Finally, the *XML token* format defines a means of representing XML-based security tokens such as SAML assertions. This extensible token format allows the customization of tokens, so, for example, although a *RACF passticket* format has not yet been defined, it can be easily put into the XML-based security token format.

8.4.1.2 Signatures: XML Digital Signatures

Digital signatures, used to ensure confidentiality and integrity in service interactions, can be implemented with XML Digital Signature (XML-DSig). XML-DSig was a joint initiative of the Internet Engineering Task Force (IETF) and the World-Wide Web Consortium (W3C). As its name suggests, it defines a means of rendering a digital signature in XML. However, people often mistakenly assume that this standard only applies to digitally signing XML documents, when in fact it can be used to sign "any digital content," to quote the specification.

8.4.1.3 Message-Level and Element-Level Encryption: XML Encryption

XML Encryption is a W3C recommendation that is not just a means to encrypt XML but also to express meta-information about the encryption performed on a digital document. This allows a document processor to be aware of what algorithms were used to encrypt the document. XML Encryption allows you to encrypt only the message subsets that must be kept confidential, thus providing a level of privacy, or confidentiality, to information within the message.

You can encrypt element names, the data contained within them, or both. When choosing how much information to encrypt, you need to ensure that the unencrypted information (that is, the element name such as Phone-Number) does not, in turn, reveal information about the likely data (for example, 888-123-4567) in the element, thus cutting down the possible dimensions that a malicious attacker has to work on with brute-force decryption.

XML Encryption and XML Signature can be used together when a document is both signed and encrypted with them. To check the signature of the data, the signed document must be decrypted by means of a transform.

8.4.1.4 Leveraging WS-Security

Both encryption and digital signing come with performance implications that need to be part of an organization's assessment of risk and countermeasures in its security policy.

Encryption and signing can be expensive computationally, especially the signature validation required at the service provider side. This cost can be even more expensive when you consider the cost of dereferencing individually signed or encrypted elements of the message. Given that a service provider is responsible for the decryption and signature validation of all incoming requests, a service requestor should not try to sign or encrypt majority subsets of a message. For example, in a message with 17 elements, signing 15 of the elements might provide an unnecessary burden. In this case, signing the entire message might be more appropriate.

Most early adopters have limited their use of WS-Security to include just security tokens for requestor identity authentication and instead rely on transport layer security techniques for message protection. This allows encryption to be provided point-to-point through transport layer techniques, providing point-to-point confidentiality on a message.

As hardware accelerators and improved algorithms emerge in combination with stronger business requirements (such as defense industry, healthcare, and others) for privacy and security, we expect that more organizations will start to use WS-Security and XML Encryption. This enables them to leverage encryption on privacy-related elements of a message for those scenarios in which they must not expose this private information until it is properly received at the final destination.

8.4.2 Trust Domains: WS-Trust

A.8.4

The Web Services Trust specification defines a mechanism for issuing and exchanging security tokens between partners. Token exchange provides the means of issuing and disseminating credentials within and across different trust domains. Basic WS-Security, as previously discussed, defines the basic mechanisms for providing secure messaging but stops short of defining trust. The WS-Trust specification provides tokens for use in WS-Security message exchanges and uses these basic mechanisms of WS-Security to ensure its own messages. Using WS-Trust, applications can also establish tokens for long-running conversations and can engage in secure communication designed to work with the general Web services framework, including WSDL service descriptions and SOAP messages.

8.4.2.1 Leveraging WS-Trust

WS-Trust defines the techniques to manage and exchange tokens through its `<RequestSecurityToken>` and `<RequestSecurityTokenResponse>` messages. When deploying an application, you need to define a particular token type that is expected by the application and that is used to authenticate the entity making the request. Because not all Web services resource invokers are able to produce such a token, there is a mismatch in requirements.

WS-Trust token exchange allows a business partner to issue a Web services request using one token type (for example, a SAML assertion for authentication purposes), even if this token type cannot be accommodated by the destination Web service. The upfront processing of the message (for WS-Security) allows other trusted elements of the architecture to take this token, validate it, and exchange it for another token type that will allow it to invoke the service. This application pattern enables you to deploy a single application, exposed to multiple business partners, with varying degrees of WS-Security functionality. A token management trust service enables this pluggable functionality.

The combination of WS-Security and WS-Trust provides a fundamental flexibility to enable security across a Web services–based SOA environment. WS-Trust provides the means to manage the security tokens enabled by WS-Security.

8.4.3 Federated Security: WS-Federation

A.8.5

The WS-Federation specification describes how to use the existing Web services security building blocks that allows business processes to work in federated groups. It focuses on the relationships between parties and the high-level architecture that supports these relationships. Two additional documents, WS-Federation Active and WS-Federation Passive profile specifications, describe how to implement individual federation solutions.

Active clients, in the WS-Federation model, are directly Web services-enabled; that is, they are able to issue Web services requests and react to a Web services response. The active profile of WS-Federation defines how an entity can carry the information required to authenticate the requestor in its request. This information is carried within the WS-Security-defined `<Security>` header of a request in the form of WS-Security- and WS-Trust-defined and managed security tokens. WS-Federation allows an active client application entity to include the required information to identify the requestor and its privileges within its request. This allows the authentication and authorization of requests, discussed previously in an implied browser-based HTTP-based environment, to be replicated in an SOA environment without browsers or direct user interaction.

The WS-Federation Passive profile specification describes a framework of how to implement federation functionality in a passive client environment that is unable to build its own Web services requests. The most commonly encountered example of a passive client is the basic HTTP browser. Because the WS-Federation solution involves the foundation of WS-Security for infrastructure support, the same components that are used to provide a passive client solution can be used for an active client solution.

8.4.3.1 Leveraging WS-Federation

The WS-Federation Passive profile describes how to implement both push- and pull-based single sign-on authentication in an HTTP-based environment. This allows a service requestor to redirect a user (service consumer) to a service provider while carrying the information required to vouch for the user's authenticated identity to the service provider—this is a *push-based single sign-on*. This profile also allows a service provider to poll for the required user identity information from the service requestor, again without direct user involvement—this is *pull-based single sign-on*. This, in turn, enables the service provider to identify the user without directly interacting with the user.

The WS-Federation Active profile describes how to include fine-grained authentication information using transport layer security and authentication techniques. For simplicity, consider the scenario in an HTTP-based environment. Transport-layer-based security uses SSL, in which the requestor identity can be based on the identity bound to the service requestor's SSL session or the certificate or, more likely, the machine issuing the request on behalf of the actual service requestor. WS-Federation Active allows service requestor authentication to a finer degree (for example, individual users at the requesting machine) than that of transport layer security techniques.

In general, if you need finer granularity user identification than when using transport layer techniques, you should use WS-Federation.

8.4.4 Session Management: WS-SecureConversation

As discussed previously, validating the signature on a message can be expensive, especially when the requestor signing the message issues multiple requests. Likewise, repeated authenticating requests from the same user can also be expensive, especially if these requests are part of a conversation between a service requestor and a service provider. The WS-SecureConversation specification describes how to leverage WS-Security and WS-Trust to authenticate a series of messages within a conversation, hence establishing a secure conversation.

A secure conversation is managed by a security context, represented by a security context token (SCT). This token contains a shared secret (symmetric key) that is, in turn, used to manage the secure conversation. This secret key can be used to sign messages that belong to a particular conversation. The specification recommends that this SCT be used as part of an additional negotiation to establish a derived key used to sign and encrypt messages, for a set of messages associated with this security context.

8.4.4.1 Leveraging WS-SecureConversation

WS-SecureConversation is still an emerging technology. In large part, this is because most early adaptors exhibit a combination of two factors: They rely on exposing HTTP-based Web services, and they are not yet fully exploiting WS-Security techniques. We expect that WS-SecureConversation will come to play a role similar to SSL within the Web services world.

8.4.5 Authorization and Policies: WS-Policy

A.8.6

In the Web services roadmap, one of the building blocks is the use of policies. The WS-Policy specification that implements this building block consists of three core specifications: WS-Policy Framework, WS-PolicyAttachments, and WS-PolicyAssertions. (The security-specific assertion specification is WS-SecurityPolicy.)

The Web services policy framework specification defines a general-purpose model and corresponding syntax to describe and communicate Web services policies that service consumers need to know to be able to access services from a service provider. WS-Policy provides flexible and extensible grammar for expressing the capabilities, requirements, and general characteristics of entities in an XML Web services-based system. Policy expressions allow for both simple declarative assertions and more sophisticated conditional assertions. A WS-Policy is a collection of one or more policy assertions (as defined in WS-PolicyAssertions). WS-Policy provides a single-policy grammar to allow different kinds of assertions to be reasoned about in a consistent manner. These assertions are specified in WS-SecurityPolicy, which focuses on grammar for defining security policies.

The WS-PolicyAttachments specification defines how policies are associated with Web services artifacts, including WSDL, UDDI, and endpoint references for deployed Web services. As with all the Web services specifications (WS-*), it is extensible and allows developers to create definitions of other resources with which a policy can be associated.

8.4.5.1 Leveraging WS-Policy

The goal of WS-Policy is to provide the information needed to enable Web services applications to express their requirements and capabilities. WS-Policy by itself does not provide a negotiation solution for Web services. WS-Policy is a building block used in conjunction with other Web service and application-specific protocols to accommodate a wide variety of policy exchange models. Policies can be used to express a number of dependencies, such as whether the service requires that the messages be digitally signed or what kind of security tokens (X.509, UsernameToken, and others) must be used.

8.5 Implementing Security in SOA Systems

This section presents some common components based on the technologies described previously that you can leverage to provide security services in an SOA reference implementation. One of the key business transformations when implementing services-oriented architectures is to identify (common) security services and evolve business processes to take advantage of these services. Initial implementations will most likely consist of existing elements of the infrastructure enabled with basic security services in a hybrid environment.

8.5.1 Implementing Basic Security Services

The basic security architecture in Figure 8.1 contains two main security components, a *point of contact* (PoC) and a *trust service*, described in detail in the following sections. Figure 8.1 also specifically illustrates two different point-of-contact elements: a transport layer PoC and a Web services PoC.

A.8.7

In this hybrid example with multiple protocols and domains involved, SOA requests are bound to SOAP over HTTP requests. This approach enables the SOA architecture to reuse large parts of the pre-SOA architecture, including the HTTP (transport layer) components. This architecture shows an external demilitarized zone (DMZ)—a neutral zone between two security domains—containing a traditional HTTP (SSL) security PoC entry to the enterprise. When the software establishes a mutually authenticated SSL connection, it also includes a coarse-grained authentication of the request.

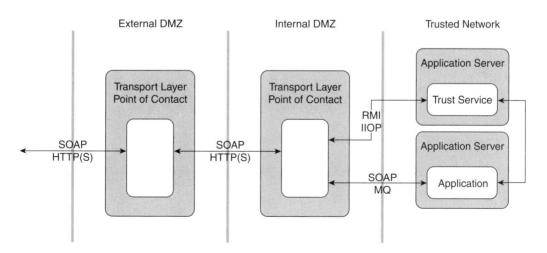

Figure 8.1 Basic security architecture.

The architecture also has an internal DMZ, whereby a Web services PoC provides introspection of the message. This Web services PoC element can leverage trust services from within the trusted network as part of the actual message validation. In this example, we show that the Web services PoC uses the RMI/IIOP protocol to communicate with the trust service, but it also transforms the incoming SOAP/HTTP request into a SOAP/JMS request.

The trust service is the architectural component that establishes the trust relationship between partners. The trust is based on the validation of the incoming message, including the authentication of identities asserted in the message, and the mapping of identities and roles as established in existing business agreements with the partners. Each of these components is discussed in further detail in the following sections.

8.5.2 Implementing Point-of-Contact Services

One of the first tasks in defining a service-oriented architecture is to understand what the service provides and establish the interfaces for the service. A PoC service is responsible for the following:

- Authentication of requests and requestors
- Establishment and management of a requestor's session (binding multiple requests or transactions by a single requestor to a single authentication associated with a given session)
- Authorization of requests within that session
- Appropriate termination of the session (due to explicit logout, inactivity timeout, and so on)

As a PoC service processes an incoming request, it is responsible for terminating any transport layer security and weeding out unauthorized requests. In a hybrid environment, the service will rely on existing transport layer security techniques:

- Terminating SSL sessions
- Authenticating the request based on transport layer security (such as SSL certificates used for mutual authentication of partners)

In a pre-SOAP environment, this HTTP-based point of contact would normally also be responsible for the following:

- Authenticating the end user or requestor based on a user's presented credentials, be they directly presented credentials such as a username and password or credentials presented by a third-party such as a SAML assertion
- Authorizing the request based on the requested URL and the user's authenticated identity

Many early adopters have chosen to keep an HTTP-based point of contact in an outer DMZ, providing only coarse-grained authentication based on the identity of the business entity in the SSL certificate. Thus, an outer DMZ PoC provides SSL sessions with various business partners and is able to block unauthorized entities (for which there is no business relationship and SSL certificate) from even passing through to the inner DMZ.

Adding an inner DMZ with a PoC service capable of introspecting SOAP messages, for example, allows the system to continue leveraging the pre-SOA environment. This specialized PoC service adds Web services–specific functionality, such as authenticating the actual requestor based on information contained in the Web services request. This inner DMZ PoC service includes routing as part of its service offering and is able to route a Web services request to the appropriate backend resource. More advanced PoCs might also be capable of transforming protocols that can expose, for example, a JMS-bound Web service internally to the external world with an HTTP binding.

In general, whether across one or many points of contact, the overall PoC service functionality includes authentication, session management, and authorization within the scope of transport and message layer security services.

8.5.3 Implementing Message Layer Security Services

Message layer security services are generally implemented in infrastructure components responsible for receiving and routing messages to an internal endpoint. Such services allow the system to protect a message to a finer degree than transport layer security, as explained in Section 8.2.3.

In general, because of the implementation cost of fine-grained message layer security implementations, message layer security tends to be coarse grained (encrypt the entire message body), with only those aspects of the message that must truly have end-to-end protection subject to finer-grained techniques.

8.5.4 Implementing Trust Services

PoC services functionality also includes message and requestor authentication. PoC services will invoke trust services to manage security tokens (and, therefore, trust relationships) within Web services requests, as explained in Section 8.3.5. Simple requestor authentication is just a matter of using the identity asserted in a security token to represent the authenticated identity. Sometimes you need more advanced functionality such as the capability to exchange tokens (when acting as an intermediary) or to provide detailed identity mapping on incoming identities (for example, mapping an identity to a role within an application). Trust services provide this functionality by managing and protecting security tokens.

8.5.5 Implementing a Federation

One additional component not shown in Figure 8.1 is a federation protocol service component because the assumption so far has been an SOA environment within a B2B-type environment. In many environments, however, direct browser-based interactions are considered part of an SOA environment. This means you might also need to authenticate users within the browser client, across your business partners, a process called *cross-domain single sign-on*. The end goal is to reduce the amount of user authentication across a set of enterprises within a particular business relationship and context. To manage this, you will require an additional service to handle all of the different single sign-on protocols. We call this a *protocol service*, as shown in Figure 8.2.

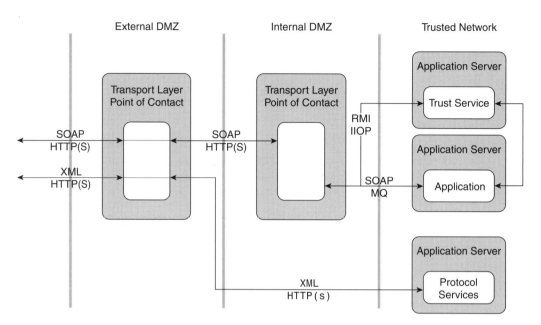

Figure 8.2 Basic security architecture using protocol services.

The protocol service generally appears as a simple backend application, accessible in the same manner as any other HTTP-accessible resource. The transport layer PoC can route requests to the protocol service so that the protocol service can then handle cross-partner single sign-on protocol flows. Note that this HTTP-based single sign-on always involves some level of interaction with a user's browser. Thus, you can continue to leverage existing transport layer PoC techniques for maintaining a session with a browser. Once you have implemented such an HTTP-based single sign-on, your users can invoke any manner of backend applications, as they are allowed.

8.6 Non-Functional Requirements Related to Security

Implementing a security model can have a significant effect on how the SOA operates. In particular, it is important to consider the relation to two other non-functional requirements: performance and manageability.

8.6.1 The Performance Impact of Security

Implementing security does not necessarily force a performance trade-off. The following guidance focuses on minimizing the performance hit of security while not impairing the actual functionality. You can also use additional techniques, such as clustering, linear scalability of components, or leveraging hardware accelerators, to offset a performance impact. To this end, you need to consider several general guidelines:

- *Focus on layered component architecture.* This enables you to appropriately tune the environment to meet performance, scalability, and availability metrics. For example, layering security functionality away from the application's functionality enables you to tune optimal security performance independent of optimal application performance.
- *Apply only a layered security approach.* Security is expensive. Minimize this cost by relying on a layered security, focusing as much as possible on transport level security. For example, it is great to have end-to-end security, but a point-to-point architecture is more common. Rather than immediately incur the cost of end-to-end security, evaluate where these points are. If the endpoints are within an enterprise's control, use transport layer security to protect the communications while on the public network. If you have to have message-level security, be sensible about the cost of this security. For example, providing confidentiality at the element level is also expensive. If possible, rely on encrypting an entire message body rather than individual elements within the message body.
- *Rely on a layered approach to authorization.* In general, you should push as much authorization functionality as feasible close to the edge of the application domain, especially in a Web services environment in which message payloads are typically quite large. If you layer your transport layer authentication decision at the edge (at the external DMZ point of contact), you can prevent unauthorized business partners from flooding the enterprise with bad requests. If you place message layer authentication at the internal DMZ point of contact, you can ensure that only a business partner's authorized users are able to access the internal system; this again reduces the number requests the application will just reject. This authorization layering enables the application to best handle the security functionality in the application level, or data authorization at the data level to which the application has direct access.

8.6.2 Managing Security

After you implement a secure SOA solution, you will need to be able to manage this security infrastructure, including managing trust relationships, security tokens for authentication, security tokens for session management, and credential stores.

8.6.2.1 Trust Relationship Management

Trust relationships are usually derived from the use of cryptographic techniques such as public key infrastructure. Simply having (and exchanging) cryptographic elements across business partners is not sufficient to establish and maintain a trust relationship. Part of a trust relationship also involves asserting and accepting requestor identities and attributes across the established trust relationships. For this reason, it is integral to manage the tokens used to convey this information.

8.6.2.2 Security Tokens Used for Authentication

Services can use X.509 certificates as the basis for security tokens to convey authentication information to sign a message. A trust service's security token functionality validates security tokens to authenticate requestors.

8.6.2.3 Security Tokens Used for Session Management

As explained in Section 8.3.7, the WS-SecureConversation specification is an extension of the WS-Trust credential acquisition model that describes how to request and use a secure conversation token for long-running conversations and sessions. The SCT provides the logical equivalent of SSL session management in an HTTP-transport-bound environment. A trust service's security token functionality should create and validate SCTs.

8.6.2.4 Credential Store Services

In addition to trust service management, trust services (or more specifically, logical security token services) can also act as credential stores. In many environments, information about a requestor is propagated throughout the environment for many different purposes (for example, audit, logging, and request authorization). Rather than carrying a large credential around with each request, it easier to carry a *credential reference*. This credential reference can then be used by the security token service to appropriately look up the actual credentials when required during request processing.

8.7 Technology and Product Mappings

Given knowledge of technologies, implementation considerations, and related non-functional requirements, you should now take a look at different categories of technologies and types of products that implement the various PoCs, including those for the transport layer, Web services, trust services, and federation services.

8.7.1 Transport Layer Point of Contact

Transport layer PoCs, as separate from the Web services layer PoCs, tend to be HTTP-type components such as HTTP servers or HTTP proxy servers. These components have become familiar elements of most organizations, whether in intranet or internet scenarios.

8.7.2 Web Services Layer Point of Contact

The different security PoC implementations include XML firewalls and gateways, Web services gateways, and other security services implementations. Most early product vendors in the Web services space released XML firewalls or XML gateways. These products are typically proprietary implementations of PoC functionality focused on XML-based requests but not necessarily those based on SOAP. These products may accommodate multiple transport bindings, supporting HTTP-based, MQ-based, and other transport protocols. *Web services gateways* are a specialized form of XML gateway that focuses on Web services–focused protocols such as SOAP or RMI-IIOP as defined by WSDL bindings.

Security services are often included within an XML/Web services gateway. The initial implementations were typically proprietary and did not support the standards-based functionality described by WS-Security. With the standardization of the (SOAP-based) WS-Security specification by OASIS and the publication of the basic security profile by the WS-I, most gateway vendors now allow for interoperability of signatures and encryption on Web services messages.

8.7.3 Trust Services

Typically, trust services have not existed as standalone components or products. In general, they are bundled as part of security or federation services as they apply to a network of systems. A more advanced offering for both trust and federation is available in IBM Tivoli Federated Identity Management™.

8.7.4 Federation Services

To date, most federation service implementations focus on passive-client (HTTP browser) based approaches to single sign-on. This approach leverages publicly available specifications for single sign-on to allow users to seamlessly access resources within an enterprise and across trusted partners. Part of the exchange of information that occurs as part of the single sign-on protocol includes the exchange of security tokens, very similar to the security tokens that trust services handle.

The IBM Tivoli Federated Identity Manager is currently the only known product that includes a component- or service-based architecture, with both trust and protocol services. The trust service of this product features, including logical security token services, are designed to be pluggable and to provide the full range of functionality previously described.

8.7.4.1 Liberty Alliance

The Liberty Alliance Project was formed to deliver and support a federated network identity solution for the Internet that enables single sign-on for consumers and business users in an open, federated way. Liberty Identity Federation Framework (ID-FF) describes profiles for B2C-based single sign-on and additional functionality. Liberty ID-FF profiles include single sign-on (SSO), single log-out (SLO), register name identifier (RNI), federation termination notification (FTN), and identity provider introduction (IPI). Tivoli Federated Identity Manager implements a multiprotocol federation gateway with integrated management support for Liberty ID FF 1.1/1.2. The added federation capability enables enterprises to quickly and securely integrate identity-driven transactions with their middleware and portal platforms.

8.8 Summary

The basic principles of applying security in any software solution are about identifying the risks, evaluating them, and then formulating a plan to mitigate them. In SOA-based systems, these security principles are the same. However, additional factors are introduced because SOA proposes distributed services and decoupled application systems. To effectively secure these resources, a gamut of technology options and variations are available with accompanying performance and operational management overheads. Mapping the security risks to the solution options requires careful planning and should be conducted formally during inception of an SOA endeavor.

 ## 8.9 Links to developerWorks

A.8.1 IBM, Microsoft. *Security in a Web Services World: A Proposed Architecture and Roadmap*, IBM developerWorks, April 2002. http://www-128.ibm.com/developerworks/library/specification/ws-secmap/.

A.8.2 IBM, Microsoft, Verisign, Web Services Security. IBM developerWorks, April 2002. http://www.ibm.com/developerworks/webservices/library/ws-secure/.

A.8.3 Hondo, M., Melgar, D., and Nadalin, A. Web Services Security: Moving Up the Stack— Security in a Web Services World. IBM developerWorks, December 2001. http://www.ibm.com/developerworks/webservices/library/ws-secroad/index.html.

A.8.4 BEA Systems, Computer Assoc., IBM, Microsoft, RSA Security, Verisign, et al. Web Services Trust Language. IBM developerWorks, February 2005. http://www.ibm.com/developerworks/library/specification/ws-trust/.

A.8.5 IBM, BEA Systems, Microsoft, VeriSign, RSA Security, Web Services Federation Language. IBM developerWorks, July 2003. http://www.ibm.com/developerworks/library/specification/ws-fed/. IBM, BEA Systems, Microsoft, VeriSign, RSA Security, Web Services Federation: Active Requestor Profile. IBM developerWorks, July 2003. http://www.ibm.com/developerworks/webservices/library/ws-fedact/. IBM, BEA Systems, Microsoft, VeriSign, RSA Security, Web Services Federation: Passive Requestor Profile. IBM developerWorks, July 2003. http://www.ibm.com/developerworks/webservices/library/ws-fedpass/.

A.8.6 BEA, IBM, Microsoft, SAP AG, Sonic Software, Verisign, Web Services Policy Framework, IBM developerWorks, May 2003. http://www.ibm.com/developerworks/webservices/library/specification/ws-polfram/.

A.8.7 Bose, S. Using Web Services Security in WebSphere Application Server. IBM developerWorks, April 2004. http://www.ibm.com/developerworks/websphere/techjournal/0404_bose/0404_bose.html.

8.10 References

Basic Security Profile. *Web Services Interoperability Organization*. http://www.ws-i.org/deliverables/workinggroup.aspx?wg=basicsecurity/.

Benantar, M. *The Internet public key infrastructure*. IBM Systems Journal, Vol. 40, 3-2001. http://www.research.ibm.com/journal/sj40-3.html.

Hinton, H., et al. *Federated Identity Management with IBM Tivoli Security Solution.* IBM Redbooks (SG24-6394-00). http://www.redbooks.ibm.com/abstracts/SG246394.html?Open.

Liberty Alliance Project. *Liberty Alliance Project Specifications.* http://www.projectliberty.org/resources/specifications.php.

Makino, S., et al. *Implementation and Performance of WS-Security.* International Journal of Web Services Research, Vol, 1, No. 1, 2004.

Menezes, Alfred, et al. *Handbook of Applied Cryptography.* CRC Press, 1996.

OASIS, SAML. *Security Assertion Markup Language.* http://www.oasis-open.org/committees/tc_home.php?wg_abbrev=security.

Schneier, Bruce. *Applied Cryptography, 2nd Edition.* John Wiley & Sons, 1996.

W3ORG, XML-ENC. *XML Encryption Working Group.* http://www.w3.org/Encryption/.

W3ORG, XML-SIG. *XML Signature Working Group.* http://www.w3.org/Signature/.

Chapter 9

Managing the SOA Environment

"The significant problems that exist in the world today cannot be solved by the level of thinking that created them."

—Albert Einstein

With the move to service-oriented architectures, the IT management landscape is changing. Existing solutions might no longer be adequate. Apart from managing the usual underlying physical and application resources, the radius now includes higher-level business applications and services. To match the increasing focus on providing business value, management solutions must evolve to measure this value.

Chapter 2, "Explaining the Business Value of SOA," describes why businesses should move to SOA and an on-demand enterprise model. The on-demand IT environment is characterized by flexible and highly responsive systems that have lower IT costs and higher utilization rates. To meet the challenges of business agility while lowering costs, best-practice business processes are being implemented to help boost productivity while increasing flexibility.

In the SOA approach, one such best practice requires additional management capabilities: service provisioning, securing services, monitoring the service status and health, understanding relationships among the services, and managing choreographed and aggregated services. This chapter describes these SOA management concepts and capabilities.

9.1 Distributed Service Management and Monitoring Concepts

Enterprise IT management and monitoring usually involves the use of well-known mechanisms and strategies in operation centers. These mechanisms can be loosely categorized into different operational models including triage, basic problem resolution, and resource-driven operations. Using these models, this section explains the evolution of the IT management models in use today and how they are changing with the transition to SOA. Each progressive step of this evolution (the management models) focuses on a higher abstraction of how a particular problem is viewed, moving from individual events to resource states (possibly aggregating events) to transaction workflows (aggregating resources), and finally to services (aggregating workflows) with service-level agreements.

9.1.1 Event-Driven Management

The first operational model generally performs event *triage*, focusing on receiving events and forwarding them on to the appropriate groups for resolution. These triage groups do little, if any, problem resolution themselves. They might review known problem logs to determine whether this event has a known solution and then implement the solution to resolve the problem. These groups are typically staffed by lower-skilled employees who might quickly rise into more senior levels after they have acquired enough expertise in a particular function.

The triage operational model can evolve into the next level of *basic problem resolution* within a short time period before transferring any events. Generally, these groups have an assigned time limit to either fix or transfer the event to the appropriate team. These groups are usually staffed at a higher skill level; more senior people might remain on this team to continue solving problems. These teams also provide input to the automation teams so that solutions to common problems can be automated as part of the environment. Variations on both of these models include a help desk to receive all initial phone calls and events. Additional business information can also be provided to the environment to prioritize by severity and business impact.

Regardless of the operational model, most IT operations centers are driven by events that trigger a call to action. These can be in the form of Tivoli Event Console™ events or new trouble tickets created through automation-integration functions. These systems can also prioritize the events, such as time sequenced, priority, business impact, or geography.

Some organizations have evolved their IT management operations to a *resource-driven* operational model. The workflows for these operations are driven by resource state changes. Resources can be real resources, virtualized resources, or clusters, and they typically are based on CICS, DB2®, UNIX®, Windows®, or capable network device systems. Operators select the next resource that needs attention and usually prioritize resources by time sequence or business impact. In these cases, the operations staff is no longer focused on dealing with raw events but on the states of resources. They have moved from strict problem resolution to some degree of anticipating or modeling problem scenarios and identifying solutions. Understanding the resource state and devising the operational tasks in managing the state requires higher staff skills.

9.1.2 Levels of SOA-Driven Management

The next level of IT management focuses on *transaction-driven operations*, in which transaction state changes drive the business workflows. Operations select the next transaction that needs attention, which is usually prioritized by time sequence or business impact. The operators no longer deal with resources or individual events; instead, they deal with the status of transaction flows. These flows are collections of events based on live or simulated transactions.

The next higher level of IT management focuses on *business service–driven operations*, in which whatever impacts business services drives the workflows. Operators select the next impacted service sorted by business priority or by *service-level agreement* (SLA) status. The key challenge in managing at this level is in understanding the business services and their components.

Many organizations are evolving through these various levels and models of IT management, moving up from simple event-driven management to more sophisticated models. This progression requires not only education and training but also organizational and philosophical changes within the organization. The transition to SOA drives these changes to focus more on business services and processes rather than isolated application views.

The key areas for SOA-based IT management are shown in Figure 9.1 and are defined in the following list:

- *Business service management* visualizes the IT environment in business service terms and manages service levels to achieve business objectives. Business service management provides intelligent, policy-based solutions to build, run, and manage critical, dynamic business processes through automation, integration, and predefined best practices. This helps reduce IT support costs by creating a value-optimized infrastructure that supports key business initiatives.
- *Infrastructure orchestration* senses and responds to changing business needs. Orchestration helps the IT infrastructure respond dynamically to changing conditions based on defined business policies. It provides intelligent prioritization of automated actions and assigns computing resources where and when they are needed. Orchestration increases utilization of existing and new resources, improves productivity of IT staff, and accelerates responsiveness to changing business needs.
- *Availability* ensures the health and appropriate functioning of IT environments. Management solutions in this area help increase the resilience of critical infrastructure elements by leveraging intelligent best practices. As a result, operators are able to respond dynamically to changing environmental conditions.
- *Security* ensures that information assets, confidentiality, and data integrity are protected according to corporate policies. Enhanced security features keep systems protected from external threats and effectively manage and protect access to information with dynamic compliance. These solutions help increase the resiliency and security of your IT environment.
- *Optimization* ensures the most productive utilization of the IT infrastructure. Optimization solutions intelligently allocate your resources so that they run efficiently and provide you with an increased return on your investment. They also provide resilient workload management between resources, which can automatically be balanced for optimal throughput and performance.

- *Provisioning* makes the right resources available to the right processes and people. Provisioning automates the allocation, change, and configuration of your IT infrastructure resources—including systems, networks, middleware, and applications—using intelligent best practices. It creates identity provisioning so that users can access the appropriate resources across multiple heterogeneous systems.

Figure 9.2 shows a more detailed view of these key management areas, including more information about the types of resources and the management roles involved.

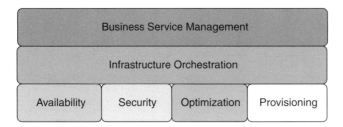

Figure 9.1 The key areas of SOA management.

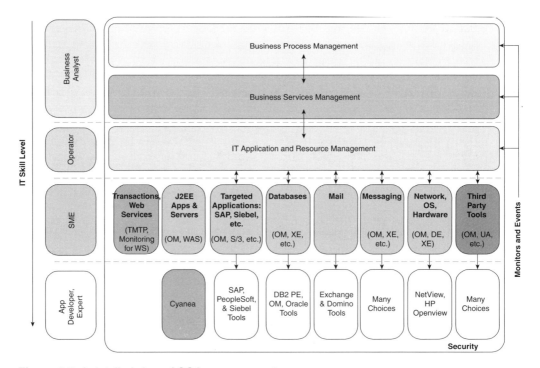

Figure 9.2 A detailed view of SOA management.

Each area of resource management can be considered independently while remaining part of the overall management framework. For example, database management requires a specific set of tools to monitor and manage the databases autonomously. These tools must be compatible with the database being managed for appropriate monitoring and control of the database.

There are similar monitoring and management requirements for transactions. However, these tools need to interact differently with the underlying functions to provide the correct levels of monitoring and control. For both of these types of tools, a common event infrastructure provides a location for operators to visualize information across the environment and allows for correlation across multiple systems. This correlation can be across physical machines as well as different types of functions. For example, consider an event caused by a transaction that is unable to access a database, and another event caused by the database running out of transaction log space. The IT management tools should be able to correlate both events to show the operator that the root cause of the transaction problem is actually the database transaction log being full.

9.2 Key Services Management Concepts

Tools for managing services supplement traditional IT management products. The concept of looking at *transactions* versus *resources* across the IT infrastructure is a relatively new one and is better suited for a model that has loosely coupled components and applications. For example, some parts of the application might lie within the sphere of control for an enterprise, whereas other parts of the application are controlled by the IT organizations of its business partners or customers. To successfully deploy and support a services-based application, an enterprise needs a transactional paradigm as well as a resource paradigm to manage these interactions. These capabilities must enable enterprises to deploy and ensure the performance and availability of new service applications, even when parts of the overall application are not under its direct control.

Although introducing service orientation addresses many of the traditional problems of integrating disparate business processes and applications, deploying services-based applications introduces new complexities that you need to manage. These include the following:

- Monitoring the services layer for performance and availability
- Ensuring compliance with service-level agreements
- Managing security policies so that service-oriented applications can communicate securely, both internally and across organizational boundaries
- Tracking the dynamic interconnectivity of the loosely coupled components of the system to understand the performance, availability, and expense consequences
- Analyzing the root cause and correcting problems based on errors at the services layer
- Developing and testing applications composed of aggregated and already operational services

- Deploying, configuring, and updating a distributed, service-oriented application across organizational boundaries in a secure, reliable, and repeatable manner
- Tracking the business impact of the use of services on the business processes

The SOA-based infrastructure and its IT management tools must address these complexities. The following sections examine the impact of the use of middleware and changing standards on the IT management toolset.

9.2.1 Managing the Enterprise Service Bus

The enterprise service bus (ESB) described in Chapter 3, "Architecture Elements," is a term for the middleware component that facilitates an SOA infrastructure. It brings together the features of several integration paradigms into a single element of the infrastructure. The ESB is responsible for delivering messages across the network, routing them as necessary, with the qualities of service required by the end points.

To achieve this, an ESB can intercept and manipulate the messages as they flow through the bus, interposing logic that requires intelligent decisions about where to route them, what quality of service to apply, and what additional message processing might be required. Its capabilities include logging, pattern recognition, metering, transformation, message validation, customized routing, and policy-driven selection of endpoints. You can apply policies to the ESB that define which capabilities apply to different services, both in terms of the business and IT infrastructure requirements.

Managing the ESB environment requires the following capabilities:

- *Service view*: The capability to discover, visualize, monitor, and manage the message interactions and relationships that make up a service. For ESB, this includes SOAP, XML, and proprietary message formats over HTTP, JMS, and MQ protocols.
- *IT linkage and management*: The ESB is hosted by an IT infrastructure that includes a variety of tools and implementations (WebSphere®, WebLogic, WPM, WebSphere Business Integration Server™, and so on). An ESB management solution must provide coverage and linkage to the EMS tools to monitor, manage, and configure the underlying infrastructure. It should also manage the backend connections such as adapters, connectors, and resource connections.
- *Security*: End-to-end security in the ESB environment is a major challenge. The SOA model will need a uniform security policy and enforcement for all the elements of the infrastructure to support the ESB. It will also need credential mapping between disparate security infrastructures.
- *Service-level management*: You need to monitor and record service levels for reporting. Service-level policies must perform actions, such as activating additional service providers, to keep the system within policy.
- *Mediation and version management*: Mediation is a new manageable entity in the ESB. Mediations must be first-class managed resources that can be monitored, controlled, and configured. The SOA model will need versioning support when new levels of a service are rolled out. You can implement this by controlling and

configuring versioning mediations that can route and transforms message traffic between older and newer versions of service providers and consumers.

- *Configuration*: The ESB environment contains a large number of infrastructures that must be configured consistently. You will need configuration support that treats the environment as a whole instead of a set of individual products.
- *Provisioning and deployment*: The objects that implement a service must be deployed in a repeatable and coordinated fashion. Again, the system must be able to automatically coordinate versioning support with the deployment of new levels of a service.

9.2.2 Evolving Standards

Services management data can be collected today through instrumentation in the middleware that supports SOA. *Application response measurement (ARM)* is a standard from the Open Group for logging start and stop points used to denote messages entering and leaving individual services. The management tools assemble the start and stop information for all the services that make up a system and provide an overall view of that system.

In the case of Web services, another instrumentation standard used to define and provide standard management data about Web services, as well as other IT resources, is the OASIS *Web Services Distributed Management (WSDM)* standard. WSDM should make it easier to manage Web services across organizational boundaries and in heterogeneous runtime environments, and it therefore offers a good solution to the needs for an enterprise SOA. WSDM should also provide better consistency and detail in the manageability information that can be obtained about Web services, such as standard metrics, operational status, and a complete list of relationships that a Web service has with other Web services and other resources in the environment. IBM's *Common Base Event (CBE)* was submitted to WSDM for standardization and is available as the WSDM Base Event in WSDM 1.0. WSDM also depends on the Web Services Resource Framework (WS-Resource) and Web Services Notification (WS-Notification) set of standards to provide a complete Web services platform for management. The security management capabilities of Web services management must include support for the following security specifications and standards: WS-Security, WS-Trust, WS-Federation, and WS-Policy. Chapter 8, "Securing the SOA Environment," provided details on all these specifications and standards.

A.9.1

A.9.2

9.3 Operational Management Challenges

Services still have the traditional management challenges in areas of security, availability, configuration, and performance. Although an SOA can be developed with many different methods and technologies, the use of common open standards enables you to consider any of these services equally as yet another resource in the management domain. However, there are still some differences from existing management models that arise from service orientation.

One such difference between services and other managed resources is that the services are application layer components, whereas most system management tools are oriented toward middleware, network, OS, and hardware types of resources. SOA services, however, can participate and be reused in multiple different business process. Thus, the requirements for managing a service vary based on the business process in which the service participates. To service consumers, the only entity that is exposed and available for them to manage is the service (an endpoint) itself and not the actual processes and components that implement the service. The service-oriented application that implements the service will most likely be out of reach for the service consumer to manage, as this is the domain of the service provider.

Another difference is that in a non-SOA environment, processes and tasks might not be composed along well-defined function boundaries in their member applications. Therefore, it might not be easy to compose or decompose these applications. SOA-based services, however, with well-defined interfaces, align the business process steps closely with an entity (the service implementation) that can then be monitored and directly and discreetly managed. This difference implies that you might need a different view—likely an easier, more flexible one—and different tools for SOAs than the functionality available in traditional systems management tools.

To consider how these differences impact your enterprise, you might need to consider the use of different management perspectives and follow a phased approach to deployment.

9.3.1 Challenges with Respect to Management Perspectives

You can look at services management from either the service provider's point of view or that of the entire enterprise. There are common management challenges for both enterprise and service provider environments. There are also unique considerations for management within each environment. The SOA approach provides additional management challenges that cover the entire lifecycle of the application, from development and deployment to the manageability and maintenance of the services.

The common management challenges for both views are as follows:

- Monitoring and managing the availability of the services.
- Providing a service registry that contains information about the services that are deployed in the enterprise and their descriptions.
- Providing the information about the services to the architects. Architects can use this information to provide solutions to problems using existing services and by defining new services.
- Management of rules that help route service requests based on the content of messages.
- Maintenance of services from a virtualized location that provides a singular service view.
- Managing multiple versions of the same services and managing the service lifecycle.

- Management of the infrastructure to help in troubleshooting operational issues.
- Monitoring of transactions provides end-to-end management capability including the various objects that participate in a transaction, such as a Web service, a session EJB, an entity EJB, or DB2.
- Maintaining and managing the relationship between the business process, services, and the IT resources. The owner of the Web services or SOA application might not control all of the services that make up the application or might have limited control of the environment in which they operate, as in the case of niche third-party services that might be integrated.
- Managing the potential for federation. The control points to enforce security and management policies should be deployed in a flexible manner and, in many cases, abstracted as services or as part of the ESB.

Service providers are faced with some unique challenges:

- The services that are provided can be utilized both by the internal line of business and by external customers. If a customer makes several requests, the service might need to block access for that customer, possibly to anticipate a faulty implementation or a specific problem with that customer.
- Usually when the services provided are critical to the customer, the service provider must maintain agreed-upon levels of service for contractual or legal reasons.
- Billing and metering of the services that different customers use.

Enterprises face the following unique challenges:

- Defining appropriate SLAs or operational-level agreements (OLAs) for each service that can be appropriately measured. This is different from a similar need for SLAs between the service provider and consumer because this SLA or OLA context is defined primarily to provide business-level monitoring to facilitate internal operational efficiency.
- Defining services with the appropriate granularity so that they can be managed and reused in the organization.

9.3.2 Phases of Deployment

As services are developed and deployed in the SOA environment, these challenges grow increasingly difficult over time. Figure 9.3 illustrates these deployment phases.

Initially, the enterprise faces *configuration and deployment* issues. During this phase, companies adjust their infrastructure to support the processes of defining, deploying, optimizing, and refining their services. This phase is especially important to service providers, requiring them to consider the security, privacy, and configuration of the services. The further refinement of those attributes is important.

The second phase involves *monitoring of the deployed services*. During this phase, the challenges include monitoring the basic availability of the services and their performance. This helps maintain the operational heath of the systems and proactively rectify quality of service issues.

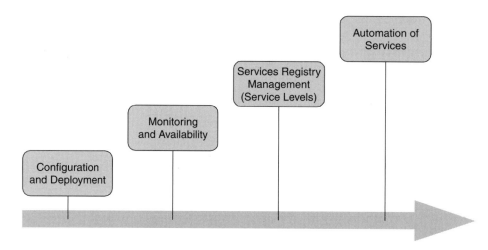

Figure 9.3 Deployment phases and SOA challenges.

The third phase occurs when the enterprise has *reusable services across the enterprise*. In this phase, the services registries for services deployed in the environment and the management of these registries become more important. These registries are also used by the service architects to create solutions for the enterprise. This is where the SLAs become more significant. This phase is also important to service providers that publish their services to external consumers.

The fourth phase occurs with the *full automation of services in the enterprise*. During this phase, services management undergoes policy-based orchestration, configuration, and automation. Automation does not imply a lack of human intervention; this phase still needs to take into account the process to handle business exceptions, as described in Chapter 4, "SOA Project Planning Aspects."

9.4 Service-Level Agreement Considerations

Today, most IT departments offer their services to internal or external consumers. Although many such organizations today have negotiated SLAs in place with their external clients or OLA with their internal clients, these agreements tend to be technically focused (such as database size and growth in gigabytes, system availability, and others). More mature organizations have SLAs with their external clients that are more business focused (for example, response time for a transaction or number of transactions per day); however, these SLAs might be inadequate in terms of measurement and reporting, or they might utilize manual activities to carry out the SLAs.

Due to the lack of products supporting the measurement of business-oriented metrics, SLA metrics are frequently technology oriented and provide little useful indication of the service quality from the consumer's perspective. Different interpretations of the service quality by the provider and consumer of the service can cause dissatisfaction among both customers and service providers. Examples of useful business metrics for services would be assured delivery dates for supply-chain services or approval response times for financial services.

A key consistent measure for SLAs or OLAs, that both the service provider and enterprises can use, is the *end-to-end transaction time*. This is especially appropriate for SOA environments, which can share services and measure the end-to-end transaction time, both with synthetic transactions and with tools such as IBM Tivoli Monitoring for Transaction Performance (see Section 9.5). By measuring the end-to-end response time, you can include the involvement of all components and related services in the measurement. This provides a consistent measurement across the environment. The consumer does not care what the server availability is as long as the transactions are completed within the defined time period.

9.5 SOA Management Products

The challenges to IT operations management and the use of business-focused SLAs can be addressed with different types of tooling. Each of these tool types addresses the needs of a different area of service management, including business performance and business service management, IT application and resource management, transaction management, Web services management, resource monitoring, and middleware monitoring. To detail the functions of these tools by areas of management, we use the example of IBM software products that fit each area.

9.5.1 Business Performance and Business Service Management

Business performance management is the process of monitoring and managing the overall organization's business performance results over time. This leads to the popular notion of an executive "dashboard" that provides presentation and analysis of the overall business metrics of the organization in a real-time or pseudo-real-time fashion. Business service management is a similar notion that focuses on the level of all individual business services in the SOA.

The IBM Tivoli Business Systems Manager™ brings the entire enterprise together to provide a business view of the environment. IBM Tivoli Business Systems Manager software is intended to be a productivity tool for operations to enable an end-to-end business view of the infrastructure and application management monitoring. It uses the monitoring software that is currently installed (such as IBM Tivoli Monitoring™), and it maps alerts and events generated by the various monitoring software products to objects in its database, and these are then displayed on the product's console.

You can use IBM Tivoli Business Systems Manager to create business views. Usually the operations staff monitors various products and consoles to complete service obligations that might relate to missed critical messages. The IBM Tivoli Business Systems Manager console can reduce the number of separate individual consoles from multiple software products into a single consolidated console. Using this single user interface, the team can proactively monitor and manage problems, determine impacts, and aid in root-cause analysis. You can use IBM Tivoli Business Systems Manager to accomplish the following tasks:

- To deliver a higher quality of end-to-end services by identifying all impacted areas from a single action.
- To manage groups of related applications that form a business system.
- To manage groups of computing resources.
- To enable true critical path management.

This product represents both the physical resources and the business system representation. The physical resources are organized in a hierarchy defined by distributed placement rules or default table entries.

IBM Tivoli Business Systems Manager receives events from the mainframe environment using a component installed in each z/OS® (formerly S/390®) mainframe system and receives distributed events from the Tivoli Event Console or from other common listener feeds.

IBM Tivoli Service Level Advisor™ enables businesses to easily, proactively, and economically manage service levels across the entire organization for maximum uptime. This software's user-friendly, Web-based reporting capability and at-a-glance dashboard show the status of current service levels and predict future trends so that you can take preventive action now and avoid problems later. When a trend toward a violation is identified, IBM Tivoli Service Level Advisor software integrates with other Tivoli products and sends alerts to the IBM Tivoli Enterprise Console®, to the IBM Tivoli Business Systems Manager console, directly to your e-mail, or using Simple Network Management Protocol (SNMP).

With its automated service-level agreement evaluation capability, IBM Tivoli Service Level Advisor software eliminates manual data analysis, saving labor, time, and money. When combined with IBM Tivoli Business Systems Manager software, you can also better align your IT infrastructure with your business processes and further increase the return on your IT investment.

9.5.2 IT Application and Resource Management

IT application and resource management is similar to existing IT management tools: They focus on the individual infrastructure elements and resources that constitute the overall IT landscape. In the SOA context, IT application and resource management also includes the relationship of these infrastructure elements and resources to business services. This area of management includes event management, provisioning and orchestration, and security management. There are several IBM Tivoli products that address additional aspects of the management arena.

9.5.2.1 Event Management

As described earlier in Section 9.1.1, events identify problems at a low abstraction level and thus must be managed across the many possible types of IT resources. The IBM Tivoli Event Console serves as the hub for IBM availability and performance solutions. The Tivoli

Event Console consolidates and processes thousands of events that occur daily in the environment. This includes events from network devices, hardware systems, middleware, and applications. The Tivoli Event Console can provide intelligent, multilevel analysis and correlation to filter out misleading or redundant events, highlight the essential information, and provide indications of the root cause of each problem quickly and accurately. It can respond automatically based on the indication of the root cause, allowing automated correction of problems without the need for involvement by an individual. This helps reduce costs by reducing the staff required to maintain the systems and by reducing the time to resolve issues.

The Tivoli Enterprise Console also includes the network management solution, which helps operators track and resolve problems down to the network layers. It provides a console that shows operations staff members only those events that they need to react to in the order of severity, and it can be tightly integrated with help desk systems to automatically create trouble tickets based on events it receives.

9.5.2.2 Provisioning and Orchestration

A provisioning system has the responsibility of directing resources to where they are needed. Provisioning can be done on many levels to satisfy application service needs, user needs, and system environment needs. A provisioning management tool defines the rules of how these resources are directed. Orchestration is the process of redirection of resources according to the rules of provisioning. As previously noted, one central idea of an on-demand system is the capability to dynamically change the environment and systems as the situation requires. Therefore, provisioning and orchestration management tools play a key role in enabling such dynamic reaction to changing situations.

IBM Tivoli Provisioning Manager™ software minimizes the need for just-in-case provisioning and helps you automate manual provisioning processes. It provisions and configures complete application environments, including support for servers, operating systems, middleware, applications, storage, and network devices such as routers, switches, firewalls, and load balancers. This on-demand automation is achieved using workflows that enable each organization to capture each of its best practices for particular processes or procedures. The extensible workflows supplied with this software can automate best practices for typical processes that administration staff members perform when provisioning and maintaining a complex application infrastructure. You can then customize and extend workflows to follow your own IT best practices.

With automation workflows, administrators can provision IT infrastructure resources with consistent, predictable, and error-free results. With this software, building or customizing standardized infrastructure configurations takes minutes instead of days. Rather than permanently dedicating infrastructure to specific applications, these resources are added to the pools of resources maintained by IBM Tivoli Provisioning Manager. When you need a resource, it can be obtained from the pool, configured, and deployed into a production environment under the control of workflows. When it is no longer required, the resource gets returned to the pool.

9.5.2.3 Security

Service security is critical to prevent fraudulent or unauthorized use of services and to provide audit capabilities for regulation compliance. The various elements of security that need to be managed have already been described in Chapter 8. You need to have these functions in a centralized security management context to allow faster deployment of services.

The products that serve in this area are the IBM Tivoli Access Manager for e-Business™ and the IBM Tivoli Federated Identity Manager™. These products provide the following key functions:

- Support for federated single sign-on and sign-off
- Web services security at the message layer
- Support for WS-Security, WS-Trust, WS-Policy, WS-Federation, and the Liberty Alliance standards

9.5.3 Other Areas of Management

There are additional areas of SOA management that focus on more specific elements such as transaction performance, Web service monitoring, and resource monitoring. These are discussed in the following sections.

9.5.3.1 Transaction Performance

During the execution of service invocations, transactions represent the activity in your service workflow. Therefore, there is a need to monitor the performance level of transactions as they are executed across your SOA system. Transaction performance management focuses on controlling and directing resources to maintain or enhance the performance of your transaction-enabled applications. It is also useful in understanding application user behavior and analyzing the performance under different scenarios and loads.

IBM Tivoli Monitoring for Transaction Performance™ is designed to help IT organizations manage their overall transaction performance. Using this software, you can record typical business transactions and then play them back with simulated users or robots to drive real transactions through an environment on a periodic basis. You can then measure these transactions for overall performance and availability. Additionally, IBM Tivoli Monitoring for Transaction Performance monitors real user performance and availability.

This software relies on the Open Group standard for application instrumentation, the Application Response Measurement, or the ARM API. In addition to working with instrumentation that is included natively in leading middleware and applications, IBM Tivoli Monitoring for Transaction Performance dynamically injects instrumentation into leading J2EE e-business applications. This approach eliminates the need for application development teams to insert ARM API calls into source code and allows dynamic discovery of transaction topologies.

9.5.3.2 Web Services Management

When your SOA implementation is based on Web services, you will also need content-specific management tools that address the needs of this environment. IBM Tivoli Monitoring for

Web Services PRPQ™ provides understanding of the relationships between services instrumented in the environment. This includes the IBM Web Services Navigator™, which provides the following key functions:

- It discovers and provides topology visualization of Web services and service relationships.
- It extracts service patterns from raw service data.
- It integrates with the Eclipse platform.
- It incorporates IBM Web Services Navigator technology and Tivoli monitoring technology.
- It is targeted to service architects and operations managers that need to understand Web services relationships, flows, and message content.
- It provides visual feedback to quickly identify relationships, extract patterns, and highlight problems.
- It is a lightweight package with a simplified installation that has no prerequisites.
- It automates the process of aggregating Web services log files.

9.5.3.3 Resource Monitoring

As explained in Section 9.1.1, resource monitoring is a necessary element of the resource-driven operational model. The IBM Tivoli Monitoring and OMEGAMON® (formerly from Candle Corporation, which was acquired by IBM) family of products provides assets to consistently monitor and manage complex and heterogeneous resources. Each of these products provides the specific management functions for each of the particular platforms, middleware, and applications that you need to support.

The IBM Tivoli Monitoring family provides assets to consistently monitor and manage complex and heterogeneous resources. The base product monitors the availability and performance status of resources to identify bottlenecks and potential resource problems. It applies preconfigured best practices to the automated monitoring of essential system resources. The application detects bottlenecks and other potential problems and provides for automatic recovery from critical situations, eliminating the need for system administrators to manually scan through extensive performance data.

In addition to the base products, specific add-ons are available to manage the individual characteristics of a given domain. These monitoring solutions are optimized to identify problems and automate repairs with specific software applications and middleware. Each solution contains a number of proactive analysis components (PACs) that describe the best practices for working with the specific application or middleware.

9.5.3.4 Additional IBM Monitoring Tools for IT Resource Management

Additional management tools are available from the IBM Software portfolio:

- *IBM Tivoli Monitoring for Applications*™ provides a powerful set of customizable and extensible application-level monitoring capabilities to help you maintain the availability and performance of ERP and CRM suites such as mySAP™ business suite and Siebel™ applications.

- *IBM Tivoli Monitoring for Business Integration*™ offers stable, secure, and proactive monitoring and management to help optimize the availability and performance within the IBM WebSphere MQ™ and IBM WebSphere Business Integration™ infrastructure.
- *IBM Tivoli Monitoring for Databases*™ helps simplify backend database infrastructure management by monitoring multiple types of database software, including IBM DB2, IBM Informix®, Oracle®, Microsoft® SQL Server, and Sybase™.
- *IBM Tivoli Monitoring for Messaging and Collaboration*™ monitors the status of Lotus Domino and Microsoft Exchange servers, identifies server and system problems in real time, notifies administrators, and takes automated actions to resolve server problems.
- *IBM Tivoli Monitoring for Web Infrastructure*™ can help optimize the availability and performance of critical resources such as Web servers and Web application servers.

9.5.4 External Product Relationships

The IBM Tivoli Enterprise Console provides the capability to receive Simple Network Management Protocol (SNMP) events from any other products, including the IBM Tivoli Event Integration Facility™ (EIF) that is used by many vendors to emit events that are receivable using the IBM Tivoli Enterprise Console. By integrating all management solutions into the IBM Tivoli Enterprise Console, you can correlate any event to provide the correct view of the environment.

9.6 Summary

This chapter presented an overview of the management concepts and key operational challenges in an SOA environment. Enterprise architects must understand the operational complexities in managing and monitoring distributed services and leverage the appropriate tools and their underlying infrastructure to address them. There are various technology components and emerging standards that paint the SOA management arena. Adopting an SOA-driven management to provide business service management propels an enterprise to a higher plateau of IT management and aligns it to be an on-demand business.

9.7 Links to developerWorks

A.9.1 IBM, *Common Base Event Specification*. http://www.ibm.com/developerworks/library/specification/ws-cbe/.

A.9.2 IBM et al., *Web Services Resource Framework*, IBM, October 2004. http://www.ibm.com/developerworks/library/specification/ws-resource/.

9.8 References

Dan, A., et al. *Web services On Demand: WSLA-driven automated management*. IBM Systems Journal, Vol. 43, No. 1. http://www.research.ibm.com/journal/sj/431/dan.html.

Farrell, J.A. and Kreger, H. *Web services management approaches*. IBM Systems Journal, Vol. 41, 2-2002. http://www.research.ibm.com/journal/sj/412/farrell.html.

IBM Tivoli. *IBM Tivoli Products*. http://www.ibm.com/tivoli/.

Kephart, J. and Chess, D. *The Vision of Autonomic Computing. Computer Magazine*, IEEE 2003. http://www.research.ibm.com/autonomic/research/papers/AC_Vision_Computer_Jan_2003.pdf.

Kreger, H., et al. *Java and JMX: Building Manageable Systems, 1st Edition*. Addison-Wesley Professional, 2002.

Leymann, F., Roller, D., and Schmidt, M.T. *Web services and business process management*. IBM Systems Journal, Vol. 41, 2-2002. http://www.research.ibm.com/journal/sj/412/leymann.html.

Naik, V.K., Mohindra, A., and Bantz, D.F. *An architecture for the coordination of system management services*. IBM Systems Journal, Vol. 43, 1-2004. http://www.research.ibm.com/journal/sj/431/naik.html.

OASIS, WSDM. *Web Services Distributed Management*. http://www.oasis-open.org/committees/tc_home.php?wg_abbrev=wsdm.

Opengroup. *The Open Group Application Response Measurement*. http://www.opengroup.org/tech/management/arm/.

Chapter 10

Case Studies in SOA Deployment

"Experience is never limited, and it is never complete; it is an immense sensibility, a kind of huge spider-web of the finest silken threads suspended in the chamber of consciousness . . . "

—*Henry James*

C ase studies help us learn from the lessons encountered during the implementation of other projects in the industry and help us recognize the concepts and elements of this technology independent of the particular implementation. The case studies in this chapter are in different vertical industries and implement different scales of SOA. The structure for each case study is fairly similar.

First we take a look at the scope of the project and the business case for undergoing the project. Next we consider the issues of development under the SOA paradigm, the goals and objectives of undertaking an SOA project, and the changes to roles, tasks, and the organization of the project. Then we address the concerns of business management as well as end users in terms of security, performance, and management of these services. We then outline the key technologies used in the implementation to achieve the SOA objectives. Finally, we examine the challenges and lessons learned from the case study.

10.1 Case Study: SOA in the Insurance Industry

The Standard Life Assurance Company is one of the world's leading mutual financial services companies. With more than 175 years of continuous services to its customer, Standard Life is the largest mutual assurance company in Europe, with more than 4 million customers and

£100 billion in assets under management as of January 2005. In this case study, the Standard Life Assurance Company evolved its infrastructure from a focus on the reuse of code at the data layer to a mature implementation of a service-oriented architecture.

10.1.1 IT and Business Challenges

Standard Life needed to meet two main business challenges: enhance its business channels while developing new ones, and anticipate and adapt to rapid changes in the environment. In the course of business, Standard Life continues to face new challenges due to the increasing rate of change and complexity of operating its business. Furthermore, the challenge in 2005 lay in the need to deliver more from less, finding creative ways to manage or reduce its cost base without affecting its current services.

On top of these two business challenges, the technical implementation for Standard Life's architecture needed to satisfy a number of design requirements and considerations so that it could achieve the following technical advantages:

- Maintain design consistency
- Offer simplicity of design
- Provide supportability, scalability, and recoverability
- Identify common code patterns
- Provide clear guidance on technical models
- Support efficient problem diagnosis
- Advise business logic placement
- Allow impact-free change
- Increase system performance
- Enable an easy-to-develop environment
- Provide useful documentation

Standard Life's SOA architecture plan, and the supporting framework and infrastructure, began with the introduction of its Application Design Patterns defined between 1999 and 2001, at which time Web services standards and tools were not yet mature. Therefore, the company needed to build an implementation that could adapt the available technologies at hand.

10.1.2 Solution Implementation

Standard Life's SOA is characterized by the use of application-level design patterns, software frameworks, and governance and management processes. The services in its SOA are implemented as XML-enabled, reusable business services available over a messaging hub. The architecture has evolved over a ten-year period (see Figure 10.1) and, following an independent review, is recognized by industry analysts as class leading and state of the art.

In 1999, Standard Life's IS department initiated a plan to move to an SOA centered on the IBM MQ Series Integrator™ (now IBM WebSphere Business Integration Message Broker™), an established technology. Figure 10.2 illustrates this architecture and its subcomponents.

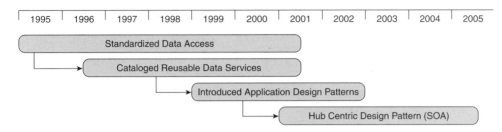

Figure 10.1 The evolution of Standard Life's infrastructure.

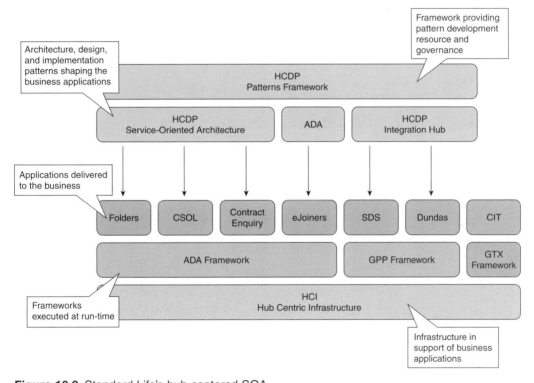

Figure 10.2 Standard Life's hub-centered SOA.

Because Web services standards and tools were not yet mature at the time, Standard Life built its software framework according to the following design considerations:

- XML schemas for service interfaces, published in a catalog (a WSDL-styled protocol)
- A runtime business services directory used for service invocation (a UDDI-styled protocol)
- A message protocol to access business services (a SOAP-styled message protocol)

In addition, it decided on the use of Enterprise Java Beans, Java Servlets, and JavaServer Pages; these technologies by then had attained a sufficient level of stability to support Standard Life's needs. With the introduction of Application Design Patterns starting in 1999 (see Figure 10.1), by its 2001 checkpoint, it had a blueprint for a new architectural model. Figure 10.2 also shows ADA, the original application design approach represented by simple design patterns that was intended as a "how to" guide for designers supported by an earlier (non-hub-centered) framework code that implemented the pattern. As Standard Life progresses to its newer HCD direction, ADA-based designs can continue to be supported.

The new model, named the hub-centered architecture (HCA), follows what is described as the hub-centered design patterns (HCDP), a new patterns framework. The HCDP (see Figure 10.3) is a set of two main pattern categories:

- HCDP SOA—A *request-reply* pattern to shape the development of internal and external clients that perform business functions by accessing reusable, channel-independent business services.
- HCDP integration hub—A *publish-subscribe* pattern to integrate applications and packages in heterogeneous platforms that isolate and decouple applications from one another.

The new HCA provides the following primary benefits:

- *Reuse*: In layers, starting with business application services at the base to framework, infrastructure, design patterns, and architecture.
- *Execution time consistency*: Applications must behave in a standard, predictable way on a standard infrastructure. This allows for better systems management (in terms of reliability and availability), makes it easier to support in production, and minimizes risk when introducing change.
- *Focal point*: Acts as a nexus for application and infrastructure improvement and innovation.
- *Change management*: The new model facilitates and manages changes to the application architectures, frameworks, and infrastructure in coordinated and planned ways. By implementing change in a consistent manner using a stable framework, Standard Life can treat all applications the same way, even when mass change is required (migrating to a new version of infrastructure to adapt to changing currency needs). By isolating the applications from the infrastructure (via the framework), it can isolate these applications from lower-level concerns such as cross-platform communications, logging APIs, and other low-level dependencies.

To understand how business services and applications are built in the Standard Life architecture, take a look at Figure 10.4, a high-level view of its SOA pattern. Figure 10.4 shows a channel-dependent layer per the particular client use of the channel-independent business service itself, with a business service interface layer between the two. The business services use XML interfaces that define recognizable business functions (for example, `Verify Identity`, `Provide Bank Details`, `Produce Statement`, and so on) and follow standard practices such as thorough documentation of usage and fault notification.

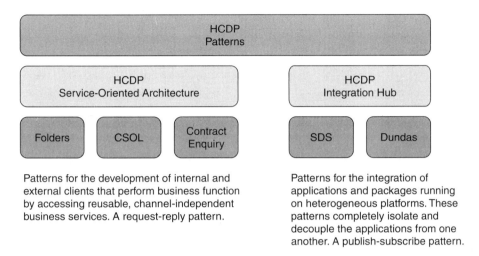

Patterns for the development of internal and external clients that perform business function by accessing reusable, channel-independent business services. A request-reply pattern.

Patterns for the integration of applications and packages running on heterogeneous platforms. These patterns completely isolate and decouple the applications from one another. A publish-subscribe pattern.

Figure 10.3 Hub-centered design patterns in Standard Life's SOA.

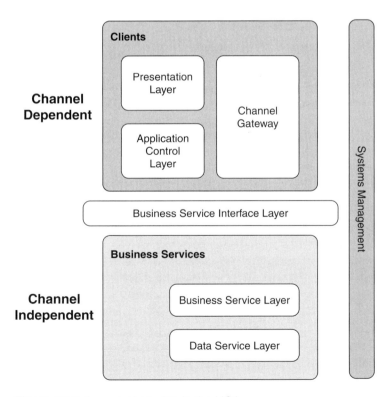

Figure 10.4 A general service in the HCA.

Standard Life built a software framework around its infrastructure, allowing applications to concentrate on the business code required within each layer rather than low-level infrastructure concerns. The framework is built around Java and COBOL interfaces, abstracting the underlying infrastructure through common APIs. In particular, the framework handles the following aspects of service invocation: operating platform issues, transport protocols, target message queues, failure handling, and time-dependent responses.

For example, this framework allows applications, when invoking a business service, to request the service by name and version. The software framework and runtime business services directory takes care of all other aspects. Standard Life's use of a business services directory (BSD) is similar to that provided by, although predating, UDDI. The BSD is accessed only through the framework and contains service endpoints with particular quality-of-service attributes.

Standard Life's SOA implementation enables the company to provide business functions over many business channels through its business services layer (see Figure 10.4). Standard Life has leveraged its catalog of reusable business services to lower costs and increase its competitive standing and revenue. New combinations of services are delivered to agents and customers. Customer service is improved by providing business functions as reusable business services that can then be deployed into any channel. This delivers on the promise of a single brand across multiple products and channels.

10.1.3 Impact of the Project

The impact of the move toward an SOA at Standard Life has lead to the following results:

- 73 service-consuming applications running in production.
- 40% of the company's backend transactions come through its SOA (an average of 1.6 million transactions a day).
- 297 business services in production and available for reuse.
- 51% of services are reused, and the instances of reuse show a development savings in excess of £2m (US$3.64m).

Standard Life's SOA implementation spans the major business units of the company. As of this writing, this includes implementations across all the main U.K. operating companies in the Standard Life Group. The company's Canadian operations also use the same design patterns, framework, and process. Overall, the approach was reusable across its environment, allowing production-ready applications to be deployed within six months.

Standard Life hired Forrester Research to review and checkpoint its approach to SOA, to take an independent account of the impact. Forrester has endorsed Standard Life's approach as either a best practice or close to one, across all their criteria for reviewing SOAs.

The concept and implementation of the company's SOA resulted in the visible external or customer-facing outcomes of this endeavor. Figure 10.5, a small sample of what is in production, illustrates the use of a portfolio of business services across many channels and applications. For example, Provide Pension Valuation is used in Folders (supporting

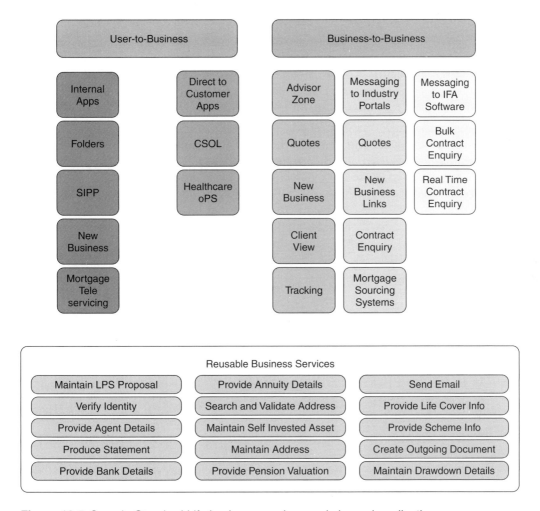

Figure 10.5 Sample Standard Life business services and channel applications.

teleservicing of customer requests), CSOL (Customer Services Online, Client view—client and policy servicing delivered for agents through the award-winning AdvisorZone Extranet), and Contract Enquiry Messaging to Industry Portals and Advisers' Back Office software solutions.

The reuse achieved by this project has been measured and represents a development saving of over £2,000,000 (US$3,640,000). This measured figure does not include the additional savings realized in operational support and service delivery functions that arise as a result of implementing a dynamic, unified enterprise architecture and the consistency of application behavior that results from building on a common framework.

Standard Life determined the preceding savings—in return on investment on its SOA—as a function of the following metrics:

- How many services are in use?
- How many are reused in two or more applications?
- How many instances of each application exist that reuse services?
- What is the value of such reuse as savings in development costs?

The chief contributing factor to the company's ROI is the reuse of services in multiple applications and instances of these applications. Therefore, there was a strong focus in facilitating and measuring reuse. To facilitate reuse, the company implemented an analysis and design-time catalog, added tools for documenting and publicizing each new service, created business service definitions and interfaces, and identified functional and non-functional characteristics that impact the services. Much of the metrics data on reuse is automatically collected from the framework during use (service name, version, used by, used for, and so on), with some data manually populated by development teams.

Operationally, the following flow of ideas explains how the IT team successfully monitors and manages reuse of the SOA model:

- A common framework enforces standardization.
- Applications are built and delivered in a consistent manner using this framework.
- Logging events are correlated end to end across different platforms within the framework.
- Data-mining tools interrogate these logging events.
- Component interaction data is available from the framework.
- Impact analysis tools interrogate component interaction information and the support system management.

10.1.4 Lessons Learned

The Standard Life IT team identified six lessons learned from this project:

- *SOA needs technology, processes, and people.* This might be obvious, but SOA isn't just technology; it also involves processes and people. Standard Life had to shift its culture to become service oriented. The company changed the skill set and trained 250 people in XML, getting analysts much more involved in the definition of XML schemas for reusable interfaces. In 2001, Web services technology was not yet mature enough for Standard Life to adopt in its organization. In its evaluation of Web services, the company concluded that it would use Web services for external messaging links to make it easier to integrate with business partners. Internally, its custom software framework masked the applications from the underlying communication protocols and other low-level concerns. Therefore, there was no need for Web services internally. Thus, there was no cost case to adopt Web services within the mature SOA that is already delivering returns.

- *SOA needs aligned architecture and operational and development groups.* Standard Life recognized the need to align architecture, development, and operational groups. In the company's experience, if any one of these groups pulled in a different direction, the overall SOA could be undermined. The company had to put in place processes that ensured a coherent approach.
- *Use a framework to deliver consistency and achieve flexibility.* The framework uncouples applications from the infrastructure, and it allows applications and infrastructure to evolve independently. Some in the organization thought that establishing a framework would mean the "de-skilling" of some teams and a lack of flexibility. However, by decoupling applications from infrastructure, it allows the applications to evolve and allows the teams to manage change in those applications. This makes the applications, and therefore the system, more flexible.
- *SOA needs management of a portfolio of services.* The IT team members found that you should not underestimate the need to manage the portfolio of services and to continually communicate the value of doing this to the organization. They found that a virtual team can work well. Earlier, when they had a single central team, they did not get the buy-in they needed to achieve their goals.
- *SOA can deliver real savings.* Although this was not really a true lesson learned, it was nice to get confirmation on what they thought at the outset. Consider defining a system of metrics during the development of your business service management and business service catalog.
- *Establish a system of metrics as part of your SOA project.* To keep the momentum, establish a metrics system as part of the approach and communicate the good news. The IT team communicated the metrics internally at many levels and even some externally. This lead to popular support of the SOA project.

10.2 Case Study: SOA in Government Services

Government systems prove to be some of the most complex types of organizations, involving many variations on organizational hierarchies (districts, departments, ministries, and so on), legislative or legal requirements, and a multitude of technical directions. This case study involves the Austrian Federal Ministry of Justice (MoJ) and its IT services provider, BundesRechenZentrum GmbH (BRZ), in an e-government project in 2002 to modernize and deliver effective government-to-business (G2B) and government-to-citizen (G2C) services. The Austrian MoJ has about 7,400 people, consisting of judges, prosecutors, clerks, and other administrators covering the district, appeals, supreme, and high courts. This does not include the 3,400 other persons who staff the nationwide system of 28 prisons.

10.2.1 IT and Business Challenges
The main challenge in this project was to connect multiple application service providers to a number of government databases to improve access to judicial records. In addition to

the issues of handling legal document access and exchange between various agencies and partners, the existing infrastructure also had a specific proprietary set of APIs, which the new system had to maintain for backward compatibility.

The key goals for the project were to overlay a new, modern, flexible infrastructure over the existing database systems, improving the interfaces for any type of service provider (an xSP), and still maintain compatibility with users of the system with older tools—all to better serve the needs of the legal community.

The MoJ created a project stakeholders model identifying the different groups involved in creating this project. The overall steering committee worked with the project leaders from each team: MoJ personnel, BRZ personnel, and personnel from IBM. These project teams developed multiple working groups that interacted with experts from each key user group they intended to support.

The MoJ provided funding and subject-matter experts. BRZ provided development personnel with knowledge of the legacy application, as well as additional subject-matter experts. IBM provided development personnel, expertise in object technology, project management staff, and the company's experiences from previous international court system projects.

10.2.2 Technical Implementation

The previous customer model of the project, which the MoJ intended to continue, provided access to the court documents through the xSPs, whereby the xSPs were responsible for providing end-user access.

Customers of the system (that is, attorneys and other government-related businesses) pay a certain transaction fee to the xSPs, a portion of which is recovered by the MoJ. The fees vary by transaction, and the data access is logged at the xSP, with the customer getting charged according to the number of bytes transmitted.

The change to the technical infrastructure included a new SOAP-based Web services application server placed in a DMZ between the MoJ intranet and the xSP's systems, accessed through the Internet (see Figure 10.6). The Web services application server then connects to the MoJs backend systems consisting of IBM S/390® mainframes. The Web services application server handles SOAP requests from the xSPs described in XML and, as an intermediary, translates these to Java Remote Method Invocations over TCP/IP to internal applications on the MoJ intranet. The interfaces to these services that the xSPs access are described in WSDL.

10.2.3 Impact of the Project

The MoJ and BRZ had the previous court case management system for over a decade, and it proved to be a great success in terms of efficiency and ease of access to information. However, with new requirements, some of the existing solutions needed upgrading. They

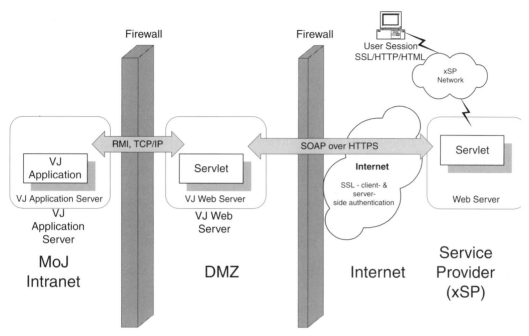

Figure 10.6 The Austrian Ministry of Justice Web services project.

identified two main problems: proprietary data formats tied to legacy applications and proprietary APIs tied to the application service provider (xSP) system.

The following applications were affected by the project:

- *Land register:* As a public register, anyone can inquire about the details of the ownership of any given plot of land. Users have been able to make this type of inquiry over the Internet since 1999.
- *Commercial register:* A service for formally registering a company for business, inquiring and updating specifics, as well as deleting information is also available over the Internet.
- *Court automation:* As part of a long-running *Redesign* project, most aspects of court proceedings (3.7 million cases per year) have been automated, specifically in the areas of civil cases (where there are around 850,000 cases per year), enforcement cases (1,231,000), criminal cases (125,000), and prosecution proceedings (655,000).
- *Electronic communication in the legal field:* Approximately 2.1 million cases per year are filed electronically, which includes 85% of civil actions and 60% of enforcement-applications. (Telekom Austria is used as an Internet service provider to connect key customers of justice like lawyers, banks, and insurance companies.)

- *Electronic learning:* Interactive multimedia self-teaching modules offer education for end-users of the system.
- *Publication of court edicts on the Internet:* Bankruptcy cases are published via the Internet in legally binding form, saving the costs of newspaper advertisements. See www.edikte.justiz.gv.at. Because of the success of this application, publications for auctions of real estate properties were added, as well as all other court publications.

The project impacted not just the MoJ and BRZ but also its partners and the general public's access and use of the system. Changes to the data format and the APIs—while maintaining backward compatibility—affected the applications within the MoJ as well as five different xSP business partners of the MoJ. Furthermore, it also affected all Austrian attorneys who work with the MoJ through the xSPs—all this while continuing the goal to support 3.7 million new cases each year.

10.2.4 Lessons Learned

The Austrian Ministry of Justice learned four lessons from this project experience:

- *Despite multiple protocol conversions, performance might not always be detrimentally affected.* Due to the nature of the distributed environment and the multiple protocol conversions at different layers, the MoJ was concerned that it could impact the performance of the actual service. However, despite the dependencies on an external provider (the xSP), the interactions through a CICS gateway to the mainframe applications, and the Java RMI invocations, it turns out that the performance impact was not that significant.
- *You might need individual solutions for different programming languages.* Multiple client technologies were used by the xSPs to implement the SOAP calls to the MoJ application servers, written in C and Java—a concern for SOAP interoperability issues. However, it turned out that the major interoperability problems actually came from the client-authenticated SSL protocol—from Web browser to Web server. The implementation team found individual solutions for this.
- *The Apache Axis and Tomcat servers at the time did not have sufficient support for services management.* The Apache Axis Web server running Tomcat, which was used to provide the SOAP service interaction, at the time did not have sufficient support for non-functional aspects such as logging, metering, and billing the usage of Web services data. The implementation team had to build a lot of these tools by hand to enable this level of Web services management.
- *Deploying services across a firewall in a DMZ requires careful balance.* A final lesson learned was that deploying the services in a DMZ requires a clear understanding of system administration functions in balance with network security; the access to resources in the DMZ required careful restricted access.

The technical issues of this project turned out to be in the realm of feasibility, although there were a few unexpected surprises. Essentially, the operation of the system turned out smoother than expected in terms of performance.

10.3 Summary

These two case studies provided views into SOA projects that are independent of the protocol mechanism; that is, one project used Web services while the other built its own system. Both examples showed how intranet and extranet applications can exist in the same architecture. The lessons learned from each project included the emphasis that SOA needs a combination of technology processes and people to make it work and that it can deliver real savings with surprisingly smooth performance.

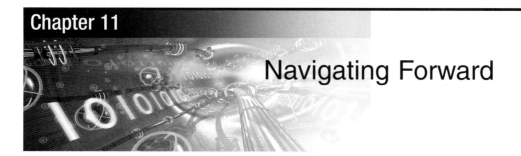

Chapter 11

Navigating Forward

"Following the light of the sun, we left the Old World."

—*Christopher Columbus*

I n this book, we navigated through a broad range of issues that you can expect when building an SOA solution. As stated at the beginning, to go into detail for all possible aspects that you need to consider when transforming your business and IT systems is too large a task for a single book. Nevertheless, we think we have provided necessary and sufficient details on service-oriented architectures and why and how they are important for any business to operate flexibly in a global economy.

11.1 What We Learned

The foremost lesson to take from our experience in SOA projects is that you will need to deal with the whole enterprise—not just the IT departments, but anyone in the company involved and working as a service provider, service requestor, or both. This approach differs from those in the 1980s and 1990s, when the enterprise data model proved to be an enormous effort, getting people lost in details and minutiae. With service orientation, the focus is on providing an infrastructure that is as flexible as needed by the agile enterprises of today.

An SOA results in flexibility and not just within your own organization. It paves the way to build service-oriented business relationships with partners, suppliers, and customers. Another result is a saturation of sophisticated applications throughout your enterprise, building a competitive advantage that can shift the whole organization toward quicker reaction to customer needs, anywhere in the world. All this leads to the architectural principles described in Chapter 3, "Architecture Elements."

As we ourselves discovered more about service orientation, we came to understand that there are success factors that stem just from having a common understanding across the enterprise—you will need this understanding and a common language to facilitate the change toward greater agility. Though you can take incremental steps toward service orientation in many areas of your software, what you really need is a business transformation process under careful orchestration and guidance throughout the enterprise. On this point, we described (in Chapters 3 and 4) the aspects related to governance (IT and business), the need for special SOA project management, and the overall architectural blueprint that acts as an outline for the enterprise. These factors combined are what provide the real roadmap toward business agility.

Applying technology correctly can pave the way for the flexibility to change and continuous business innovation. This requires an infrastructure that supports self-defined, loosely coupled interfaces. Additionally, it calls for the use of tools from emerging technologies that incorporate existing assets through automation, virtualization, and integration. These tools also need to support self-defining, declarative semantics, as well as strong analysis and compositional techniques based on software engineering techniques like aspect-oriented programming.

As outlined in Chapter 4, "SOA Project Planning Aspects," the concepts, the services, and their inter-communication all need to be standardized in order to achieve loose-coupling and flexible interoperability. In addition, there also needs to be a change in how the organization develops these SOA-based systems. We showed that new roles come into play in the SOA model. We also encountered a need for closer cooperation between IT and line-of-business representatives.

We learned that most existing IT architecture can be a choke point for business innovation, as monolithic systems and applications cannot be easily reused, and that each generation comes with its own monoliths and assumptions. Merger and acquisition activities and the requirement for new ways of doing business electronically have proportionally grown the need for integration. Ad-hoc integration solutions that were used to link dedicated systems together are often custom-made solutions that create connections that are difficult to change and maintain.

Hence, a new architecture is required that overcomes these deficiencies. We showed in this book how the concepts of SOA—though not a totally new approach in principle—can help create an infrastructure, a development environment, and an integrated approach between IT and business groups within an enterprise and beyond. These SOA concepts provide the necessary base for flexible IT supporting an agile business.

To a certain degree, a lack of standards limits the capability to deliver meaningful interoperability. However, our collective experience has shown that the applicability of Web services and related industry standards can allow organizations to cross the barriers of programming and operating systems built up over the past decades.

The final lesson we learned is that the strength of your architecture is key to its success. A strong plan saves you from doing a big-bang replacement of systems with potential high risks of failure. Instead, a strategy of small improvements can help justify cost. Factors that play an important role here are common standards for communication and description (as given by SOAP, WSDL, and other WS-standards), as well as an understanding of industry and cross-industry semantics and the taxonomy of services (refer to Chapter 5, "Aspects of Analysis and Design").

11.2 Guiding Principles

This book represents, as with any other printed document, only a snapshot of time based on the accumulated knowledge and insights from ongoing projects at enterprises, in development, and in research laboratories. As with any new discipline, service-oriented architecture and the supportive on-demand operating environment will continue to evolve as subjects of further development.

Summarizing, we can say that an SOA enables flexible connectivity of applications or resources by doing the following:

- Representing every application or resource as a service with a standardized interface
- Enabling them to exchange structured information (messages, documents, business objects)
- Mediating the message exchange through a service integration bus
- Providing on-ramps to the bus for existing application environments

This allows quicker combinations of new and existing applications to address changing business needs and improve operational effectiveness by managing the topology of the application network.

The principles of SOA might sound like a simple approach; they might indicate a lack of sophistication or a "boil-the-ocean" approach. But this does not mean it is simplistic. An SOA, rather, is a smart way of allowing gradual and continuous improvements based on easy-to-understand patterns and a set of commonly accepted standards.

Based on our analysis of the collective experience of many IBM teams in more than 70 client projects in this area during the last two years, we can name seven guiding principles to consider when entering the SOA adventure:

1. *SOA requires CEO- and CIO-level commitment* (see Chapters 1, 2, and 4). SOA is not just a product for which standard IT ROI equations apply, nor is it just a new IT technology to apply. But to justify the transition toward SOA, consideration of both IT and business benefits are required.

2. *The business team and IT team work hand-in-hand* (see Chapters 4 and 5). SOA is all about flexible business processes that IT offers the means to implement. Adequate

forms of business process modeling and industry or enterprise decomposition are the first critical steps leading to a well-defined set of services.

3. *Avoid the "big-bang" approach* (see Chapters 3 and 4). This means to start small by selecting a well-defined application or business process area. Then use the SOA blueprint to establish an initial target architecture, and finally, leverage existing data and backend processes using adaptor technologies.

4. *Fully embrace the use of standards* (see Chapters 3 and 6 through 9). Here we especially refer to open standards (for example, the Web services standards) and open source, providing a new and proven approach for a collective endeavor toward a greater target to master global business requirements in a quickly shrinking world.

5. *Governance is critical for success* (see Chapter 4). We recommend, as a first step toward establishing or enhancing the end-to-end implementation process, that you "seed" your SOA center of excellence. This is where you should initiate your first SOA project to create the first incarnation. This also means a need for well-defined processes and documentation and establishing architectural guidelines early on (see Chapters 3 and 5 through 9). In addition, an organizational infrastructure has to be set up to ensure optimal reuse and integration of all aspects of the application lifecycle including deployment.

6. *The first step is the hardest, so plan ahead* (see Chapter 4). For successful project management of SOA projects, it is key to leverage best practices and patterns experience (such as tooling, consulting) and to use experienced practitioners to define the first set of infrastructure and business services (for example, to determine what is the right granularity for services). Finally, a set of integrated tools or an SOA workbench that allows business and IT people to communicate on common objects can help bridge the "language" gap—that is, translate business requirements into technical implementations.

7. *Adopt innovative software engineering principles* (see Chapters 3 and 5 through 9). This includes open-source development principles as well as new software engineering techniques such as service modeling (analysis and design), event-based models driven by business situations, and transformations into implementations patterns, supported by adequate tools.

11.3 Future Directions

As of this writing, most of the aspects, tools, methods, and standards described in this book are in a state of early adoption and, in some cases, have been defined and their usefulness proven.

In the areas of modeling, aspects of security, and service assets development, we will soon see new ideas that follow the thoughts we have outlined as being based on experiences from real-life projects of various customers. This shows that the principles of SOA are applicable to many solutions in many industries. However, to become more efficient and react quickly to business needs, there is still a market to establish of industry frameworks, common taxonomies, and semantics for specialized services and tools.

With the model of an on-demand operating environment in mind, you can expect to see special services to come that not only relate to business applications and integration for B2B or electronic markets, but also utility services that allow you to create an entire market of service providers on the Web. In addition, there are many ways to implement SOA that are agnostic of the programming platform, with various possible technologies you can choose to implement.

11.3.1 Technology Standards

Some standards have been well established for a while, thankfully, such as the SOAP messaging protocol and the WSDL description language. There are others, however, that are still at the proposal stage, while still others are starting to reach maturity within standardization organizations like OASIS and the W3C. We hesitate to indicate which proposed standards, due to the fairly rapid rate of progression of standards today. You should examine the Web sites of these organizations for their Web services proposed standards to ascertain their current status.

A.11.1

11.3.2 Web Services Monitoring and Visualization

Current research on Web services monitoring and visualization, including event-driven architectures that support these tasks, is starting to emerge from research labs. More sophisticated policy and management tools can help the SOA administrators and operation analysts to better care for the flexible, self-organization environment of SOA-enabled organizations that operate on a large, even global, scale.

11.3.3 Semantic Web Services

Semantic Web services are another topic that is gaining weight, especially when you have to deal with increasing numbers of connections, foreign units, and periodically emerging new approaches, products, and ideas that all need to be communicated and tested so that they can be used as designed. Semantic services provide a deeper understanding and provide context for how the information or the service is supposed to be used. Such semantic information enables architects and designers to know how to more effectively incorporate these services into their applications and architecture. A corollary is that new forms of directory and search engines will likely emerge from this activity.

11.3.4 Open Development Platforms

The development tools for SOA will be based on common, open platforms in which various individuals' roles can match the instrumentation and cooperate, just as the various SOA roles depend on each other. Open software development platforms, such as Eclipse, thus will become more integrated with business modeling and business process tools. This avoids or minimizes locking into proprietary development platforms, a significant obstacle particularly when engaging multiple organizations or companies in your SOA applications.

11.3.5 Services Assets

There is now an evolution toward support for model-driven development, and for finding and reusing service assets (as described in Chapter 6, "Enterprise Solution Assets"). Communications between IT and business groups are becoming more sophisticated and automated, resulting in easier and less error-prone interactions.

11.3.6 SOA Programming Models

A.11.2

As discussed in this book, service-oriented architecture is not new, and its concepts allow gradual transformation and integration of existing systems. Additionally, with regard to the existing skills in a large array of programming languages used to build existing IT systems, there is a need to learn how to create services around and in those systems. This affects not just COBOL or CICS, C++ or C#, Visual Basic® or Java, but in some cases, it even extends to applications in FORTRAN and PL/1. We expect programming model support for any such system very soon, even more than the object-oriented aspects have been taken in by those systems in the past. In this context, there are technologies such as SDO that provide a unified framework for service data access.

11.3.7 Virtual Services Platform

IT infrastructure might see similar changes toward virtualization of system and network resources so that they can have business services reach all the way down the abstraction levels to quantifiable storage units and processing nodes. In this context, grid computing introduces autonomic provisioning of service resources that leads to actual distributed computing, so that business services can initiate and interact across the entire corporate network (perhaps even globally).

11.3.8 Event-Driven Architectures

As services become more commoditized and the IT infrastructure allows more and more flexible solutions to be realized, the notion of events gains importance. We see in the enterprise service bus (ESB), as described in Chapter 3, a very suitable means to allow event-driven solutions. The loosely coupled nature and the strict use of self-describing interfaces, service brokers, and common event infrastructures enable you to concentrate on the events as they occur in real business life. Whether planned and calculated or totally unpredictable, in an appropriate architecture, they are manageable in a way similar to the emergency plans and rules.

11.3.9 Model-Driven Architectures

Business information itself might need to evolve and integrate to take advantage of the dynamics of SOA. With the greater emphasis on model-driven architectures, the concepts common in software modeling today can go up the chain into the activities of business analysts. Building this stronger correlation to business activities allows the business units of an organization to become more directly involved in the IT architecture and planning of the SOA.

A.11.3

11.3.10 Utility Services

When services become a common utility globally, business analysts may be asked to find new metrics, processes, and concepts to quantify and describe the many different types of business activities. What we see nowadays in strategic outsourcing, in which selected business partners are bound in long-term contracts, will soon become a market of point solutions that are as easily interchangeable, as seen in manufacturing industries. It is very likely that due to the globalizing pressures on enterprises, the aforementioned standards, taxonomies, and semantics will quickly reach a maturity similar to that available in the manufacturing industry today.

11.3.11 Industry Adoption

In terms of reuse and portability across environments, there is a software analogy to the parts market in the manufacturing industry: The software market can also become one in which standardized service implementations allow interchangeability and replacement more easily. As specific taxonomies and industry semantics evolve, industry services frameworks are being developed for vendors and consumers of services, provided as online services, as "parts" implemented inside an enterprise IT system.

11.4 Summary

As you can see, SOA can be a large subject rather than just one specific topic. It reaches across many existing problems that both business and IT have faced for a long time. Although it provides a paradigm of how the two worlds can work together, this does not come without significant effort. The promises of overall business agility and versatility may be the real motivators for this merger. As a departing thought, we would like to reiterate the true impact of this new paradigm: *SOA can transform the very life structure of not just IT but the functions of the entire organization.*

11.5 Links to developerWorks

A.11.1 You can see an up-to-date list of technology specifications and standards related to SOA and Web services at http://www-128.ibm.com/developerworks/webservices/standards/.

A.11.2 IBM's programming model for SOA enables software developers to create and reuse IT assets, using component types, wiring, templates, application adapters, uniform data representation and an enterprise service bus. http://www.ibm.com/developerworks/webservices/library/ws-soa-progmodel/index.html.

A.11.3 This three-part series by Alan Brown and Jim Conallen explores the nature of Model-Driven Architectures in depth. http://www.ibm.com/developerworks/rational/library/3100.html.

Glossary

access control list (ACL)

A mechanism for determining the access level and permissions that a given computing resource, such as a file or database field, provides for a given identity.

agility

The capability to lower the enterprise's center of gravity and move with suppleness, skill, and control. See also **business agility**.

application programming interface (API)

A set of routines and function definitions that abstract the implementation details and make it easier to develop and build software applications.

application server

An application server is a server-side program in a distributed network that is dedicated to hosting the enterprise application's business logic. It provides the middleware infrastructure as part of a multitier application, consisting of a user interface server, a business logic server, and a database or transaction server.

Association for Cooperative Operations Research and Development (ACORD)

A global, nonprofit insurance association whose mission is to facilitate the development and use of standards for the insurance, reinsurance, and related financial services industries.

authentication

The validation and verification of the identity of a user, device, or some other computing entity, often as a prerequisite to allowing access to resources in a system. Authentication merely ensures that the entity is who it claims to be, but it says nothing about the access rights of the entity.

authorization

The process of granting or denying access to an individual or computing entity. This allows access to various resources based on the entity's identity. See also **access control list (ACL)**.

business agility

The capability of an enterprise to respond with speed to market opportunities, external threats, or customer demands by changing its business processes that are integrated end-to-end across the company and with key partners, suppliers, and customers.

business process

A set of logically related tasks performed to achieve a defined business outcome. A process is a structured, measured set of activities designed to meet the business objectives.

Business Process Execution Language (BPEL)

An XML-based language designed to enable task-sharing for a service-oriented architecture environment—even across multiple organizations—by orchestrating and choreographing individual Web services. Using BPEL, a developer formally describes a business process in such a way that any cooperating entity can perform one or more steps in the process the same way. In a supply-chain process, for example, a BPEL program might describe a business protocol that formalizes what pieces of information a product order consists of and what exceptions may have to be handled. BPEL does not specify how a given service should process a given order internally.

business process modeling (BPM)

An analysis and design activity performed by business consultants within a company to model both the current state of an enterprise and the intended future state by using BPM tools. Usually, to move from the current state to the future state requires IT transformation.

business-to-business (B2B)

A set of business processes, usually automated, between trading partners. It is performed at much higher volumes than business-to-consumer (**B2C**) applications.

business-to-consumer (B2C)

A form of electronic commerce in which products or services are sold from a company directly to a consumer.

choreography

A mechanism for orchestrating multiple services together by specifying (usually by graphical tools) the linkages and coordination between them to create a business process. It also defines the flow of information among the set of services, participants, and activities.

Common Object Request Broker Architecture (CORBA)

A set of industry standards published by **OMG** that defines a distributed model for object application systems.

component

A modular unit of functionality accessed through one or more interfaces.

component business model (CBM)

An enterprise model consisting of autonomous and manageable components. Each component is a grouping of the people, technology, and resources that deliver specific business value and potentially are able to operate independently. This helps decision-makers to "disentangle" the organization, cutting through historical boundaries arising along organizational, product, channel, geography, and application lines. It is an end-to-end way of looking at the business through all the layers—not just the business layer but the application layer and IT infrastructure, too. The consolidated view of all the layers is the foundation for recommendations concerning the enterprise.

component-based development (CBD)

An approach to the design, construction, implementation, and evolution of software applications. Software applications are assembled from components from a variety of sources; the components themselves may be written in several different programming languages and run on several different platforms.

componentization

Decomposition of an architecture into interchangeable pieces or components to assemble an application from reusable components within frameworks. SOA and Web services go a step further by encapsulating components in a standards-based service interface that allows components to be reused outside their native framework. Componentization is not limited to software; through the use of subcontracting and outsourcing, it can also apply to business organizations and processes.

confidentiality

A mechanism to ensure that data in transit or in storage cannot be read except by authorized systems or people. Confidentiality for Web services is often achieved using encryption, implemented either at a transport level using **SSL** or at a message level using XML encryption.

demilitarized zone (DMZ)

A computer host (called the bastion host) or a small network inserted as a "neutral zone" between a company's private network and the outside public network. This zone protects the private network from possible intrusions.

digital signature

A type of electronic signature that is used to guarantee the integrity of the data. When linked to the identity of the signer—using a security token such as X.509 digital certificates—a digital signature can be used for nonrepudiation since it links the signer with the signed document.

Eclipse

An open platform for tool integration built by an open community of tool providers. Operating under an open-source paradigm and with a common public license that provides royalty-free source code and worldwide redistribution rights, the Eclipse platform provides tool developers with ultimate flexibility and control over their software technology.

Eclipse Modeling Framework (EMF)

An open-source framework based on **Eclipse** that targets **MDA** development by providing facilities such as customizable graphical editors and Eclipse plug-ins.

electronic business using eXtensible Markup Language (ebXML)

A set of **XML**-based standards for business data sponsored by **OASIS** and UN/CEFACT, the United Nations' electronic business unit. ebXML was created to prevent fragmentation of electronic commerce into multiple, incompatible XML dialects and to provide a migration path for existing users of EDI, the pre-Internet e-commerce standard.

electronic data interchange (EDI)

A standard format for exchanging business data. A message contains a string of data elements, each of which represents a singular fact such as a price, product model number, and so forth, separated by a delimiter.

enterprise application integration (EAI)

The software and architectural principles to bring together (integrate) a set of enterprise applications aimed at modernizing, consolidating, and coordinating the enterprise's IT landscape.

enterprise information integration (EII)

The process of integrating structured and unstructured information sources into a unified information source.

Enterprise Java Beans (EJB)

A specification developed by Sun Microsystems that defines a Java API for server-side enterprise components that execute within a **J2EE**-compliant applicant server. The specification also details remote communication protocols, persistence, transactions, concurrency control, naming services, and deployment descriptors.

Enterprise Service Bus (ESB)

An open standards–based distributed messaging infrastructure that provides a secure, reliable, event-driven, and interoperable framework for integrating enterprise applications in an implementation-independent fashion by leveraging the principles of **SOA**.

enterprise solution asset (ESA)

Architectural assets that are reusable across enterprise projects and that help accelerate solution implementation. ESAs are used to formalize architectural decisions and articulate best practices.

eXtensible Markup Language (XML)

A general-purpose markup language developed by the **W3C** for the definition, transmission, validation, and interpretation of data/information between applications and between organizations. The extensibility allows the creation of specialized markup languages and domain definitions with their own customized tags by using a formal grammar and vocabulary (called an **XSD**).

extract transform load (ETL)

The processes that enable companies to move data from multiple sources, reformat and cleanse it, and load it into another database, a data mart, or a data warehouse for analysis or onto another operational system to support a business process.

graphical user interface (GUI)

A mechanism for interacting directly with a computing device using graphical display capabilities (such as menus, widgets, icons, and controls) to make computer applications easier to use.

grid computing

The virtualization of distributed computing and data resources such as processing, network bandwidth, and storage capacity to create a single system image, granting users and applications seamless access to vast IT capabilities. Just as an Internet user views a unified instance of content via the Web, a grid user essentially sees a single, large, virtual computer.

Hypertext Markup Language (HTML)

A markup language designed for the creation of Web pages and other information viewable in a browser.

Hypertext Transfer Protocol (HTTP)

The underlying communication protocol used by the World Wide Web. The protocol defines how messages are formatted and transmitted and what actions Web servers and clients (such as browsers) should take in response to various commands.

Hypertext Transfer Protocol Secure (HTTPS)

A secure version of **HTTP** in which a secure socket layer that encrypts the session data is used instead of plain text socket communication.

IBM Rational Application Developer (RAD)

An integrated development environment (IDE) tool to quickly design, develop, analyze, test, profile, and deploy Web, **Web services**, Java, J2EE, and Portal applications. Optimized for IBM WebSphere software and supporting multivendor runtime environments, it is powered by the **Eclipse** open-source platform so that developers can adapt and extend their development environment to match their needs and increase their productivity.

IBM Rational Software Architect (RSA)

An integrated design and development tool that leverages model-driven development with the UML for creating well-architected applications and services that allow you to unify all aspects of software design and development. It includes all of the features of **RSM** and **RAD**.

IBM Rational Software Modeler (RSM)

A customizable, **UML**-based, visual modeling and design tool that enables users to clearly document and communicate various system views to architects, systems analysts, and designers.

IBM WebSphere Application Server (WAS)

See **WebSphere**.

IBM WebSphere Business Integration (WBI)

The business integration solution suite from IBM for process integration, workforce management, and enterprise application connectivity.

Insurance Application Architecture (IAA)

An architecture published by IBM for the insurance industry. It includes a business model, a design model of components, interfaces, and messages, a generic design framework for product definition and agreement administration, and design models for the creation of data warehouses.

Internet Inter-Orb Protocol (IIOP)

An open-standard protocol published by **OMG** to be used for communication in **CORBA**-based systems.

Java 2 Enterprise Edition (J2EE)

A standard from Sun Microsystems for a platform-independent Java environment for developing distributed, multitier architecture applications. The standard details modular enterprise components, using several technologies such as **EJB**, **JDBC**, **JSP**, **servlets**, and **XML**, that can be executed on a J2EE-compliant application server.

Java 2 Standard Edition (J2SE)

A collection of Java **API** that provides an environment for developing Java applications.

Java API for XML-Based RPC (JAX-RPC)

A Java-based programming model for the development of **SOAP** applications. It simplifies development by abstracting **SOAP** protocol-level runtime mechanisms and providing mapping services between Java and the **WSDL**. It is also referred to as **JSR** 101.

Java Connector Architecture (JCA)

A J2EE-based technology standard for connecting application servers and enterprise information systems (EIS).

Java Database Connectivity (JDBC)

A Java API for interacting with any database by providing methods for querying and updating data. It is oriented toward relational databases.

Java Messaging Service (JMS)

A Java API for interacting with messaging-based systems. The API supports both the point-to-point (and queuing) and publish/subscribe interaction models. It is the primary standard to provide a reliable foundation for loosely coupled, asynchronous messaging within a distributed environment.

Java Specification Request (JSR)

A document that formally describes proposed specifications and technologies to be added to the Java platform. Formal public reviews of JSRs are conducted before they become final and are dictated by the Java Community Process (JCP).

JavaServer Faces (JSF)

Java-based technology that leverages existing, standard **GUI** and Web-tier concepts without limiting developers to a particular markup language, protocol, or client device. It consists of APIs for representing user interface components and managing their state, handling events and input validation, defining page navigation, and supporting internationalization and accessibility.

JavaServer Pages (JSP)

A JavaServer-side technology that enables developers to dynamically generate **HTML, XML,** or other markup languages. This allows Java code and certain predefined actions to be embedded into static page content.

key performance indicators (KPI)

Quantifiable measurements based on financial and nonfinancial metrics that reflect the critical success factors of an organization. These are used in the **CBM** to assess the present state of business and to prescribe the course of action.

mediation

Functionality provided by an **ESB** on **XML** messages and documents that flow through the bus. Mediation facilities include data transformation and content augmentation, dynamic routing, and customized handlers.

message queue (MQ)

The method by which a process (or program instance) can exchange or pass data using an interface to a message-based system. It is also used in reference to IBM's WebSphere MQ product, which provides transactional message queuing and **JMS** facilities for many platforms.

message-driven bean (MDB)

An **EJB** designed to handle asynchronous service invocations. It is invoked by a **J2EE** container when a **JMS** message arrives at the endpoint associated with the bean.

message-oriented middleware (MOM)

The term for application communication software that connects systems in a network by carrying and distributing messages between them. The messages may contain data and/or software instructions. MOM infrastructure is typically built around a queuing system that stores messages pending delivery and keeps track of whether and when each message has been delivered.

meta-object facility (MOF)

A set of standard interfaces from **OMG** that can be used to define and manipulate a set of interoperable metamodels and their corresponding models.

model-driven architecture (MDA)

Model-driven architecture is a software design methodology proposed and sponsored by the **OMG**. It defines levels of abstract, platform-independent models that can be used to generate more concrete models using an appropriate specification language. The generation from an abstract model (usually represented graphically) to a platform-specific, concrete model is done by using automated tools.

New Generation of Operation Support Services (NGOSS)

An open standard published by the TeleManagement Forum for business solution framework and architecture.

Object Management Group (OMG)

An open membership consortium that produces and maintains computer-industry specifications for interoperable enterprise applications. It is aimed at setting standards in object-oriented programming as well as system modeling.

object-oriented analysis and design (OOAD)

A methodology for modeling an application by representing it as a collection of cooperating objects.

On Demand

IBM's vision of an enterprise orientation whose business processes are integrated end-to-end across the company and with key partners, suppliers, and customers and that can respond with speed to any customer demand, market opportunity, or external threat.

On Demand Operating Environment (ODOE)

A comprehensive set of product and solution offerings from IBM that enables an **On Demand** enterprise. These solutions are categorized into integration, automation, and virtualization. Integration refers to creating business flexibility by integrating disparate, unconnected business and IT processes. Automation refers to reducing costs and increasing business responsiveness through IT and business linkage. Virtualization refers to improving working capital and resource utilization.

ontology

A formal and rigorous conceptual schema about a domain that is typically represented as a hierarchical structure containing all the relevant entities and their relationships and rules within that domain.

Open Application Group Integration Standards (OAGIS)

A standard created by the Open Application Group (OAGi) to create a common business language and canonical model for application integration in organizations.

Open Grid Services Architecture (OGSA)

Standards published by globus.org that represent an evolution toward grid services architecture based on Web services concepts and technologies. See also **grid computing.**

operational-level agreement (OLA)

A contract with the focus on operational issues with respect to the maintenance of the service and providing new services.

orchestration

Interactions and process flow among services in a business process. See also **choreography**.

Organization for the Advancement of Structured Information Standards (OASIS)

An international consortium that drives the development, convergence, and adoption of e-business standards. The consortium produces Web services standards and standardization efforts in the public sector and for application-specific markets.

port type

An interface which is a logical grouping of operations and represents an abstract service type, independent of transport protocol and data format.

public key infrastructure (PKI)

A system of digital certificates, certificate authorities (CA), and other registration authorities that verify and authenticate the validity of each party involved in a transaction.

publish

The publish operation occurs when a service makes its **service description** available to a service requester. Where and how it is published can vary depending on the requirements of the application.

quality of service (QoS)

A measure of a service's non-functional characteristics such as availability, performance, reliability, security, and integrity. It is used to match the needs of a service requestor with those of the service provider.

Rational Unified Process (RUP)

An iterative, architecture-centric, software engineering process developed by IBM Rational by incorporating the software engineering best practices. It establishes four phases of development, each of which is organized into a number of separate iterations that must satisfy defined criteria before the next phase is undertaken. In the inception phase, developers define the scope of the project and its business case. In the elaboration phase, developers analyze the project's needs in greater detail and define its architectural foundation. In the construction phase, developers create the application design and source code, and in the transition phase, developers deliver the system to users.

Remote Method Invocation (RMI)

A **RPC** protocol published by Sun for accessing Java object methods remotely within a distributed application system.

remote procedure call (RPC)

A protocol used in the client-server model that allows one application (the client) to request a service from another application (the server) located on another computer in a network without having to understand network details.

resource definition framework (RDF)

A family of specifications maintained by the **W3C** for a metadata model that provides an ontology system to support the exchange of information and knowledge on the Web using **XML** as an interchange syntax. It integrates information and content from library catalogues and worldwide directories to syndication and aggregation of news.

reusable asset specification (RAS)

A set of concepts, notations, and guidelines for describing the reusable assets of business systems. The specification focuses on specific reusable assets within (and occasionally across) architectural views and how to document each asset.

RosettaNet

A nonprofit consortium working to create, implement, and promote open e-business standards and services.

Security Assertions Markup Language (SAML)

An **XML** standard by **OASIS** for exchanging security assertions between security domains, the identity provider, and a service provider, for creating and exchanging authentication and authorization information.

service

An application component deployed on network-accessible platforms hosted by the service provider. Its interface is described by a **service description** to be invoked by or to interact with a service requester.

service consumer

The role in a SOA played by programs that send service request messages and subsequently consume service response messages according to the descriptions published by **service providers**.

Service Data Object (SDO)

A data programming architecture and **API** for the Java platform that unifies data programming across data source types (relational databases, entity **EJB** components, **XML** sources, Web services, **JCA**, **JSP**), provides robust support for common application patterns, and enables applications, tools, and frameworks to more easily query, view, bind, update, and introspect data.

service description

The details of the service interface, including its data types, operations, binding information, and network location. It could also include categorization and other metadata to facilitate discovery and utilization by service requesters. The service description may be published to a registry such as **UDDI**. See also Web Services Description Language (**WSDL**).

service provider

The role in a SOA played by programs that receive service request messages and subsequently send service response messages to **service consumers** according to descriptions published by those programs.

service registry

A repository of service descriptions where service providers can publish their **service descriptions**. Service requesters can find services and obtain binding information (in the **service descriptions**) for services during development for static binding or during execution for dynamic binding. See also Universal Description, Discovery, and Integration (**UDDI**).

service-level agreement (SLA)

A contract between a service provider and a service requester that stipulates a specified level of service. It could contain agreements on support options, enforcement or penalty provisions for services not provided, a guaranteed level of system performance, availability, and other **QoS**.

service-oriented architecture (SOA)

A framework for integrating business processes and supporting IT infrastructure as secure, standardized components—services—that can be reused and combined to address changing business priorities.

service-oriented modeling and architecture (SOMA)

An IBM methodology that provides in-depth guidance for the identification, specification, and realization of services. It uses techniques of domain analysis, **BPM**, **CBM**, and **OOAD**.

Simple Object Access Protocol (SOAP)

A **XML**-based messaging protocol maintained by **W3C** that is used to encode the information in Web service request and response messages before sending them over a network. SOAP messages are independent of any operating system or protocol and can be transported using a variety of protocols, including **HTTP** and **JMS**.

single sign-on (SSO)

A user or session authentication process that allows a user to provide one name and password and have credentials propagated to access multiple systems and applications.

Unified Modeling Language (UML)

An accepted **OMG** standard that provides a general-purpose modeling and specification language for specifying and visualizing complex systems. It has traditionally been used to specify, visualize, construct, and document **OOAD**-based application projects.

uniform resource identifier (URI)

A generic term for all types of names and addresses that refer to objects on the World Wide Web. A URL is a type of URI.

Universal Description, Discovery, and Integration (UDDI)

An **OASIS** standard for a platform-independent, **XML**-based registry to publish and discover network-based software components and services.

virtual private network (VPN)

A method of accessing a private network in a secure way over public communication lines and networks.

virtualization

A set of technologies and tools that can help you aggregate pools of resources to achieve a consolidated view throughout an IT environment. Virtualization technologies provide a logical—rather than physical—view of data, computing power, storage capacity, and other resources.

WBI Server Foundation (WBI-SF)

A comprehensive edition of the WebSphere Application Server that provides enterprise extensions such as a process engine to run **BPEL**, adapters for a wide range of enterprise information systems, and enhanced **QoS**. See also **WebSphere**. Formerly, it was called the **WAS** Enterprise Edition.

Web Ontology Language (OWL)

A semantic markup language for publishing and sharing ontologies on the World Wide Web. OWL is developed as a vocabulary extension of **RDF**.

Web services (WS)

A family of technologies that consist of specifications, protocols, and industry-based standards that are used by heterogeneous applications to communicate, collaborate, and exchange information among themselves in a secure, reliable, and interoperable manner. It is the primary technology for enabling and realizing **SOA**.

Web Services Description Language (WSDL)

A standard language for defining a Web **service description**. It uses XML and XSD to describe the **port type** and its operations, the message formats, and the protocol bindings.

Web Services Distributed Management (WSDM)

An OASIS standard for distributed management by defining specifications to represent manageability interfaces of resources as Web services (Management Using Web Services) and to describe Web services as resources with manageability interfaces (Management of Web Services).

Web Services Interoperability Organization (WS-I)

An open industry effort chartered to promote Web services interoperability across platforms, applications, and programming languages. The organization brings together a diverse community of Web services leaders to respond to customer needs by providing guidance, recommended practices, and supporting resources for developing interoperable Web services.

WebSphere

A **J2EE**-based application server platform that is the foundation of the IBM WebSphere software platform. It provides support for dynamic e-business and **SOA** by providing an application deployment environment with application services that provide enhanced capabilities for transaction management, as well as security, performance, availability, connectivity, and scalability. Sometimes it is abbreviated to **WAS**.

WS-Addressing (WS-A)

A specification that defines XML elements to identify Web services endpoints and to provide end-to-end endpoint identification in messages. This enables messaging systems to support message transmission through networks that include processing nodes such as endpoint managers, firewalls, and gateways in a transport-neutral manner.

WS-Federation

This specification defines mechanisms to allow different security realms to federate using different or like mechanisms by allowing and brokering trust of identities, attributes, and authentication between participating Web services.

WS-I Basic Profile

This profile is a specification defined by **WS-I** that provides interoperability guidance for core Web services specifications such as SOAP, WSDL, and UDDI.

WS-Notification (WS-N)

A family of related white papers and specifications that defines a standard Web services approach to notification using a topic-based publish/subscribe pattern. It includes standard message exchanges to be implemented by service providers that want to participate in notifications, standard message exchanges for a notification broker service provider (allowing publication of messages from entities that are not themselves service providers), operational requirements expected of service providers and requestors that participate in notifications, and an **XML** model that describes topics.

WS-Policy

A specification that provides a general-purpose model and corresponding syntax to describe and communicate the policies of a Web service. It defines a base set of constructs that can be used and extended by other Web services specifications to describe a broad range of service requirements, preferences, and capabilities. It provides a flexible and extensible grammar for expressing the capabilities, requirements, and general characteristics of entities in an XML Web services–based system. Policy expressions allow for both simple declarative assertions as well as more sophisticated conditional assertions.

WS-Reliable Messaging (WS-RM)

A Web services specification that describes a protocol that allows messages to be delivered reliably between distributed applications in the presence of software component, system, or network failures. The WS-RM protocol defines how to identify, track, and manage the reliable delivery of messages between exactly two parties, a source and a destination. It also defines a SOAP binding that is required for interoperability.

WS-Remote Portlets (WS-RP)

A specification that defines how to leverage SOAP-based Web services, which generate markup fragments within a portal application. By defining a set of common interfaces, WS-RP allows portals to display remotely running portlets inside their pages without requiring any additional programming by the portal developers. To end users, it appears that the portlet is running locally within their portal, but in reality, the portlet resides in a remotely running portlet container, and interaction occurs through the exchange of **SOAP** messages.

WS-Resource Framework (WS-RF)

A family of specifications for accessing stateful resources using Web services. Because Web service implementations typically do not maintain state information during their interactions, their interfaces must frequently allow for the manipulation of state—that is, data values that persist across and evolve as a result of Web service interactions.

WS-Security (WS-S)

A Web service specification that describes security enhancements to SOAP messaging to provide quality of protection through message integrity, message confidentiality, and single message authentication. It provides three main mechanisms: security token propagation, message integrity, and message confidentiality. It provides a foundation for further security specifications such as **WS-Trust** and **WS-Federation**.

WS-Trust

A specification that defines a language that uses the secure messaging mechanisms of WS-Security to define additional primitives and extensions for the issuance, exchange, and validation of security tokens. WS-Trust also enables the issuance and dissemination of credentials within different trust domains.

World Wide Web Consortium (W3C)

An international consortium in which member organizations develop and build consensus around Web technologies through specifications, standards, and guidelines.

XML Path Language (XPath)

A language that describes a way to locate and process items in XML documents by using an addressing syntax based on a path through the document's logical structure or hierarchy.

XML Schema Definition (XSD)

A **W3C** recommendation to formally describe the schema and elements in an XML document. It defines a structure for the custom elements and their corresponding attributes, their relationship to each other, and what types of information/data may be contained in them. This can be used to verify that the content of an XML instance document adheres to a particular schema.

XML Stylesheet Language (XSL)

A **W3C** specification for a family of languages, such as **XSLT** and **XPath**, that describes how **XML** documents are to be formatted or transformed.

XSL Transformation (XSLT)

A declarative language to describe how to convert an XML document from one structure into another structure by specifying a set of templates and rules.

Index